PARTIAL MAP OF THE

CANADA

Donated to

Augustana University College

by

JAMES HENDRICKSON

THE UNKNOWN COUNTRY

THE
UNKNOWN COUNTRY

Canada and Her People

BY BRUCE HUTCHISON

Illustrated

LONGMANS, GREEN & COMPANY
TORONTO

First Canadian Printing - October, 1943
Second Canadian Printing - December, 1943
Third Canadian Printing - October, 1944

Designed by Robert Josephy

PRINTED IN CANADA
T. H. BEST PRINTING CO., LIMITED
TORONTO, ONT.

To my father, who became a Canadian
and found his happiness tending the earth
of Canada

Foreword

At the start this book had a plan, but the writer soon forgot it and is confident the reader will not discover it. Perhaps that does not matter. This is not a guide book or a travel book. The reader who tried to follow its broken and casual journeyings across Canada would certainly lose himself. No attempt is made to cover the whole of the country, and vast stretches of it are deliberately left out. This book is an attempt rather to give the stranger a general glimpse of the surface of Canada and something of the substance, the people, the problems, the history, and the future beneath the surface. It is not a student's book, but the facts of Canadian life, as given here, will stand up, even if there are some slips in detail. It is written to provide not an academic investigation but what Cartier called the "ready way to Canada," or at least an easy way. It is written in the belief, reinforced by much traveling among them, that Canadians and Americans really know very little about Canada; that Canada is, among the important nations of the world, the least known in its real content; that the future relations between Canada and the United States will inevitably form one of the basic factors of world politics; and that these relations are widely misunderstood and often misrepresented. If the reader knows even a little more of Canada after reaching the end of this book, the job will have been worth doing, and the original plan well lost.

CONTENTS

Photographic Illustrations Will Be Found Following Page 196

THE UNKNOWN COUNTRY

My Country

No one knows my country, neither the stranger nor its own sons. My country is hidden in the dark and teeming brain of youth upon the eve of its manhood. My country has not found itself nor felt its power nor learned its true place. It is all visions and doubts and hopes and dreams. It is strength and weakness, despair and joy, and the wild confusions and restless strivings of a boy who has passed his boyhood but is not yet a man.

A problem for America they call us. As well call a young thoroughbred a problem because he is not yet trained and fully grown. A backward nation they call us beside our great neighbor—this though our eleven millions have produced more, earned more, subdued more, built more than any other eleven millions in the world. A colony they have thought us though we have rebelled and fought and bled for the right to our own government and finally produced the British Commonwealth of equal nations. A timid race they have called us because we have been slow to change, because we have not mastered all the achievements nor all the vices of our neighbors.

They have not known Canada. Who but us can feel our fears and hopes and passions? How can aliens or even blood brothers know our inner doubts, our secret strengths and weaknesses and loves and lusts and shames?

Who can know our loneliness, on the immensity of prairie, in the dark forest and on the windy sea rock? A few lights, a faint glow is our largest city on the vast breast of the night, and all around blackness and emptiness and silence, where no man walks. We flee to little towns for a moment of fellowship

3

*and light and speech, we flee into cities or log cabins, out of
the darkness and the loneliness and the creeping silence. All
about us lies Canada, forever untouched, unknown, beyond our
grasp, breathing deep in the darkness and we hear its breath
and are afraid.*

*No, they could not know us, the strangers, for we have not
known ourselves.*

*Long we have been a-growing, but with strong bone and
sure muscle—of two bloods, French and British, slow to be
reconciled in one body. We have been like a younger boy in the
shadow of two older brothers, and, admiring their powers,
watching the pageant of England and the raging energy of
America, we have not learned our own proud story nor tested
our own strength. But no longer are we children. Now our
time is come and if not grasped will be forever lost.*

*Now must we make our choice. Now must the heaving, fluid
stuff of Canada take shape, crystallize, and harden to a purpose. No people of our numbers has ever occupied such a place
before in the flood tide of history, for we are of two worlds,
the Old and the New, one foot in each, knowing England,
knowing America, joined to each by blood and battle, speech
and song. We alone are the hinge between them, and upon us
hangs more than we know.*

*Wondrous and very sweet is our name. Canada! The very
word is like a boy's shout in the springtime, is like the clamor
of geese going north and the roar of melting rivers and the
murmur of early winds.*

*Can we not hear the sound of Canada? Can we not hear it
in the rustle of yellow poplar leaves in October, and in
the sudden trout-splash of a silent lake, the whisper of
saws in the deep woods, the church bells along the river, the
whistle of trains in the narrow passes of the mountains, the
gurgle of irrigation ditches in the hot nights, the rustle of ripe
grain under the wind, and the bite of steel runners in the snow?*

Have we not felt the texture and living stuff of Canada?

Have we not felt it in the damp, springy forest floor, in the caress of the new grass upon our face, in the salt spray off Fundy or Juan de Fuca, in the hot sun of the prairies, in the beat of blizzards and the fierce surge of summer growth?

And the colors of Canada, those also have we seen. We have seen them in the harsh sweep of prairie snow, in sunlight and shadow vibrant across the heavy-headed wheat, in foaming apple orchards and in maple woods, crimson as blood, and in bleeding sumac by the roadside, and in white sails of schooners out of Lunenberg and in the wrinkled blue face of mountains. And we have smelled the clean, manly smell of Canada, in pine forest and settlers' clearing fires, and alkali lakes and autumn stubble and new sawdust and old stone.

Yes, but we have not grasped it yet, the full substance of it, in our hands, nor glimpsed its size and shape. We have not yet felt the full pulse of its heart, the flex of its muscles, the pattern of its mind. For we are young, my brothers, and full of doubt, and we have listened too long to timid men. But now our time is come and we are ready.

CHAPTER ONE

Chez Garneau

A song awakened us before daylight. A man was singing lustily in French below our window. In the darkness we could hear the jingle of sleigh bells along the village street as he drove past and, above the bells, the mellow voice, booming out of a mighty chest. It was an old French song, such a peasant song as the troubadours must have sung in the lost France where these Quebec people came from, long ago. Slowly the song faded with a dying tinkle of bells, far down the Island of Orleans, towards the St. Lawrence.

We lay there in our huge, carved bed, under the eaves, and listened to the last faint sound, trying to picture the unseen man on the sleigh, whose fathers had sung carelessly like this, here on their Island, for three hundred years; trying hard to forget that this was 1941 and no songs in the world any more.

Then the great, cranky bell of the church clanged out, suddenly, fiercely, with sharp tongue and morning temper, rousing the villagers to worship. The priest would be there in the freezing church, pulling the bell rope as it had been pulled regularly every morning, without fail, since 1717. When the clanging ceased, grudgingly, we could still hear the thin sound of sleigh bells, far off, and a last frail shred of song.

Now Madame Garneau was moving about downstairs, lighting the new, white-enameled stove, just shipped on mail order from Quebec and the finest on the Island. In a little while we could feel the heat of it, ascending through the big trap door

6

which opened into our bedroom on a cunning arrangement of rope and pulleys. It was still dark when I went down to shave in the bathroom, which had been installed a good century after the house was built, so that the more intimate features of it were separated from the dining room by a thin panel only, and an extraordinary publicity and a fearful sound attended its use. It made you think of the St. Lawrence ice breaking up in the spring.

M. Garneau was sitting at the kitchen table in the corner, where a tiny electric light glowed day and night on a high shelf, before a colored china figure of the Virgin and her Child, with a bowl of artificial pink flowers beside her. M. Garneau read his Bible to prepare himself for Mass, his heavy fingers slowly tracing out the words. Every morning he goes to Mass before breakfast, trudging through the deep snow of the village street, to chant responses to the holy words of the curé. Yet M. Garneau is not a specially religious man. He is just an ordinary poor farmer of Quebec, with a weatherbeaten, dark, shrewd Norman face.

Madame was cooking breakfast over her new stove, to be eaten after Mass. She bowed shyly to us—a tall, lean woman like a picture by Rembrandt. Her face was placid, with the immense and solemn dignity of the land, but strangely sad. I remembered how she had told us simply of her grief—*"pas des enfants."* To live without children in Quebec, to live without hope of leaving your house, your land, to a son of your own, is hardly to live at all. It was God's will, and no prayers to the Virgin and her Child could alter it.

M. Garneau greeted us jovially in the kind of childish French that we could understand. *"Bon jour, madame et monsieur! Beaucoup de neige aujourd'hui!"* He pointed to the window and in the first morning light we could see the snow, drifted deeply against the porch. *"Ah, oui,"* Jean said brightly in her remarkable French, *"beaucoup de neige."* And with a special effort of memory she added: *"Il fait froid."* M. Garneau grinned at me, for Jean's atrocious speech, her blithe assault on the language, was already a kind of bond between us.

That was the queer thing that we could never get quite used to—not a word of English was spoken in this old house in the very heart of Canada; hardly a word of it on the whole Island of Orleans, a few miles from the busy City of Quebec. But that is the first thing we had to understand if we were to understand our country, and the first thing that an American must understand, if he wants to know what sort of neighbors live beside him, guard his northern frontier, require his aid in war and peace, as he requires theirs.

Canada is not English—that is the first thing to understand. Half of it has no British blood. A third of it speaks French. It is a North American country, its people a North American people, as old on this continent as the people who are called Americans. Two great races are here. One came from France but has been separated from its first homeland for nearly two centuries and knows no land but this. The other came from England but not until it had lived for several generations in the American colonies and become part of the New World. It is because these blood streams have not yet merged, because their cultures have remained so well balanced and each so vigorous, that Canada is still a dual personality—a country not fully formed, not crystallized yet into final shape and substance, young and awkward but with youth's strength in its lanky body, youth's restlessness and uncertainty and love of life in its heart. No guidebooks have pictured it, no historian has told its story, no poet has sung its song. To the world it is unknown; to itself, like the mind of young manhood, still a mystery.

These were the first people of Canada, among the first white people of America—people like the Garneaus, whose fathers had lived in this house for nearly two centuries and on this Island in the St. Lawrence since 1648. They never expect, they never want to live anywhere else, and if there were children to plow this land after them, to cook at this stove, to pray before this queer shrine in the corner, life would be complete and perfect.

When they started down the road in the snow towards the church, where the big bell was clanging again in the belfry, we had a chance to look about their house and guess how they lived.

It was an old house, not far under three centuries, built of stone, the walls two feet thick and the roof supported by vast beams, roughly hewed, mortised together with oak pegs and dark with age. In the cold, clean attic under the roof everything was in place—Madame Garneau's spinning wheel, her loom, her huge painted chests of mittens, gloves, hooked rugs, linens and woolen goods which she had made in the winter and would sell in the summer. At one end of the attic the stone chimney thrust up through the floor and through the roof, ten feet wide.

The two bedrooms in the eaves were filled with huge and ponderous pieces of furniture, and our bed, with curious pointed ends capped by carved fleur-de-lis, would have held a family of four at least. There was a small stove in the corner, painted aluminum color, with neat round birch logs in a basket beside it. The wooden walls were yellow and green, shiny and smooth as satin. The whole interior, indeed, was painted up like a child's dollhouse, in greens, yellows, and reds. You felt as if you were living in a toy shop at Christmas time.

But all this was a setting only for the real jewel of the household—that masterpiece, the parlor. It was separated from the rest of the house by handsome glass doors (a recent improvement, by their newly varnished look) and it was seldom entered except when the priest called or a corpse was laid out, or the whole Garneau tribe gathered, fifty strong, for a reunion at New Year's. Then the glass doors were flung wide, revealing the inner spectacle.

Jean and I peeked into the parlor, with a guilty feeling, and as we opened the long-sealed doors, a gust of icy air blew outwards like the wind from a cave. It was a cave of treasure.

In one corner stood a tall brick fireplace, painted a glistening red and never used, lest the flames mar the paint work. The firewood was laid on it neatly, but no one would ever touch a match to it. On the mantel shelf above were myriads of seashells, collections of wax fruits under round glass covers, colored photographs of parents, brothers, sisters, aunts, uncles, nieces, and nephews. And more of them on the upright piano— a vast clan of Garneaus, some living down the river, some as distant as Montreal, one in Winnipeg, but no children of this house. *Pas des enfants.*

In the corner bulked a huge, distended but immaculate easy chair that no one surely had ever sat in. There was upright dignity, sobriety, and good breeding in the other straight-backed chairs, each with its covering of a gay hooked rug. Giant red roses sprouted out of the greensward of the carpet, and on the carpet lay a strange yellow pelt of fur, like the skin of a collie. Yes, as Madame told us later, caressing it with her worn hands, it was the skin, the last mortal remains of a beloved dog named Jacques.

We did not step past the threshold of the parlor and quickly closed the door with a feeling of sacrilege, and we looked at each other, trying to imagine the babies exhibited there to the admiring relatives, the New Year's parties when a new year might bring happiness instead of new wars, the corpses of Garneaus stretched out there, with candles beside them, awaiting burial.

We went out on the porch and looked down the street. The village clung to this narrow road, every house grasping it for support and comfort—the oblong, hip-roofed houses of Quebec, with fat, comfortable chimneys at each end and a little porch in front, the true Canadian architecture, brought from France but so deeply rooted in our soil as to be almost native.

Like a Christmas card it looked, the village of St. Pierre, with its double line of gaily painted houses laughing at the snow. A red sleigh jingled by and the driver, in a rough fur coat, like a grizzly, raised his whip to us respectfully. The people were coming out of the church now, black shapes against the snow far down the road, where the last houses of the parish straggled into the white fields. Presently the Garneaus trudged up the steps, stamping the snow from their boots.

Madame wanted Jean and me to eat by ourselves in the dining room, which was a continuation of the kitchen, but when we refused, she seemed pleased. *"Un honneur,"* said Jean and Madame blushed. *"Doucement,"* Jean added expansively, imagining this to be a compliment. M. Garneau looked surprised, then winked knowingly in my direction. Jean's French had brought this man and me close together.

We all sat at the table beneath the little electric light and the shrine of the Virgin in the corner. After crossing himself, M. Garneau attacked his porridge with interest and considerable sound, pausing to suck the thick milk from his long mustache. Then came eggs from Madame's chickens (they had laid straight through the winter, she said with pride) bacon from her pig (ah, he was a fat one, that, and used to gorge on the windfall apples) and strawberry jam (plenty of manure of the cow, you understand, makes the strawberries grow large and juicy). All these things we praised as best we could, Jean excelling herself with murderous adjectives, and Madame colored with pleasure. Monsieur repeated that there was nothing like the manure of the cow to make things grow, but for the hot-bed, the manure of the horse, naturally. With that he attacked a plate of bacon and four eggs.

Presently he pushed back his chair, loaded his pipe with his own tobacco—the powerful native *tabac* of Quebec, which smells like a dragon's breath—and prepared to talk of more serious things. He tried to speak slowly for my benefit but every new thought would start his words flying again, until

Madame would raise her bony hand and he would grin and slow down. I missed half his words, but got his drift all right.

There was something wrong with the world, said he, and the basis of it was the unsound distribution of wealth. *"Mal distribué,"* he kept repeating. Not that this Norman peasant with his ten-acre farm, his sound house, his horse and plow, his cow and chickens, wanted socialistic reforms or any non-sense of that sort. Ah no, the land was his. "My land!" he said over and over again, clenching his fist, as if to grasp in it the rich soil that his fathers had cut out of the wilderness and left to him.

"My land!" and you thought of that first day in 1535 when Jacques Cartier looked out from the rail of the *Grand Hermine* and, seeing the jungle of wild grapes down to the water's edge, called this the Isle of Bacchus. You thought of the Indians who used this Island, calling it Minigo, as a temporary prison for their captives, holding them, like lobsters in a crate, to be massacred and tortured at leisure. You thought of the first settlers here, and Eleonore de Grandmaison, the first woman—such a woman as Madame Garneau rocking on her chair, with folded hands—and the Hurons who fled here from the Iroquois to seek the protection of the French, building themselves the first Christian temple of bark. You remembered the story of the massacre, when the Iroquois swept down in their canoes and carried the Hurons off, flaunting them before the guns of Quebec City, and the end of the Huron, Jacques Oachonk, who chanted Christian hymns while the Iroquois scalped him, poured hot sand on his skull, and twisted his ligaments with red-hot gun barrels—chanted so loudly that they could hear him a mile away.

"My land!" said this Norman peasant, sitting in his comfortable kitchen with its new stove and electric light, and you saw just such a man as watched the English fleets of Kirke and Phips and Wolfe sail up the river to bombard Quebec. They fled when Wolfe landed here, burying their money in the ground, but they came back. Wolfe had taken Quebec, New France had fallen, Canada was part of the British Empire, but the Islanders came back, and nothing, neither the English nor hard times, nor the evils of the economic system, nor modern war, nor the total madness of the world could take the island from them.

No, not the land, not the flat Island land lying like a great whale in the river, but the arrangements of men were at fault, said M. Garneau. Ah yes, but wait a while. He pointed at me with the stem of his pipe, a crafty look in his narrow, black eyes. After the war things would be different. He burst into another torrent of words, but Madame raised her hand again and he stopped, sighed, and started to pull on his gum boots and his cap with the 'fur ear flaps. His cow was waiting to be milked, but it was not often that he had a chance to talk to strangers. Halfway to the door he paused and came back to the table and pointed the stem of his pipe at me again.

Ah, yes, he said, standing there in his gum boots, the fur flaps dangling about his ears, ah, yes, it was all very well for the politicians to make their promises. Oh, they had come down here to the Island of Orleans, the fat politicians from the city, and promised the farmers everything, and made fine speeches. But when they were elected what did they do? He thrust his hand into his pocket and winked at me and grinned and muttered, *"Argent!"* And I remembered this same gesture, precisely this same talk, from a miller in an ancient French mill beside the Marne, while the great mill wheel turned and splashed beside us. The Frenchman has brought his humor, his cynicism, his hard realism and cheerfulness across the ocean. He has not changed much in this country through more than three hundred years. He is, in Canada, the uncorrupted, simple Frenchman who never heard of the Enlightenment, the Revolution, the wave of anti-clericalism, and, at last, the Fall.

Finally M. Garneau pulled his cap down over his ears, buttoned his coat, and started out with a milk pail, and we heard him whistling as he went down the path to the stable. Quaint, the guide books call such men as this, and railway posters try to make them look like French peasants, like the people of France whom they have not known nor seen nor had contact with since the Battle of the Plains, in 1759. No, they are not of France. They are not of England. They are of Canada, and so much the basic stuff of Canada that each man can trace his family back to the great battle or beyond, and no man is so poor that one of his ancestors is not known somewhere in the history of war or trade or politics. No waiter who serves you at table, no boy who shines your shoes or woman who washes your laundry, but can point to the family name somewhere in the story of Quebec.

Yes, quaint they call these people, as if they were a small oddity, a tourist attraction, museum pieces—these people who, with a few hundred muskets, could hold half a continent against the Iroquois, who could exist here against cold and hunger and the graft of the French court and the whims of the King's women. A problem they call these people because their quality is too strong to be easily absorbed, altered, or lost—unassailable, this rock of another race and culture in our common, tepid American sea of uniformity, monotony, and mediocrity. Charming, simple, quaint—so the guide books call them and any tourist will agree—and the French-Canadian smiles politely and takes your money. But he is smiling *at* you.

Her husband milking at last, Madame felt free to produce some of her work for us to see. Out of a big, blue-enameled chest she hauled a roll of carpet, so large she could hardly lift it, and spread it out across the floor. Even after it reached to the edge of the living room most of it was still unrolled. It lay in vivid cross stripes of reds and greens and purples, merging softly into each other, fresh out of her loom, and beside it a dozen hooked rugs, each with a vivid picture of Quebec villages, sleighs and flowers worked into it from nothing but old rags, brightly dyed. On the table she spread a pile of knitted and beflowered mittens and gloves and napkins made from the linen of her own flax. She stood smiling down at these results of her long winter's work, and leaned over to feel the texture of the carpet, to smooth out the rugs with her rough, cunning hands. She would have no trouble selling them all, she said, in the summer.

Here was a peasant woman who had no book learning, who had never been a hundred miles from the Island and yet knew something hidden from nearly all of us; knew the value of *things;* knew that nothing is owned or possessed until it is used and put to work; knew what is real wealth and what is shadow and aggravation and burden—knew it better than the economists or philosophers, and far better than the rest of America, to which most possession is but the illusion and counterfeit of ownership. Each thing she valued at its true worth, not for its price, name, reputation, or fashion but for its use and quality—actualities to be touched, handled, used, and made to serve. The loom, the spinning wheel, the new electric pump in the basement, the fine new stove, the surging waterworks of the bathroom—each of them was a servant not a master, each doing a job for her, each, like a friend, binding her down to the household, to the soil, to life.

The little plaster Jesus in His mother's arms, the electric light burning beside Him, was assurance of a better life yet to come. But one world at a time—they knew that, these people, as well as the dying Thoreau knew it. Here was a mixture of lusty worldliness and unquestioning faith that we tortured Anglo-Saxons can never understand. And they are wealthy, too, in real wealth, independent, lacking nothing of real value on an income that we would consider penury.

These are the things that distinguish the French Canadian from the rest of America—his grip on things, on the earth, on reality, where we have come to accept shadow for substance, radio jokes for the simple, profound humors of the day's work, desiccated breakfast powders for bread, and the synthetic celluloid fornications of the screen for life.

In the afternoon, when it was too dark for work, the neighbors called—Adjutor Charpentier, a young, sandy-haired, lanky fellow in his courting wardrobe of bowler hat and mail-order overcoat; with him his girl, tiny Marie Fiset, who wore her home-made dress as if she had come off the boulevards, and Amélie Garneau, Madame's niece, who waits on table in Quebec City and likes strong perfumes.

They were a little embarrassed by us and sat on the edge of their chairs, and Adjutor blushed furiously when I asked Jean if she thought the young man was going to marry Marie. We had forgotten, after a day in this house, that anyone could speak English.

They sat for a couple of hours, speaking seldom, rocking in their chairs, giggling at some obscure family joke quite beyond us. Madame passed around some of her apples and fudge, and I offered cigarettes, which the girls refused, and that was ample entertainment. There we sat, munching apples, talking about the weather and the snow and the prospects of the spring, as these Islanders must have talked for centuries. Only a few miles away, its squat dark tower visible from the Island, stood the Château Frontenac, more luxurious than King Louis's Versailles. Madame listened, half smiling, hands folded. Always she rocked on her chair, listening to the young folks. Their voices and laughter were precious in this childless house.

In the evening I wallowed up the street and through a new drift of snow towards the light of the priest's house. It stood behind the church—the ancient, steepled church of St. Pierre that they began to build in 1717 and built over and over again until it looks almost new now, with its white plastered outside and shiny towers. As I staggered through the deep snow, heading for the single light, it was easy to feel the ghosts of that old church around me—Antoine Carpentier, who cut the stone for the walls, and Pierre Langlais, who was paid £35 for making the doors and window arches, and old Burke, the Irish curé, who, unable to speak much French and encountering a difficult word, would growl out at his leading parishioner: "You say it, Gosselin!" And the rich seigneurs who had their own pews and special rights of worship, and all the hundreds of unknown, poor Islanders who had come here in life for baptism and communion and in death for burial.

The priest's house was long and low-roofed and, from the outside, rather imposing, but when the door opened I saw that it was bare, without carpets, cold, wholly ascetic. The curé himself opened the door—a tall young man, iron-gray of hair, with handsome, lean face in which the passions had been fought down and ruthlessly burned out. In the room to the left an old man sat, slumped in his chair and he seemed to have been weeping. The parishioner had come for comfort to the curé and was not denied it.

The curé closed the door to that room and led me into another at the right of the hall. He sat down at his desk and quietly filled his pipe, waiting for me to speak. Unhappily, he knew no English but he listened patiently to my bad French and replied as simply as he could, asking me eagerly about Western Canada, the outer immensities of his country that he never hoped to see, for his flock was here, old men called on him in the night, and he would never leave. Here, in his black robes, this priest of a tiny village represented the undying power of the Roman Catholic Church in Quebec, the church's most faithful child. Nothing can prevail against the curé. He is the center of life in the village as his church is the gateway of life and death. Just such men as this young man before me had come out to New France with the first white soldiers, carried their little wooden crosses and beads on foot and by canoe into the forests, into the west, down the Mississippi, lived with the Indians, died of their diseases, suffered their torture, their filth and their obscenities.

Such a man as this, I thought, was Jogues, who went to an Indian feast though he knew it was an invitation to death, and whose head stood rotting on a Mohawk palisade. Of the same sort was Brébeuf who made no cry and uttered no sound though the Iroquois baptized his head with boiling water, hung red-hot axes on his naked shoulders, lit a belt of pitch and resin about his body, and cut out his heart. "Grant me, oh Lord," Brébeuf had prayed, "so to live that you may deem me worthy to die a martyr's death. Thus, my Lord, I take your chalice and call upon your name. Jesu! Jesu! Jesu!"

A martyr's death he was granted, as fine a death in the stinking Iroquois village as Latimer's at Oxford, and a speech as noble as Latimer's: "Play the man, Master Ridley, and we shall this day light such a candle by God's grace in England as I trust shall never be put out!" Never put out was the light of the French missionary, who built up such a legend of courage, of wisdom, of charity and stern justice that not all the agnosticism of this age, not all the sins of the big cities, the upsurge of new economic forces, have prevailed against him. The village curé, patient, clever, sometimes misguided or worldly, always fully conscious of human frailty, is the real ruler of these people.

We talked there for about an hour, of Quebec, and the war, and of the Island, and almost pathetically he kept asking me about those other countries that he would never see, nodding thoughtfully as I tried to tell him, smiling politely at my jokes. I left him at his door, a tall, solemn figure in his black robes, a young man who might have known wealth, luxury, women. I waded through the snow and he went back to his parishioner, the troubled old man who needed his comfort.

Next morning Madame Garneau had us up early to catch the snowmobile for Quebec City. It came along just as we were finishing breakfast, and M. Garneau, sighting it through the window, rushed out wildly in his shirt sleeves, and hailed it from the porch. We bundled aboard this contraption which has skis in front and caterpillar treads behind, the only mechanical device which can travel the island roads in winter. It was already full of farmers bound for town, and Amélie, Madame's niece (superbly turned out, painted and perfumed), sat on my knee and I didn't mind.

M. Garneau piled our grips in, talking fast. He was very proud of the snowmobile. It seemed to represent progress on the Island. It was part of the mysterious process of change which he had glimpsed vaguely—part of the revolution which long ago had shaken the world and now penetrated even here. But Madame stood on the porch of the house, hands folded in front of her, calm, immovable, her placid face watching us. She waved once and nodded gravely. Not for her the new machines, the new ideas. She stood there unshaken and unafraid, strong as Quebec itself, part of the past, rooted deep in the soil that Frenchmen have tilled here for three hundred years, part of the warp and woof of countless looms in countless little white houses like this. But a grim, sad figure after all, a childless woman—"pas des enfants."

The snowmobile started. Madame raised her hand slowly. Her husband waved and shouted and grinned after us. The machine heaved and lurched through the snow and everybody inside began to talk and laugh in an atmosphere stifling with the smoke of tabac. Yes, they will mechanize these people some day, with machines like this, bring them our civilization, teach them our clever ways, and our vague disease of glut and surplus and satiety.

Mother of Canada

City of Quebec they call you, as if stones and mortar and a name could hold that urgent spirit! Fair and lovely and quaint, the strangers have called you, but who save your children can know you, Mother of Canada? Who save your sons shall know the meaning of the smile on your wrinkled face, the touch of your aged hand, they who have gladly died for you, from the Long Sault to Vimy Ridge?

From your womb came we all, came every man who calls himself Canadian, came this whole nation of Canada, from sea to sea. And you have watched your children grow, how patiently, how long! What sons have nursed at your unfailing breast to learn wisdom and courage and the love of this land, to fight the savage, to plow the earth and build railways and rear up other cities of another tongue, to sail across the sea and fly in alien skies that you might still live here, in your old way!

How long have you watched the River, who was your mate from the beginning! Watched him, with leaping heart, bring the ships from France in the spring, when you were hungry and sick and betrayed; watched him, with dim, longing eyes, as he carried the last sail away in the dying autumn; watched, unafraid, the enemy fleets of Kirke and Phips and Walker, and the last English fleet of Wolfe, who was to take you, but never to possess you. War the River brought you, and siege and bombardment and pestilence, yet he was your mate and you loved him. Always the River lay beside you in ceaseless rise and fall of tide, and you clung to him for life.

You have been no saint, O Mother! You are old now, older

than four centuries, but there is still a twinkle in your eye that is not English, not altogether respectable either, and comes from the hot nights of ancient France. For lovers you have had —how many!

Cartier first, that bearded, black sailorman from St. Malo, and you shivered here together among the Indians that first winter, all but dying of scurvy and hunger. Then Champlain, the moon-faced man, cold to look at as a painting on a saucer, but with a lion's heart. He brought out a child bride when he built your first habitation, but it was you he loved, and his unmarked bones are hidden somewhere beneath your battlements. Frontenac loved you, too, and dressed you in fine raiment and fought for you on battlefield and in King's throne room, and died here in his lonely château, died in your arms, tired, old, forgotten. His wild heart he willed to his frigid countess in France, sealed in a lead box, but she sent it back, and it lies with his body somewhere, known only to you. And Montcalm, whose life was like a white banner of honor before men, loved you well enough to die fighting in the field yonder and might have saved you, too, but for your betrayers, those strumpets of the French court. And Montcalm, too, lies under your stones.

Oh, you have had lovers who were men! Rivals you have had also—Du Barry, Pompadour, Montespan, who could plunder you for a little while. But they are gone long ago and you remain, still making men's hearts beat faster as they pass by.

You had priests, confessors, spiritual comforters—Laval, the first lonely bishop, poor as his church mice, tolling his bell alone at dawn, and countless priests, missionaries, monks, nuns. You were faithful to the church, but never too holy for this life, and you have drunk it to the lees. How many different times and things and men you have known—those first days when the Indians howled at your gate; the lean days of five sieges; those wicked days when you lived like a great lady of France with your court, your silks and satins, carriages, feasts,

*intrigues, and duels; the top-hatted, stuffy days of Confedera-
tion when the Canadian nation was built here within your
gates; and now the days of your comfortable old age, when
you have become a legend, a name, and a monument, and
strangers, knowing no better, call you quaint.*

*Still you are our Mother. Still you watch the river bearing
his tides of ships and men and events ceaselessly up and down
—your ancient mate, the St. Lawrence. Now behind you are
new sounds, the sounds of men marching and drilling and flying in your skies. Deep sounds, rumbling in factories, woods,
mines, and fields, the sounds of your nation coming of age.
Your work bears at last its full fruit. Your sons are grown to
manhood now. You have waited long for them and now they
are ready. Oh, Mother, can you hear?*

CHAPTER TWO

The Rock

James Wolfe first saw the rock of Quebec from the river. It was the twenty-sixth day of June, 1759. Thirty-two years old Wolfe was then, youngest general in the British Army, already far wasted with disease and ordered to capture half a continent before autumn.

Long he looked at the rock over the rail of his ship, this frail young man with chinless face and sad, brooding eye. From the river you may see it so today, for the rock changes little through the ages—a few steeples added, a tower or two, some houses and stone walls in dark, serrated line against the sunset. Thus many men, in different centuries, have seen it.

Untouched and virgin was the rock when the first white man, Cartier, gazed up at it in the forgotten summer of 1535, and knew it immediately as one of the strongholds of the earth —this vast, pointed upthrust of cliff, bare and stark, a place where a few bold men could defend a nation. Champlain saw it after the lapse of a century and wisely built his first frail fort upon its side, founding the nation with a few flimsy huts. Three times invaders saw it, captured it once when Champlain was too sick and hungry to hold it, turned away twice, beaten.

Now Wolfe knew that to take the rock would be to take Canada, to make North America English, under that resplendent, fat, and ineffable monarch, the third George.

From the rock an older general watched the Englishman. Louis Joseph de Montcalm-Gorzon, who had soundly beaten the English in four successive campaigns already, kept his telescope trained confidently on the English fleet, but behind the smile of that handsome, gentle face was the knowledge that Quebec had been half lost already, its stores depleted by crooked politicians, its walls weakly built by crooked contractors, its money gone to buy silks and perfumes for the French King's mistresses. "What a country!" writes Montcalm in his last dispatch, "where rogues grow rich and honest men are ruined!"

He will not have to watch the river much longer. "War is the grave of the Montcalms." It is a saying almost as old as France.

Once Wolfe attacks upon the flat shore below the rock and the French drive the redcoats back into their rowboats. Humiliating indeed is the first venture of the young general who must deliver a continent up to King George.

Wolfe, pondering on the deck, gazing at the black thrust of the rock, conceives his final plan. It is a bad plan, any soldier will tell you. Military historians forever afterward will disparage it. But Wolfe makes it, alone in his cabin, telling no one of it, writing his orders by his own hand, writing a last letter to his mother, making his will and looking for the last time at the miniature of his sweetheart in England. Then he sits down among his officers to read aloud Gray's "Elegy." "'The paths of glory,'" whispers young Wolfe in that dingy cabin, "'lead but to the grave'!" and he adds: "Gentlemen, I would rather have written that than beat the French tomorrow."

At this moment Gray, who wrote it, is eating roasted chestnuts by the bed of Lady Cobham, dying of dropsy in London. Neither Gray nor anyone else in England knows what Wolfe is planning to do this night. It is the twelfth of September, wet, windy, and cold.

Wolfe's ships slip up the river past the rock. Before dawn the rowboats come down with the tide, and when Montcalm's sentries hail them, the reply is given in French and they suspect nothing. These, surely, are supply boats from Montreal. The troops that the suspicious Montcalm has sent here have been ordered back by Vaudreuil, most blundering of governors.

Wolfe's Highlanders and redcoats leap upon the shore at Anse au Foulon and scramble up the slippery hill west of the rock. At dawn their thin line is flung across the Plains of Abraham, of old Maître Abraham Martin, the river pilot. Maître Abraham, you cannot save them now.

With the first light Montcalm, knowing now this is the end, knowing his orders disobeyed, his plans betrayed, his Canada lost, charges on his black horse, sword drawn. The English, firing as one man at forty paces, cut the French and Indian line to tatters. It flees helter-skelter back toward the walls of Quebec, carrying the wounded Montcalm with it, who, when told by Dr. Arnoux that he cannot live, says: "So much the better. I shall not see the surrender of Quebec." And having written a respectful letter to Wolfe, he is thrust by a few monks and nuns into the hole made by an English shell, for no one has time to dig a grave.

Wolfe is dead also, a bullet through his chest, just able to see that the French are beaten, muttering: "Now God be praised, I die in peace."

The little skirmish has lasted about half an hour; both generals have died, as if their parts had been written for them by a Greek tragedian; and America belongs now to the glorious monarch. A very badly planned battle, all the military historians agree.

Today children are playing baseball around the monument, on the spot where Wolfe died in peace. Ask them the way to Quebec and they will not answer unless you speak in French, for they know no English. The 60,000 Frenchmen conquered by Wolfe have grown to more than 3,000,000, about a third of the Canadian nation and, at the present rate of fertility, will some day be the largest part. In two hundred years Champlain's first settlers have multiplied a hundred times, a feat of reproduction perhaps never seen on the earth before. To be in comparable position, the United States would have to contain some 40,000,000 people who spoke their own separate language, made their own separate laws, and lived their own separate lives. Wolfe's victory has turned out to be no conquest but a union, not yet complete.

On Maître Abraham's field the modern Canada, the nation of two races, had begun. The battlefield is a good starting place for your own march upon Quebec.

Enter it, like Montcalm in his last hours, through the St. Louis Gate—not the original but rebuilt with broad arch and tower on the original plan—walk down St. Louis Road and the Grand Allée, and you will know at once, though you have seen all the cities of the world, that you have seen none exactly like this. Any tourist pamphlet will recite its names, streets, monuments, buildings, legends, views; and Monsieur Carrel, in his well-known guidebook, has drained the English dictionary quite dry of adjectives and grafted them to the French idiom in a truly astounding fashion. But no one, so far as I know, has ever caught the peculiar essence of Quebec, which falls into no recognizable category, being of two worlds.

Even Kipling could mutter only a few clipped phrases of astonishment, and novelists failed more dismally than soldiers in their attempts to capture Quebec. Probably because there is no place in the New World, at least, to which it can be precisely compared. Boston, perhaps, holds as much history, but Boston is an aged spinster, growing fat with good living, virtue triumphant but to lovelife unknown. Quebec, though older, is French and no spinster, has known life, lived it and relished it all and still looks out with bright, knowing eyes from the rock.

Quebec has that rare thing known in Europe, but almost unknown in America—the perfection of planning which comes of no plan, which has grown like a plant unfolding, street by street, stone by stone, planless and perfect. You would change no stone of it, from the obese English citadel on the peak of Cape Diamond to the meanest house in Lower Town.

They have changed it from time to time. They have painted it and primped it and sold it to tourists, but few travelers have seen past the surface to the substance of Quebec. Fewer have understood that this is the expression of a French genius for communal living and human society which died in France with the Revolution, just as the Island of Orleans still holds the unspoiled genius of the pre-revolutionary French peasantry.

Quebec must be seen in all weathers and seasons. Its streets must be trudged in sunshine and in snow—when the first grass is breaking green on the slopes of the Citadel, when the maple trees are scarlet along the cliffs, when it is all buried deep in white winter. And then it is no use trying to put it into words any more than five centuries of poets could catch the peculiar and subtle rhythm of London, and every man is astounded, even now, to discover this new and nameless thing for himself.

Only in a few places—in an English cathedral, perhaps, or in an old Paris street, or in a forgotten white village by the Danube—is it possible to capture the pungent flavor of enduring life; of individual men's lives left somehow in the stones that they have shaped, the streets they have laid, the houses they have built, so that it can be sensed and breathed, communicating itself, as one living man to another—so that you may know the touch of their vanished hands by the touch of their enduring stone, the cast of their mind by the things they have made, the look of their eyes by some sudden glimpse of a ruined wall or an old garden. In all America, Quebec alone holds this ultimate magic.

You may go to M. Carrel's illustrated guide and learn all the names, places, dates, and legends, with a rich added ration of hyperbole, all for thirty-five cents. But, having done so, forget the details, forget the prodigal M. Carrel and look at this strange growth whole.

Half of it lies on a flat beside the river—the Lower Town by law of gravity and by law of social caste. Half of it lies on the tableland above—the Upper Town, where the Upper Classes have always lived. Winding, panting little streets toil up the cliffs to join the two—streets of oldest Europe and not of America—and to the sheer cliffs cling strange buildings as if they had fallen from the top and paused halfway down, wedged in the rock. Over all, always, from every angle, day and night, looms the dark shape of the rock, rising suddenly out of the river, with the round walls of the Citadel ringing its head like a dull crown—English, stolid as a steak-and-kidney pudding.

Best of all you can see it from the tower of the Château Frontenac which, despite its flunkies and miles of rich corridors and the kind of effete luxury which the poorest traveler now demands, has managed somehow to fit itself, with French towers, inner courtyards, and narrow gateways, into the general planlessness and French abandon of the city.

From the tower you can look far down the flat and glistening river to the Island of Orleans, where life is lived as if on a different continent and in a separate age. Liners pass up and down the river now and fussy little ferry boats, running over to Levis, but it is not long, as time is measured, since this brimming basin was filled with high-sterned ships, square-rigged, bristling with guns, and with the canoes of Indians and voyageurs, for this was the center and heart of New France, all the way down the Mississippi to New Orleans.

Directly below, so that you could toss a biscuit upon it (which the Château Frontenac will obligingly supply if you ring for room service) is the Lower Town—such a jumble of old houses, chimney pots, grime, narrow streets, women screaming in old windows, children playing in dark canyons of brick, as would be a slum anywhere else in America, but here, as in the old streets of London or in the squalor of St. Antoine, has a kind of patina and glory of its own.

Down there was the Indian village of Stadacona, when Cartier came, and from the river bank yonder the natives swarmed out in their birchbark canoes to greet his ships, and tried to frighten him away by dressing up like horned devils. Halfway up the cliff there, now swarmed over by dirty buildings, Champlain built his Abitation, a crazy gim-crack botch of gables, galleries, moats, and drawbridges, which hardly looked like the beginning of a great nation. Only eight of its twenty-eight inhabitants were alive the next spring.

Just below you, on the cliff's edge, partly on the site of the hotel, Champlain finally reared the Château St. Louis, a grim building of pitched roofs and square flanking towers which was burned a hundred years ago. But not before it had housed a passable imitation of Versailles, with courtiers in silks and ruffles, governors, soldiers, grafters, concubines. It was there that Frontenac lived alone, his countess refusing to come with him from France; there that he received, with guards, flags, banners, arms, and magnificence of Fontainbleu, the blind-folded English envoy who asked his surrender; there that he told the New Englander, Phips, that his guns would answer all invaders; there that he died alone, betrayed by his King and his country. Gorgeous and fantastic adventurer, who could dance at an Indian campfire or grace a quadrille, could love, fight, drink, eat, and swagger through the battlefields, courts, and châteaux of Europe and through the trackless forests of Canada! On Frontenac the appreciative modern world has conferred its highest honor. A cigar has been named after him.

Over to the right, from the tower window, the greensward runs up to the top of the rock, to the edge of the low citadel walls. To the left, the pinnacles, walls, buttresses, spires, and steeples of the city lie in strange tangle of masonry.

But today the last snow of a late spring is falling, and the whole city is dim, the river a blur, Lower Town almost lost. And sitting in your tower room, you think of Cartier in his winter camp beside the river, his men all dying of scurvy, until a friendly Indian tells him to brew tea of spruce needles. You think of Champlain shivering in his absurd Abitation that first winter, watching for the first sail in the spring. You think of Frontenac in his château, with plumed hat and jackboots and rapier by his side, watching the last sail go down the river in the autumn. You think of all those lonely winters for nearly two hundred years when this was New France, waiting for news from home. Looking down on it from the tower, in the snowstorm, you have a feeling of warmth and security, as if you were safe for a moment from the hunger and the cold and the misery of your species. From just such a window, on such a day, Marie Antoinette must have advised the breadless mob to eat cake.

In front of the Château, on the lip of the cliff, they have built a terrace where it is the pleasant custom of the townspeople to stroll at night, with a French instinct of neighborly curiosity. They usually wait for the warm weather, but the early spring is the best, on a night when a hundred smells of new growth, warming earth, cooking, and habitation ascend from the cliffs and from Lower Town, and the broken ice, moving up with the rising tide and down at the ebb, makes wild shapes on the clean streak of moonlight across the river.

Lovers will be strolling on the terrace then, as they used to stroll in ruffles and plumed hats. (And we have it on the authority of M. Carrel as a connoisseur and, what is more, as a Frenchman, that "few cities can vie with Quebec in the beauty of its women.") A few old men will be about, muttering on the benches. There will be none of the fashion and wealth to be seen on the great promenades of the world, on the Paris boulevards, or beside the Danube in Budapest, or even in Atlantic City, but the terrace of Quebec will have a comfortable family air about it, and in the twilight, without any great feat of imagination, you may hear the rustle of silks, and see the occasional plumed hat and hear the tinkle of a distant saber, long gone.

At the end of the terrace you can climb up the wooden steps to the walls of the Citadel, a genial and ridiculous old fortress, fat and stuffy in the Victorian style, but with regal chambers within. The King of England stayed there in the spring of 1939, and an American reporter (female) was able to enter by stealth and note that the furniture included an old-fashioned and homely crockery receptacle under the bed. That was thought to be news in the spring of 1939.

The inner heart of Quebec has always been the square at the other end of the terrace, where Champlain stands in heroic bronze, doffing his hat, on the site of his old château. (Where are his bones, this founder of Canada? Lost in the masonry somewhere, lying under some wall or dark basement or crowded street.) From the first days of the town this square has been a common meeting place, where a gallant would greet a lady by sprinkling her fingers with holy water, where gossip was exchanged and news announced. Now the cabbies snooze in their shiny *calèches* (usually pronounced "calash") with high white wheels and single, lazy horse—each driver a beautiful liar with his own specialties in the legendry of Quebec.

Across the square, facing Champlain, is the English cathedral, so English with its square unornamented body, its pointed steeple, that Wren should have built it, for the design was evidently stolen from him. All the basic differences in the two races are here, fixed in the stone of the English church and of the French churches all about it—the glum, unsmiling look of the English, who hide the most sentimental nature in the world under a concerted national look of solidity, building their churches like their faces, permitting only a few carved wrinkles of respectable amusement, an occasional cautious chuckle in Gothic; and the French, whose laughter is hewn in marble, whose plump and comfortable bodies bulge out in fat, spangled towers, whose tripping tongue and bubbling accent are captured for a moment in the richness of jeweled altars, vaulted roofs, and painted ceilings.

From the square you stroll down the winding street, cut into the rock of the cliff, past the little park, where, in a hotel now gone, the nation of Canada emerged in written constitution (the work of a few bearded men in frock coats), and near by a family of sleepy antique cannons loll, with open mouths over the ramparts. Then, by further curves and steep, cobbled hills, you reach Lower Town. It is there, in these narrow streets, where children play and good wives gossip, and storekeepers argue, that you feel the absurdity of Quebec.

Absurd, I mean, that people should walk these streets in modern clothing or, worse, drive through them in automobiles. Every man should be in plumed hat and jackboots. Every woman should wear billowing silks, carried in coach or sedan chair. So they lived here once. A century and a half they lived here before the English came, three times as long as most cities in America have existed; lived in rich medley of courtiers, sailormen, soldiers, black-frocked missionaries, *coureurs-du-bois* in leather coats, fresh out of the woods, voyageurs, singing off the river, and solemn priests and hooded nuns and great ladies for whom duels were fought and men died on the field of honor. Only the French could do it, would have thought of doing it, would have erected and maintained here, amid a handful of people, on a rock above the river, with Indians howling around, a little Paris of their own.

No wonder the English were astounded when they came and, conquering, found themselves conquered. No wonder the young naval officer, Horatio Nelson, had to be torn away by his shipmates, carried bodily to the ship's boat, out of the arms of his French-Canadian sweetheart.

Down here, in this strange, pathetic little brown church, wedged between larger buildings beside the cliff, Frontenac and the others came to worship. Notre Dame des Victoires they called it because their prayers were answered and the fleets of Phips and Walker sailed away, unavailing against the rock, but not before cannon balls had burst through the roof. Inside, at the rich altar, still burn the candles in their red glasses, and in the dim light people still kneel and pray—roughly dressed fellows off the streets, old women and children. A little girl comes in, calmly crosses herself, kneels for a moment, leaps up again and skips out of the House of God as naturally as she would romp out of a schoolroom, and a young man in leather windbreaker and corduroy pants, whom you would take for a truck driver, moves reverently past the Stations of the Cross, praying silently, with eyes closed, before each.

In the little square outside, which used to be the market, with the merchants' houses standing around, there is nothing to mark this for one of the historic spots of America, except a bronze bust of Louis Quatorze, covered today with snow—no climate, this, for the Sun King, who never understood the New France, nor suspected that one day it would send its blood and treasure, under an English king, to rescue the Old. The square is deserted, grimy, ragged, and you must search it out for yourself. It is better thus, than ornamented and renovated and presented to the tourist like a painted corpse.

Further down the winding street, if you care to look for the bronze tablet which marks it, is the place where the gallant Montgomery died. "The troops," said Montgomery's battle order, "will advance to the attack of works incapable of being defended by the wretched garrison." Wretched indeed was the garrison of Quebec that night of December 31, 1775—a few French and English huddling in the city that Wolfe had recently captured. The French, thought Montgomery, would be glad to escape their conquerors and join the revolting Thirteen Colonies, but Montgomery's old friend, Guy Carleton, was defending Quebec that night (where they had often drunk together at the Golden Dog) and the French had made up their minds. When Montgomery led his charge through a snowstorm, fifty English and French, fighting together at the Sault au Matelot, met the five hundred Americans with such a fire that they turned and ran. Montgomery lay dead in the snow of the dark street. New France had decided to stay with England and would fight again, within forty years, against other American invaders.

From Lower Town, from its canyons, gulfs, and gorges, you can look up at the living stone of the cliff that thrusts itself through the streets, overhangs the houses, and is as clean, untouched, and virginal in the middle of the city as on the day when Cartier first saw it. It is something like the up-ended rock of Edinburgh, but Edinburgh is Scottish, with lean, tight-lipped old castle, standing alone. This is all French and as friendly as a sidewalk cafe. But do not inquire too deeply. On the bluffs above you is such a welter of spires, roofs, pinnacles, steeples, walls, monuments, and statues as only a guide book can distinguish—such a jumble of stone and mortar and labor that I never attempt to learn the names of its pieces, but am content to wander among them, aimlessly, as through a wood.

I always pause, however, at the tiny restaurant of M. Trudel, for I remember him in those spring days of 1939 when we waited here for the King of England. The plight of M. Trudel became through the press something of a national scandal, for all his relatives flocked to town and filled his house— Dominique with wife and three daughters from Sorel, Guillaume from Trois Rivières, with new bride, and countless cousins and aunts; and M. Trudel, having imported $25 worth of lobsters from the Bay of Fundy, for his special customers to celebrate the royal fête, had to hide them in the icebox and keep it under lock and key. Alas, when the King, long-delayed by fog, finally arrived, and M. Trudel opened his box, the lobsters were not fit for special customers any more. Guillaume tried them, but was ill, and the rest of the family refused to touch them, despite M. Trudel's urgings. In the end, though he was loyal to his sovereign, M. Trudel considered the royal tour little less than a financial disaster.

The modern streets of Quebec, the business streets, are to be avoided. They can only bring disenchantment, but the market I never miss. In the open square the fowls, pork, mutton, and vegetables are laid out in open carts, and the air is filled with the joint smell of them and with the shrill cries of farmers and their women and bargaining housewives, and perhaps you will see a well-dressed businessman filling a suitcase with green peas or onions for supper. Best of all, in the spring, the maple sugar is sold in bricks, or in little chalices made of white birchbark.

Through the maze of back streets you always end up at some outcropping of the rock, and you can crawl up it by narrow stone paths or by occasional iron stairways. Presently you will bump into the old city wall, rebuilt since Montcalm complained of it, but still girdling Quebec like a belt. Just outside it are the Parliament Buildings, square and lean, with solid towers, built since the great age, the old abandon of design and decoration compressed by the blight of Victorianism. But there are some fine murals inside and splendid red and green rooms, where Quebec politicians make their politics.

Politics they make very seriously in Quebec. These people have been brought up to politics, to law, to the classics. Every well-to-do farmer or tradesman wants his son to be an *avocat*, a doctor, or a priest. Most of the old aristocratic families are heard of no more; a lusty middle class, a comfortable and earthy bourgeois class, has risen to rule Quebec, and a poor country lawyer is the leader of the race, but still the classical tradition persists, and young French-Canadians find that they cannot compete in the crudities of modern industry with the young men of the English-speaking provinces. Yet, beside an educated French-Canadian, with his exquisite speech, his courtly manners, his fluid gestures and mobile face, the flowing cadence of his speech, any other North American must feel like a barbarian.

M. Langlois, a gorgeous old lad with white mane of hair, explained it to me with a sigh. "Our education, our life," said he, "is based on the premise that religion is the center of man's existence. Therefore, religious education comes first. Idealism is ahead of materialism. But our young man, trained in the classics, in the humanities, in religion, competes with a fellow who has studied engineering and business. Naturally, he is outdone. But we are learning."

Yes, learning our ways, learning business and industry, studying in technical schools. But will it mean the loss of something much more valuable? You wonder. Meanwhile the French-Canadian feels a sense of inferiority, and every so often a shrill cry of race is heard in these parliament buildings. A mountebank appears, carries the old torch among the villages, tells the habitants that the English are ruining them, that the English have all the best jobs, the capital and the power, and for a little while there is wild talk of an independent Quebec, a free French nation on the shores of the St. Lawrence. It is sure-fire, but never lasts.

Your French-Canadian is too shrewd not to know on what side his bread is buttered. By a law of 1774 the English, wiser than they were in the Thirteen Colonies, guaranteed the French-Canadian's religion, his language, his laws; and he knows they would be safe under no other flag. No state of the Union would ever enjoy such freedom and privileges as Canada has granted Quebec.

The two chief races of Canada have lived apart, seldom intermarrying, but they have learned to live in peace in a common country; and, though they were divided as never before by the first World War (which the French never considered their business) they are more united than ever by the second— a fact seldom noted by foreign journalists who visit Montreal for a day, talk to a few discredited politicians, and announce a deep schism in Canada. At this writing no schism has appeared, but the contrary. Yet if Canada should adopt a policy of complete military conscription and Quebec should oppose it as before, the old trouble might recur.

To the mountebank the French-Canadian listens and he may

cheer, and will accept a cigar or a drink on election day, but he is as canny and suspicious as a Scot. Here politics is a kind of game, a contest, an amusement for long winter evenings, and oratory is a skill as highly regarded as cricket in England or baseball in the States. French orators can say things that we would not say because in our mouths and our language they would sound ridiculous. When that greatest of orators, M. Lapointe, was swinging his people behind the war, no one was surprised when tears surged down his cheeks. Everybody wept with him.

There is also in the Frenchman a reverence for authority that no other North American knows. This country was founded under a feudal system in great seigneuries, where the seigneur could demand work, gifts, and taxes from the habitant land owners. Only a few months ago was the last remnant of this system repealed, the last rights of the old feudal landholders ended, with compensation. The French-Canadian has known no slogan like Liberty, Equality, Fraternity, has been untouched by the Revolution in France, has been scandalized by France's disorders, its anticlericalism, its materialism, and finally its fall. He has lived longer under a king than any other citizen of the western world, including the English, who once cut their king's head off.

The old seigneur has gone, but a tight and vigorous ruling class has taken his place, a class of rich men and professional politicians. Politics here is generally believed by Canadians to be more corrupt than in other parts of the country, but its ways are so devious, so much a part of another race, that the outsider never really understands it. The French-Canadian says his politics is only a little more frank than that of other provinces, a little more realistic, a little less hypocritical. Certainly it is based on a complete recognition that the elected are entitled to rule, the faithful are entitled to the jobs, and the party must be maintained like a well-organized commonwealth of its own.

Nowhere is the rich and distinguished man so respected. Instead of envying or condemning talent and success, the French-Canadian acclaims it, feels pleasure in it, feels that it honors him and his race. English Canada abolished titles of nobility years ago. The French-Canadian admires them and probably would like to see them restored, for his society is built up in clear stratification, orderly and sound, with the priest and the politician and the highly born unchallenged at the top.

Old M. Langlois sighed. Why, he asked, cannot the French remain the cultured, religious people, the protectors of the classics, the artists and dreamers while the English build the factories, work the machines? It is a pleasant fancy, but the modern world drives the French-Canadian out of his study, his classical university courses. Ah yes, it is true, says M. Langlois, the young no longer honor even the church as they should, but it is of no significance really. These young agnostics of twenty will be faithful sons of the church at forty, when they have sons of their own. Of course, there are "movements" in Quebec, some labor talk, but the labor unions are led by priests. What harm can come of them? A few priests may have "tendencies" but, if so, can be moved by the bishop to another parish.

The French-Canadian calls himself generally a Liberal in politics. He is the chief surviving Tory of the world.

I walk back to town by the narrow streets but substantial houses of Upper Town—respectable, stern houses, cheek by jowl, flush with the pavement, shuttered and mysterious, with the French touch of little courtyards, the English flavor of walled gardens. It is all clean, compact, solid, a city where a man expects to remain, to live his life out in the same house, while all America moves on and on, leaving behind a wake of slums.

Always as I walk these quiet streets I feel that behind the walls is a life, strange, exotic, rich, that I shall never see or know. Probably there are only ordinary people on the other side of these shutters, sitting down to a roast of beef and an apple pie, but I will never believe it. Still, somewhere there, if you could only peer through the keyhole, are candlelight, hooped skirts, swords, shoe buckles, fans, flirtations, and splendid adulteries—as in the Duke of Kent's square, ugly house, where that stout Georgian kept his mistress, amid routs, levees, and balls, so openly that it was no longer a scandal. Or in the forgotten house of Angélique des Meloises, the mistress of Bigot, that grafting treasurer who had ruined New France— Angélique des Meloises, the very name is a catalogue of intrigues, assignations, closed coaches, duels, feasts, and carnivals. Alas, they ended abruptly: Bigot went to jail in France and Angélique had to keep him in his old age, but her house is still there, with a kind of sweet scent about it. Montcalm thought it a fit place to die in.

It is the houses, not the monuments, squares, and public buildings that hold the life of Quebec, that intangible thing by which you may know a city (and there are not half a dozen in America), a living organism made of memories and joint toil and common suffering. But it must forever escape the stranger so that, looking at the shuttered window, the bolted door, he can only sense it, like a distant perfume, like the sound of voices behind a garden gate, forever closed to him.

Back of that again is the life of churches, of monasteries, convents, hospitals, of ascetic men living in prayer, and nuns toiling in kitchen, chapel, and sewing room, and in the Ursuline chapel a flame lit by Madeline de Repentigny in 1719 still burning—a teeming life, well ordered as a bee's hive, unchanging and content, but well hidden behind these walls so that you walk past them and shudder a little at their austerity, at the godlessness of your own ways.

The stranger always sees ghosts in Quebec. Guide books are filled with them. Female poets are constantly holding séances in the streets and public squares. No newspaper reporter but summons up the spirits of Frontenac and Champlain, who must grow rather tired of it.

Unhappily, I have never seen them. I have tried to summon them, but they do not come. Only in guide books can I find them and in bronze statues. Yet, in a spring evening on Maître Abraham's field, or on the brisk dawn of an autumn day, when the river is all splashed with red and yellow, I can believe that those wild spirits are still somewhere about. And perhaps old Frontenac, white and grizzled now, looks at Quebec, and at the nation beyond, and he says to Champlain: "Well, by God, Sam, it was worth the trouble after all!" And Champlain, the placid man, smiles contentedly and goes on digging in his little garden, his child wife by his side.

Canadian Spring

Spring rides into Canada upon the warm Japan Current. He lands quietly, without public greeting or knowledge, on the southern tip of Vancouver Island, one night in early March; or he may take a notion to come bursting in suddenly at the end of February, in raincoat and galoshes, but wearing violets and daffodils and primroses in his hat. With a wild shout down the western wind, he goes to work.

There are cones to be hung like Christmas candles on the great fir trees of the coast woods, and giant, shaggy sword ferns to be uncurled, and the tender, coiled stalks of maiden-hair, like the tight fists of newborn babies. There is the first white lily to be thrust up in a spinster's garden at Cadboro Bay and carried to town in triumph for display in the dingy windows of the Victoria Daily Colonist. *All the rock gardens require a fast, rough job of painting in quick daubs of purple and yellow. A thousand retired and tweeded British Colonels must be knocked up one morning early and warned that the trout are running in the Cowichan. The sea serpent of these parts, genial and obliging Cadborosaurus, must be awakened and reintroduced to the front pages of the local press. Old men must be hustled forth into Stanley Park to shiver a little as they begin their immemorial campaign of outdoor checkers on a board twenty feet square.*

Then, with a sigh and a sniff at the first rose, Spring is off for the interior country, following the gold-rush road to Cariboo. At Ashcroft he stops overnight to warn Joe Wong, the Chinaman, that he had better set out his tomato plants in the warming Dry Belt soil, each with a little paper tent over it.

Hastily he sprays the huge, red-barked pines with manly perfume and the sage brush with a clean, burning tang, and next day he sweeps the bare, round hills with a thin water-color wash of faintest green. And at last he releases a tide of pink apple blossom into the Okanagan Valley, standing by Kalamalka's bank to watch it churn and foam and billow for a hundred miles.

Now eastward again, he toils into the dark defiles of the Rockies, where the yellow avalanche lilies are waiting for his touch to leap out of bed a foot from the receding snow. That done, he heaves and grunts in many a slide of rock and gravel as he unlocks the winter ice, and presently the Fraser is roaring westward to the sea, fat and oily with its burden of mud, cutting a sharp, dirty line far out into the Gulf of Georgia.

In one leap Spring is on the prairies and racing eastward on the hot breath of a Chinook wind, telling the farmers to test the moisture of the earth, to repair their broken tractors and look to their stores of seed wheat. By the time he has reached the Great Lakes, the first green stalks of grain will be thrusting through the winter crust far behind him, and in Winnipeg the early crop of tin cans and ash heaps will be leaping up suddenly through the snow, and one day, long after he has passed by, Spring will be given a ponderous welcome on the editorial page of the Free Press.

Now the Lakes must be freed, the great economic lung of Canada started breathing again, the cigar-shaped grain ships thawed out of their winter's prison, and to the north, in the vast badlands of little trees, a million ponds must be melted, dog sleds must be stored away, canoes repaired, and hibernating settlers left blinking in the doorways of their cabins.

Next (oh, hurry now, for the time grows short!) the hardwood forests of Ontario must be set tardily at the year's work, jagged mountains of ice must be pushed out with a boom from the cold lips of Niagara, the long-growing whisker of icicles shaved off the chin of the canyon and sent hurtling down the St. Lawrence to the ocean.

With one stroke Spring wipes the glistening winter rime from the Gothic towers of Ottawa, sets the heavy carillon bells clanging above the river and, flitting into the dim House of Commons, he whispers into the ears of 245 politicians that it is time to discard winter underwear, to forget votes and divisions and rules of order, and go home. After that Politics, Spring's sworn enemy, can get no more work done.

From Parliament Hill, Spring steals down to Laurier House, puts the Prime Minister's beaver cap and grizzly bear coat into mothballs, remembers to release the imprisoned mosquito hordes of Rideau and Chaudière, and gently wakes the aged senators, who snooze in the Rideau Club.

Now he wades across the river into Quebec, listens for a moment to the first sound of wagon wheels in a melting village street, dawdles for a little among the birches, to try out upon their mottled trunks his new palette of black, white, purple, and faintest pink, and grudgingly goes to work in earnest on the maples, until into every farmhouse and backwoods shack a small boy comes rushing to shout: "Sap's runnin'!"

After making sure that the holes are bored, the spigots thrust into the oozing sapwood, the sap boiling with sweet smell in every iron syrup pot, Spring sighs a little to leave it all and sets out doggedly, on foot, for the Maritimes. There you may see him entangled in fish nets and lobster pots and brightly painted buoys, or swinging a calking hammer against the hull of a schooner, hard by a field where the new lambs are bawling. And in the evening you will find him in some cozy inn, at the edge of Fundy's Bay, glass in hand—rum, by preference, thick and dark, smuggled from the West Indies—telling some old sea dog that once more the job is done.

CHAPTER THREE

The Wood Choppers

When we swung out of the timber, on the rounded hill high above the St. Lawrence, the wind off Mount St. Anne hit us all at once, as if a door had been opened. The old mare hurried on, hoping to finish this disagreeable chore and return to her warm stable. Our little red sleigh lurched and creaked in the frozen ruts of the road. Jean and I snuggled deeper into the buffalo robe and pulled our fur caps down over our ears. Young Morel stood up in the front of the sleigh without a shiver, though he wore only a light windbreaker and nothing over his ears—a red-faced giant, beefy but hard, the kind of tough, jolly Frenchman whose fathers fought the Indians here and civilized Canada.

It was still winter up in the hills though spring had come to the banks of the river—deep winter in late March and, in our red sleigh with the bells jingling, we felt as if we were going to a Christmas party a hundred years ago. This was backwoods Quebec, not tourist country. This was the country of the wood-choppers, who have lived from the beginning not as farmers but in, by, and of the forest, until they are almost a part of it and have changed little and are unspoiled. Few Canadians have ever seen them.

We could see them now as we drove through the ragged string of villages wedged between the hills, which are jointly called St. Féréol. Most of the men were out in their front yards sawing wood with thin bucksaws, held taut by the semicircle of a bent sapling. They did not stop sawing as we passed. No man can stop sawing long in this climate. Life is sustained by cord-wood in the big, grinning Quebec stove, by pulpwood sold to the paper company, by logs for the sawmill. Always they saw and chop and burn, and the forest never fails.

How they live at all is a mystery beyond an Anglo-Saxon. Only the thrifty French could do it, with some woodcutting in the winter, a few months of work for the paper company in the woods and the toil of a few narrow, niggard acres in the summer. Among these people you are probably as far from the world as you could be in any inhabited part of America. Some of them have never been further than Quebec City, thirty miles up the river, some not that far.

In such villages in other parts of Canada you would find a settled melancholy, dull patience, and stark ugliness, but here was obviously an air of cheerfulness and family pride among these lost and ragged clusters of habitation. In the villages— a poor huddle of a dozen houses—the women were out paying afternoon calls with curious and strict formality, and some-how, tramping through the snowdrifts, they wore their cheap clothes, fresh out of a mail-order catalogue, with all the smart-ness of Montreal. They were French and knew the ancient secret. I tried to raise my fur hat to them (a loan from young Morel), but it was far too cold for that. Yet the women of St. Féréol strode along the rutted road, chattering comfortably, with flowered hats of the latest style perched on the tops of their heads.

A priest in flat black hat and flowing black robes slipped past on skis, going swiftly like a witch on a broomstick. An old man, on his way from the kitchen to an errand in a little house at the rear, paused modestly until we passed, then resumed his journey. Everywhere the men, in caps with fur-lined earflaps, overalls, and rubber-soled, high boots, sawed away at the heaped-up birch poles, and chopped woodpiles almost as large as their houses. The children stood silent and wide-eyed at the roadside to watch us. Everywhere we passed bobsleds loaded clumsily with logs and poles. There were dogsleds, too, frail contraptions, each hauled by a single dog and bearing a man or a few parcels from the store.

Mile after mile stretched the narrow road between the Christmas trees, but always far off and far below lay the broad bluish streak of the river, and always in every hollow a little band of houses huddled together like sheep, out of the wind.

The houses were taken straight out of a picture book. The oldest were of stone, of the beautiful early French design, long and low, with great chimneys at either end, and the newer buildings, made of wood, were full of fantastic conceits which nobody but a Frenchman would attempt. All the doorways were ornamented with fretwork, brightly painted, and the window frames were colored in combinations of red, yellow, blue. In every window potted plants were blooming and through the white lace curtains peered the faces of women, watching us. Few strangers pass this way, only the heavy-laden wood sleighs.

Like a picture book, yes. And the main village of St. Féréol, cuddling up to the lean spire of its stone church, looked like a composite of all the village pictures, on all the colored advertising calendars of the world. It looked, in the distance, except for the snow, like Stow-on-the-Wold, like a hundred spired villages in the Cotswolds, in France, in Switzerland, or in Austria. But up close, the villages and houses, so picturesque at a distance, were generally in need of paint and a little run down. This is poor country. The woods will keep you alive, buy your wife a dress out of the catalogue, but no more.

The mare kicked up her heels as we turned back, knowing she was bound for home, and we nearly froze before we got there. Down by Morel's Hotel, the grass was beginning to turn a little green and they thought the maple sap might be running tomorrow.

The ancient hotel of M. Morel *père* has stone walls two feet thick, standing these hundred and fifty years, and great warmth, shiny new paint everywhere, and a kind of genial, chaotic hospitality. The first thing Jean said, in her appalling French, was that she had studied very well the language when she was a little boy at school and added: "The room of the eating, where is it that she declares herself?" She declared herself downstairs, we were glad to find, with a wondrous gallery of colored prints picturing the battle of Omdurman, the blood of the wounded fairly flowing over the walls, ivy growing up along the ceiling, and a stuffed pheasant strutting in the corner. And, of course, the inevitable pea soup which only a Quebec housewife really understands how to make, the only truly national Canadian dish so far invented.

After that, we sat in the parlor which declared itself above, with a stuffed white owl, a gigantic waterfowl, unidentified, a colored print of King George V made when he was under forty, a reproduction of "The Angelus," and a radio. Always a radio, in the smallest cottage, with French coming over it from Montreal. Ideas are flowing in here, into the towns and smallest villages. What these ideas are doing to Quebec, how they are changing the old values and the old virtues, how much they are helping to unite the two races of Canada and break down old barriers—this is one of the great imponderables and unknowables of Canadian life.

A couple of young French-Canadians were living at Morel's —engineers from the big paper mill down the road. They talked, in flawless English, about the mill, about their work, about costs, markets, methods of manufacture. Here was the basic change that sweeps the old French province—young men learning to compete with the English-speaking Canadians in their own business, in manufacturing, in modern technics.

All up and down the St. Lawrence the smoke of English-speaking capital billows up beside the French church spires, hard by the little narrow farms which, cut and re-cut, handed from father to son, all run down to the river edge. Back in the hills the streams and rivers are dammed for power by English-speaking corporations. Quebec, which was agricultural, peasant, as simple as St. Féréol, is being industrialized by the enterprisers of the other provinces. French people leave their farms to live in the new industrial towns and cities, and there they find that life is not what they used to think. It is infinitely more complex and difficult and glittering. There are pleasures they never heard of, and economic problems, class problems, wage problems unknown back in the village, where the curé could settle anything, from birth to death. Instead of the curé there are here agitators who stir them up against the owning class and against the English-speaking Canadians. Soon Quebec begins to develop a self-conscious proletariat, where it had once only a carefree peasantry.

The church grows worried. Some of the people in the towns are skeptical and question the old teachings. The ruling classes are worried also. The politicians find all sorts of new pressures, new cries, and new notions. An attempted New Deal by a group of charlatans, fattening on this blind new urge, has plunged the thrifty province into debt.

What is happening to Quebec, the most conservative, peaceful, innocent part of the whole New World? Civilization is coming to Quebec, that is all. The civilization of machines. From the window we would see the dark smokestacks of the mill and hear its whistle. Up and down the river, and back into the vast wooded interior, whistles are blowing and men are herding together as they have herded in every other aging civilization, as they herded into Rome.

These young engineers could drive to Quebec City any evening in half an hour to see a movie. Soon a new highway would cut the drive down to twenty minutes, if you hit it up to eighty miles an hour, which would be quite safe, they said. A few miles away, up in the hills of St. Féréol, men were squatting on dog sleighs.

Back of us here, a few miles from the river, is still the country of legend and poetry. Not far off, as the crow flies, is Peribonka, where Louis Hémon wrote *Maria Chapdelaine,* perhaps the only true Canadian classic, a story so simple, unadorned, and perfect that it lingers forever in your mind like the memory of an old song, learned in your childhood. It tells of these people's lust for the land, of the first plowing and the smell of clearing fires and the sudden-surging spring. It tells of the first settlement in these woods, of men cutting down trees, hewing out stumps, sowing their first seed, and dying in their little cabins, with a priest kneeling beside them. It tells of Francois Paradis, who walked through a blizzard to see his sweetheart, until the wolves got him.

It was not written of another age, but of this. The Bédard family, for whom Hémon worked as a farm hand (refusing more than $8 a month because he lacked experience, having newly come from France), is still at Peribonka, and the original of the immortal Maria, now plump and middle-aged, has been seen there by many visitors, as if you could summon up the original Evangeline, or Tom Sawyer, or the last of the Mohicans. She will live as long as Canada.

Hémon died before he could write another book, died at the right time for an artist, when he had reached perfection and before he could fall below it—a single book, one masterpiece. But life remains still as he knew it, once you leave the river and the mill town, and always the proliferating French race pushes on still further, gnawing back the forest.

This is the primitive Quebec that Henry Drummond knew —that Irish doctor who suddenly discovered, better than they knew it themselves, the life of the French habitant, whose poems in habitant dialect remain the true picture of an era and a people. As we sat in the parlor of M. Morel a pretty housemaid with a dark, roving eye, swept the floor, humming at her work. Here was Drummond's Nice Leetle Canadienne:

> *Don't matter how poor dat girl she may be,*
> *Her dress is so neat an' so clean,*

Mos' ev'rywan t'ink it was mak' on Paree
And she wear it, wall! just lak de Queen.
But if she love you, I spik it for true,
She will mak' it more beautiful den,
And sun on de sky can't shine lak de eye
Of dat nice leetle Canadienne.

Have you never heard of Bateese Trudeau who went to "leeve on State"? It is the story of Quebec's continual migrations into Maine and Massachusetts—and the story of one who came back with the handsome American name of John B. Waterhole, but returned a second time, broke, and simple Bateese Trudeau now for good. And who knows Canada if he cannot recite "The Wreck of the Julie Plante," when "de night was dark lak' wan black cat" and:

De win' she blow lak' hurricane,
Bimeby she blow some more,
An' de scow bus' up on Lac St. Pierre,
Wan arpent from de shore.

Alas, they were all corpses on the river sand next morning, the gallant captain, the crew, and the Rosie Girl, that unhappy cook who had been a chambermaid on a lumber barge on de Grand Lachine Canal. And every Canadian remembers the closing advice to go and marry some nice French girl and "leev on wan beeg farm," for

De win' can blow lak' hurricane,
An' spose she blow some more,
You can't get drown on Lac St. Pierre
So long you stay on shore.

It is as much a part of our Canadian legend, this story of the "Julie Plante," as is "Alouette," that deathless song of the plucked lark. Three Canadians cannot get drunk together without bellowing "Alouette, Gentille Alouette!" one of them standing on a table to shout the verses, the others roaring out the chorus. The words are absurd, without meaning, and yet mean Canada, from the tundra of the north to the battlefields of the Old World, and they dim the eyes of every Canadian who hears them in a foreign land.

This backwoods country is the home also of the French songs that came out of Normandy and are as old as Charlemagne, of *"Sur le Pont d'Avignon"* and that haunting lilt, *"À la Claire Fontaine,"* which was sung in Europe before America was discovered and is still sung in the Quebec shack, uncorrupted. They have always been a singing people, singing to the beat of their paddle on the river, singing on the long portages, and in Indian villages and on the balconies of Quebec.

Happily men like Marius Barbeau in the National Museum at Ottawa have gathered these songs on gramophone records, sung by the old professional singers who used to make their living at it, and they will never be forgotten. Yet to the English ear, a few stray lines written by the Irish poet, Moore, after a canoe trip down the St. Lawrence, seem to hold better the magic of the river:

> *Row, brothers, row, the stream runs fast,*
> *The rapids are near and the daylight's past.*

There are the voyageurs, paddling and singing in the dusk, from Gaspé to Michilimackinac.

It is the country of legend and superstition also, where a man may be turned into a *loup-garou,* a bewitched ox or dog, where the devil has often been seen paddling through the air in his huge canoe, where goblins may get into your stables and tie your horse's mane into knots and you must drive them out by hanging up a palm branch blessed by the curé on Palm Sunday. Why, everyone knows that, on the island of Bic, Indian ghosts dance where the Micmacs were burned by the Iroquois in their caves; and who has not heard of the curé of L'Islet, who was given a black demon horse by the good Lord to help him build a church, and when a workman unbridled the beast, he flew away into the mountain, making the Devil's Hole, where all kinds of accidents and misfortunes occurred until a cross was erected there? And Frank Oliver Call, who collected such folklore, tells how the men of Trois Pistoles went out on the river ice to kill 700 seals, and when the ice was carrying them, helpless, out to sea, the women rushed to their church to pray, and the wind, suddenly changing, blew them all safely home again.

The young engineers at M. Morel's smiled at these old tales, but miracles of healing, at the shrine of St. Anne, two miles away? Ah, those were different. Those were miracles. Next morning being Sunday, both of the young men rose at 6 A.M. for Mass and came home to bed again afterward.

We strolled down from the hotel through the village of Beaupré, which, despite its mill, maintains its virginity fairly intact—the long, single street, paralleling the river, the fretted woodwork of many colors, the mansard roofs and, here and there, the original stone houses, long and low with double chimneys, and finally a wondrous house with stunted tower, latticework and fretwork like old embroidery, indescribably hideous but affable, giggling and good-hearted, like a respectable retired prostitute.

The mill and the resulting prosperity have brought new houses but they lack the true beauty of the very old or the friendly ugliness of the middle-aged. They are all ghastly, square, protuberant, with weird iron stairways leading to the second stories, and without the redemption of humor or fancy. Across the little river the mill company's new townsite, cut in two by the huge, stilted flume, is filled with English cottages and we were startled to hear children shouting in English at their play. It was a new sound. The English executives and some workmen have come to Quebec, even while the French-Canadians are pushing ever further into the other provinces. The French and English children played here together, between the legs of that monstrous insect, the flume. Perhaps it was a portent.

At the far end of the bridge, across the little river, is the shop of Madame Fournier, *pharmacie et épicerie,* where the children's nursery rhymes of all the world must have been written. It is the shop in Wonderland where Alice bought her candy, and it is littered with sweets, biscuits, and toys, and colored rubber balls are suspended from the ceiling, and the shelves are crammed with whistles and pencils and scribblers, and an old lady in spectacles blinks wisely behind the counter. One by one, as the bell on the door tinkles, the children file in shyly, each with a red toque and mittens, to choose lollypops out of the big glass jars.

As we sat there, drinking a cup of Madame Fournier's tea, the sleigh bells jingled in the melting snow of the village street. It was the last touch needed to complete the illusion of childhood.

An old man, with a plume of white hair and a bristling outer fringe of white whisker, sat in a corner smoking gravely, and his son, a youth in his twenties, was drinking pop. The son talked to us in English, told us of his job in the mill and how he had driven his own car as far as Toronto. When he began to talk about the progress of the war, his father still listened, without a word, peering at him suspiciously under bristling white eyebrows.

"He doesn't speak English," the son said. "My brothers and me, we speak always English when we don't want him or my mother to understand. Boy, does it make them sore!"

He turned to the old man in a kind of apology. *"La guerre,"* he said. The father understood then what we had been talking about, and at once his eyes lighted up, he clenched his fist and jumped to his feet. Then, for ten minutes by the pendulum clock in the corner, he gave us his opinion of Hitler. There was nothing cheap or hackneyed about it, no mere calling of names. The old man had the eloquence of his race, with nuances and overtones of invective too subtle for me to grasp, and I suppose I missed the best of it. At least I understood the final passage as he shook his finger under my nose—"butchery for the sake of butchery, blood for the pleasure of blood, murder for the joy of murder!"

Then he sat down again and puffed his pipe calmly, as if nothing had happened.

"He used to be a deputy in the legislature," his son said, rather proudly. "He used to hate the English. Now he hates Hitler worse." And there was another portent.

M. Morel *père,* a vigorous, red-faced man in his fifties, came along in his car then (he called it "la may-sheen") and drove us down the river, past the mill to St. Joachim to see the old church there. In the vestibule a small boy was unloading firewood from a sleigh hauled by a big dog. An old woman, all in black, prayed in one of the huge pews, her lips moving silently.

M. Morel pointed proudly at the organ loft, the golden apostles at the altar, the carved and painted wood everywhere. It was *très belle,* he said, and *très ancienne.* He spoke of it with as much local pride as a member of a Rotary Club would speak of a new city hall or civic abattoir.

We drove on down to Le Petit Cap, a high nose of land, jutting boldly into the St. Lawrence, where there is a kind of summer retreat for priests—a huge barracks, wooden-beamed and rough-hewn, utterly bare inside, with a room for the Cardinal of Quebec which lacks ornament or comfort of any kind.

A little boy brought out a key almost as large as himself and led us through the snow to a white chapel which stood alone in a glade of elms and was more like an English church in an English churchyard than anything I have ever seen on this side of the Atlantic. Opening the door with the big key, the boy pulled the bell cord, for our amusement, and a fierce peal quivered for a second in the woods and rolled out across the river, far below.

In this little church, with its whitewashed walls, cold after a winter of disuse, you caught for a moment something of the peace, the confidence and the enduring power of the Faith, far from the big mill, the modern highway, the worldliness of Quebec City. How long this bell has pealed over the river! How long will it continue to ring in the spring and hang silent in the winter woods?

Next morning M. Morel *fils* appeared to drive us to the city. Yesterday he had been the rough woodsman standing in the sleigh, untouched by the cold. Today he appeared in gray fedora, silk scarf, new overcoat and spats, with a new automobile. You would not have found a better-dressed man on Fifth Avenue, nor a better-looking. He could speak no English, but his pretty wife could, having lived in Montreal. She wore the latest fashion and so did her little girl, who, let us hope, will be but the first of another big generation of Morels.

The road up to Quebec, never far from the river, passed always, as in France, down the swarming main streets of the villages, and there seemed to be a village every half mile— unmistakably French, with high galleries where you could sit gossiping with the neighbors, and a church and a florid silver tower, and Apostles and Christs in gilt everywhere. Then a few roadside shrines and finally, at St. Anne's, the giant basilica.

Some Breton sailors built the first shrine here to make good a vow they had taken when they were threatened with shipwreck. When the second shrine was being built in 1660 a stone mason, crippled with rheumatism, uttered a prayer and was miraculously healed. Since the wrist bones of the Saint herself were presented to the parish by Bishop Laval in 1670 the miracles here have become known to Catholics all over the world. In the old church, which was burned, you could see the hundreds of crutches abandoned by those who were instantly healed. Above the towered and rich basilica, a miniature city of little chapels, massive convents, churches, and golden statues has sprung out of the soil. Everywhere the church, everywhere the French instinct for florid ornament, which prompts these people, with perfect reverence, to put cluster lights around the golden figure of Jesus.

The narrow village streets were crowded today, for it was Sunday, and after Mass the young people were all out visiting, the boys in their new store clothes, the girls a trifle overdressed —for us—but not for them. They could wear it.

Ornament they love, and festival. On Corpus Christi Day, through these streets they would move in procession, carrying the Host, with crosses and candles and chants, with priests in their vestments and choirs in their surplices, and little girls in white dresses, scattering flowers, and every house would be decorated with flowers, and everywhere saplings would be thrust into the ground. Or at Christmas the great midnight Mass here and in every city, town, and village would fill every church, and afterwards every house would provide a feast.

As we drove through the villages today the church bells were ringing—always the bells, up and down the river, the bells that the homing voyageurs used to hear at their weary paddles, that every stranger still hears as he comes up the river, that you may hear from the deck of your liner as it slides between the lush banks, where the cows are grazing, a few yards from the deck. Always the sound of bells on the river.

As we left it all behind I remembered what Louis Hémon had written in his story of Maria Chapdelaine—this young Frenchman who, coming here, had leaped across the separation of three centuries and felt the blood of these people in his veins:

Three hundred years ago we came, and we have remained. They who led us hither might return among us without knowing shame or sorrow, for if it be true that we have little learned, most surely nothing is forgot.

We bore oversea our prayers and our songs; they are ever the same. We carried in our bosoms the hearts of the men of our fatherland, brave and merry, easily moved to pity as to laughter, of all human hearts the most human; nor have they changed. We traced the boundaries of a new continent, from Gaspé to Montreal, from St. Jean d'Iberville to Ungava, saying as we did it: Within these limits all we brought with us, our faith, our tongue, our virtues, our very weaknesses are henceforth hallowed things which no hand may touch, which shall endure to the end.

Strangers have surrounded us whom it is our pleasure to call foreigners; they have taken into their hands most of the rule, they have gathered to themselves much of the wealth; but in this land of Quebec nothing has changed. Nor shall anything change, for we are the pledge of it. Concerning ourselves and our destiny but one duty have we clearly understood: that we should hold fast—should endure. And we have held fast, so that, it may be, many centuries hence the world will look upon us and say: These people are of a race that knows not how to perish. We are a testimony.

For this is it that we must abide in that Province where our fathers dwelt, living as they have lived, so to obey the unwritten command that once shaped itself in their hearts, that passed to ours, which we in turn must hand on to our descendants innumerable. In this land of Quebec naught shall die and naught shall suffer change.

Nobler words have seldom been written in English. These were written in Quebec by one who had become a Canadian.

But Quebec will change. It is changing. The machine is coming to Quebec, and the thing we call civilization. Yet still the bells peal along the river, above the whistle of the mill.

Letter from Montreal to Young Lady with Violets

MY DEAR JOAN:

For twelve years now, and some weeks, since you were born, you have lived next door to us in Saanich, and it is hard to remember any time when you were far away; harder to realize that, at this moment, you are on the other side of the continent, picking violets, while we watch the snow fall here in Montreal, blotting out the hump of Mount Royal, covering all the statues and church steeples with white frosting. Yet we have proof of it, alas, in the box which you sent us. It was full of your violets, picked a few days ago on Vancouver Island.

The violets in the box, I am compelled to tell you, are withered, but as evidence they will serve. The violet clump under the old plum tree still thrives and flowers in December, and that is what we wanted to be sure about. You will not remember it, but the violet clump is only a happy accident. You were too small to remember anything then, and your only contribution to the garden was your habit of sowing green peas and carrots in all directions, if we were unwise enough to let you get your hands upon the spring seed packages. Well, a man named Smith gave us the violets; and, though the name is not uncommon, we have always thought of them as the Smith violets, a rare family. For you will note that they are of remarkable size, with little orange-colored eyes in the center, of a specially brilliant hue, and their scent can be detected fifty feet away. A whiff of it still lingers in them, withered as they are, here in Montreal, where a blizzard is raging in the street outside our window. (What a wide and varied country ours is, my dear Joan!)

Mr. Smith says he brought the violets from New England and tells a fabulous tale of their origin in England long ago, but we were too busy in those days to pay much attention to the antiquities of gardening. We were young as gardeners then and you were barely three years old. So I hardly think you will recall the day that Mr. Smith drove out to our newly acquired acres in Saanich and presented us with the violet roots, wrapped in a grimy newspaper. You were engaged at the moment in strewing scarlet runner beans in eccentric circles on the vegetable garden. (We had not yet discovered the stratagem of giving you rice to sow, which would not germinate.) So we were pretty short with Mr. Smith. We couldn't afford to leave you long alone in the garden.

When Mr. Smith had gone, we looked wildly about, and, seeing a patch of vacant earth beneath the old plum tree, we scooped out a little hole and tramped the violets in and forgot them. Then, next spring, you suddenly appeared in your ragged tweed coat (made over from a pair of your father's old golf trousers), and at your heels was your first dog, Nipper, whose father was a bulldog and whose mother, you said, was a "rough-haired terror," and clutched in your plump, red, and earthy hand was a bunch of violets. You had found the forgotten plants under the plum tree.

No, you do not remember that. Nor the joint commercial enterprise undertaken with your brother when you gathered all the Smith violets and, wrapping them in bits of ribbon, peddled them throughout the neighborhood (price one penny or a cookie), grasped so tightly in your hot little hands that they were withered before the last sale.

Thus the Smith violets became your violets, and you are picking them again, while we live here in a steam-heated room in Montreal and the snow drives against the windowpanes. You *are sniffing the sweetness of them in the evening and watching their impudent, orange-colored eyes that belie their shy look. And as you stand up, with a bunch of them in your hand, do you still see the globules of rain on the fine twigs of the plum tree and, looking at them closely, observe the outlines of the earth and sky reflected in them, like a glistening little world, all complete? And are the robins calling already, and the frogs croaking down in the swamp, and have you seen the turtle in the lily pond yet?*

Do not answer, my dear Joan. And send us no more violets to remind us of our exile here in the snow of Montreal. Let them grow there as they will, in the ground they settled and made their own with help much better than ours. And when you stand up, your hands full of violets, and see the world imprisoned in a hanging drop of rain water, observe how small it is, and remember that we are only at the other side of it, and will return one day, perhaps before the last of the Smiths has retired for the season. Send no more violets to Montreal, for it only makes us homesick, makes us realize suddenly how big a girl you are getting to be, and that soon we shall have no one to pick the first blossoms under the plum tree.

CHAPTER FOUR

Ville Marie

Montreal is the second French city of the world, much too large for the country behind it, swarming with over a million people out of Canada's entire eleven millions, far gone in the dropsical American disease of size, and its urgent skyscrapers, like weeds in a garden, are crushing out the last relics of a great and noble history.

Quebec, though thirty-four years older, is spry, bright-eyed, fascinating, unmistakably the grand dame. Montreal is losing her figure, tries to hide it under diamonds, fur coats, and rouge, and she appears in public with a shaven poodle on a leash, escorted by a stout gentleman who owns a railway, some banks, and an indifferent digestion.

But Montreal is still as much the metropolis of Canada as New York is of the United States—not by size alone, but by consent, by tradition, force, history, and sheer character. Everybody goes to Montreal. Through the Windsor Station, as through the Grand Central, flow all the tides of the world, and in the old Windsor Hotel, which somehow has refused to be hurried, you eventually meet everyone.

The money of Canada has drained for three centuries into Montreal. The toil of farmers on the prairies, of trappers up north, of lumberjacks in the New Brunswick woods, of fishermen on the West Coast has built up here our only great city, with a great city's daily habits; our chief accumulation of wealth, rich living, and true metropolitan attitude; the city's cast of mind and, you might say—if the word had not been seduced and bedeviled in the advertising columns—its glamour. Montreal is one of the half dozen cities in America that can be compared with the seasoned and settled cities of Europe, the rest being only small towns with growing pains.

You pass the shuttered houses of Quebec and dream of old-fashioned gallantry and forgotten loves. You pass the ostentatious houses of Montreal and glimpse visions of modern riches, butlers, maids, flunkies. You see the master class, an overstuffed but genteel luxury, something like that of Park Avenue and Long Island, but with an entirely different flavor, a certain added elegance and floridity which is French.

You are likely to forget, in your wonderment, where all this came from. It came out of the labor of millions of poor Canadians, far from Montreal, by a cunning arrangement of geography and economics, and it lives, this splendid life of Westmount and Mount Royal, on top of a teeming slum, as luxury does everywhere.

The lady with the diamonds and poodle never strays far enough from the spacious sweep of Sherbrooke Street to see anything unpleasant, but be fair to her. She is a patron of the arts. She maintains great institutions of learning and a costly system of churches and charities. She possesses perhaps the only real manners, in the old-world sense, to be found in any sizable quantity in Canada. Beside her, Toronto or Vancouver, equally prosperous, look like the wives of men who have just made a fortune in oil.

If you see her in the Windsor dining room, or at the Ritz, drinking wine with her luncheon, perhaps accompanied by one of her beautiful daughters, you will be fascinated, despite her expanding girth. You will gawk and stare at these two ladies of Montreal, sipping their wine, exchanging their gossip (in French, of course) with such a tinkling music of language, with gestures so exquisite, with such a perfect wearing of clothes and sparkle of jewels, with such a touch of felicity as will be found nowhere else except in the movies, where it is rehearsed. And, watching these incredible creatures, you long for a life more fortunate, more exciting, more splendid than you can ever hope to see. Unfortunately, Montreal has other daughters who do not drink wine with their lunch and have never set foot inside the Windsor.

To catch a quick and convenient glance of Montreal, take the early morning train up to Ottawa. It is kind of a rite with us, a communal custom, the morning train to Ottawa. Everybody will be on it, and it is your perfect chance to study the Canadian ruling class.

It is the only place in Canada where you will be sure of seeing every lady in fashion, every man well tailored, for as a people we don't know much about clothes. We have invented none of our own and have been content to imitate the Americans, who don't know anything about them either. But at least on the Ottawa train everyone will be strictly in style: sleek Montreal bankers who have generally managed to run Canada; corporation lawyers; perhaps one of those witty French-Canadian advocates who can make our courts sound like a trial in a good stage play; a few of the abler French-Canadian politicians, plump, pink, healthy, with ties a trifle too vivid; and transplanted London businessmen in short black coats and striped gray trousers.

I like to sit and watch them, as the train races up the valley of the Ottawa, and ponder the Canadian character. This is not it, of course. This is the thin, glittering surface of it, supported by a deep sea of plain, poor people, but you can start here and look downward.

You will find no real answer, no clear definition of the Canadian. You could easily write a dozen definitive adjectives beside the name of the Englishman and everyone would recognize him; or beside the Frenchman, German, or Chinese. The American is not quite as clear, having so many elements, but he is clear enough. The Canadian, however, leaving aside the distinctive and clear-cut people of Quebec, is still a blur, just emerging now into clear lines. In a world which is supposed to be all organized, classified, pigeonholed, and card-indexed, you see in Canada the interesting phenomenon of an important nation, the world's sixth trader, the second member of the British Commonwealth, still in the very middle of gestation. The character of the final offspring no man can guess.

The Englishman often thinks the Canadian just another American, who somehow didn't join the Revolution. No Canadian can travel in England without being taken for a Yankee, because of our speech. The American comes here and finds us British, a little stiff in spots and with a slightly English accent —though God knows we are nasal enough in Ontario and the Maritimes, clipped enough in the prairies, and with only a vague flavor of English speech in British Columbia. Of course, we are neither English nor American. We are, rather to our own surprise, Canadian.

The American can feel the sudden difference as soon as he changes at Montreal West from the New York to the Ottawa train. Not merely in speech (though it is certainly different, usually more rapid, with a broader a and a much harder r), but in the attitude, tempo, outlook, and, perhaps, in the more subdued manner.

No two peoples in the world, of course, resemble one another so closely and none have got along so well together, but the common assumption that Americans and Canadians are identical is definitely wrong and not particularly helpful. What the whole difference is, no one has ever been quite able to say. The Canadian certainly is more conservative than the American, less demonstrative and less frank on first acquaintance. He is not so bold and emotional either, and not so restless or so nervous as a rule. The Canadian is not quite so democratic and open in social contact and he is more aware, I suspect, of the inequality of men, which is denied by the Declaration of Independence but confirmed in every street and every apartment house of this continent.

The Americans are much more of a race than we are, much more of a type, nearer complete achievement in breeding. They have a far deeper sense of nationality, community, and interdependence, having stood on their own feet, without overseas support, much longer than we. They are far more of a nation, as any frank Canadian must admit.

Not only that. The Americans have an energy, a bursting exuberance and nervous force which always amazes and rather frightens us. When I go to Washington, when I have been with Americans on such adventures as a presidential election train, I am overwhelmed and left limp, as is any Canadian, by the astounding activity and speed of these people. I admire it, as all Canadians do, and fear it. I have the feeling that it will snap at any minute from sheer exhaustion, and when it is still going strong at midnight and I am tottering, I stop trying to understand it.

The Canadian has a greater reverence for tradition than his neighbor, sometimes too much. He has also a greater respect for law and order, has never known a lynching in modern times, nor gang wars, nor high-class crime. He is slower to change and slower to get excited. A Canadian electorate is about as inspiring as a dead mackerel compared with the drama of a presidential campaign. This is not good for our Canadian democracy.

The British Throne is an interesting, if not a vital index of Canadian character. The Throne suits Canadians not because it is British only, but because it works satisfactorily. It is a successful instrument of government, modified drastically to meet our needs. If it were not practical and useful it wouldn't last ten years in this country. In addition to this pragmatic reasoning, the Canadian, for all his Americanism, usually regards the Throne still with a certain secret emotion, not as anything divine, compulsory, or even clever, but as a kind of outward and visible sign of courage and decency and honor, which he would like to believe are inside him. These things it is not good form to mention, but they must have some convenient repository.

The Canadian character is a blend of three distinct elements —British, French-Canadian, and American. The American influence, naturally, is winning out. How could it fail? Upon the basic stratum of British and French-Canadian conservatism, every day a thin new layer of vigorous Americanism is washed in by the waves of radio, movies, magazines. Nothing can stop this northward-flowing tide of ideas where only about 5 per cent of the people were born in Britain and only half are of British extraction. We are becoming a British nation more by institutions, policies, forms of government, laws and living ways than by blood.

An Englishman can seldom become a Canadian. The English people's chief strength is that they can never be nor want to be anything but English. An Englishman of middle age who settles in Canada is likely to eat here the rest of his life, but to live in England. That is what made England great. It will not make Canada great. The English youth, however, turns into a Canadian, and his son belongs outright to the New World. The Scotsman, as everywhere, adapts himself instantly to the new country and usually ends by governing it.

A certain type of superior Englishman causes only irritation here. We don't want him to tell us what to do, even if he happens to know better than we. Perhaps it would be more accurate to say that generally we are attracted less to the individual Englishman than to the character of the English race, which is so much a part of us. This admiration—never so high as during the present war—is wholly good except when it occasionally degenerates into a conscious colonialism, a kind of butler's mind, which is a very disagreeable thing to encounter.

A few colonial Canadians thus find it hard to face the fact that Canada is not another England, but not many. Yet none of us can visit our ancestral homes in England without deep emotion. No Canadian sees England for the first time without a sudden realization of Canada's youth, its rawness, and disorder and the centuries of labor needed to tame it.

To Canada the Englishman brings the virtues of discipline, public obligation, and "the right thing," which we need, and, if he frequently irritates us and sometimes drives Canadian governments almost frantic, Canadian boys, again and again, have gladly died for England.

The Americans we have liked and disliked by turns in our early days, but, until lately, we have seldom understood them. We have liked their ability to get things done, envied their vigor and great projects, and rather disliked their habit of slapping one on the back when sober. But we have seldom understood the real, solid substance of American life because we have generally seen in magazines, movies, and radio only the froth. No nation has been more misrepresented than the United States, with all its instruments of information. The wonder is that, through all this, Canadians and Americans have been the best international friends ever known on the earth.

Above all, the Canadian character is the result of twenty years of disillusionment. It has a sense of frustration and failure and lack of a clear road, a concerted national drive. It has a sense of fumbling, a desperate desire to get somewhere, to be something.

All these words don't help much. I do not know and I suspect that nobody knows what makes the difference north and south of the border, but it is there. Making a broad guess at it, Canada is different because the mark of the frontier is still plainer on us, because we are still a little closer to the soil and the forest, a little poorer and more simple and unsophisticated, less brittle, less jumpy, and not so clever.

If we would recognize these differences instead of attempting to ignore them or sweep them away with after-dinner speeches; if we would admit on both sides that Canadians and Americans are not precisely the same, it would do much to bring us together. It is the expectation that both peoples will behave precisely alike on all occasions that has made for occasional annoyance in the past and may do so again.

You are not annoyed when a Chinaman eats with chopsticks, because it is his custom, but you won't dine with a fellow countryman who eats with his knife, because he is supposed to observe your code of manners. It will make North America the stronger and richer if Canadians develop their own character, are not absorbed and completely overlaid by American culture, but are allowed to make their distinct contribution to the whole.

Montreal, which has been lost in the rush of these speculations, manages to stand out against the American tide a little better than most places. It is, to begin with, a unique habitation, sprouting out of an island in the middle of the St. Lawrence, with a lush green mountain in the middle of it. Cartier, the first white man, came up here in 1535 and found a weird community of savages living in their own fort, behind powerful wooden walls, growing their own food with organized agriculture, and calling their town Hochelaga. Paul de Chomédy de Maisonneuve landed here in 1642, sprang ashore, and fell down on his knees in a prayer of thanks for such a townsite, and at an improvised altar a priest said Mass and predicted: "You are as a grain of mustard seed that shall rise and grow till its branches overshadow the earth."

There, at the junction of the St. Lawrence and the Ottawa, beside the Indian village, Maisonneuve and his forty-three settlers built their town of Ville Marie, hugging the side of Mount Royal. All trade out of the west, north, and south soon flowed through Ville Marie, by the logic of geography, and has never ceased to flow.

Out of Montreal went LaSalle, searching for a route to China, and returned to have his seigneury west of the town called Lachine—in irony at his failure. Out of Ville Marie went the hunters and trappers and traders. Out of Ville Marie went young Dollard with sixteen followers who, after taking communion and vowing to die, held up the Iroquois at the

Long Sault, fought for eight days in a ruined stockade against seven hundred warriors, were killed to the last man but saved the town—surely one of the world's great tales of courage, but unknown, unsung, because Canada has not yet found its poet or its voice.

Now, looking at the Island of Montreal as Cartier did, from Mount Royal (which supplied the city's modern name) you could hardly guess that it was the product of cavaliers, voyageurs, Indian fighters, and missionaries. At first sight the dark chimneyed sweep of the city on the river flat, with the broad glint of the river, the thin line of bridges, and the Green Mountains of Vermont faint to the south, is like the appearance of many other American cities.

Then you notice the upthrust of church spires everywhere, the green copper domes and frail steeples, through the billows of green foliage. Montreal is different because it has architecture, and most of it the work of the Catholic Church. Only a few North American cities have any concerted scheme of architecture; Montreal is rich and prodigal with it, has statues at every corner, noble buildings on every street, like an old European city but, still hugging its mountain, it has never quite lost touch with the forest that Maisonneuve found there long ago.

The trees still grow in streets like Sherbrooke. McGill University is still lost in verdure a few yards from the main business thoroughfare. The mountain foams up in the core of the city, almost as green and virginal as when Maisonneuve planted a wooden cross there (now replaced by a steel one, a hundred feet high, blazing in the night sky as a warning to the godless).

The guide books of Montreal are fat and full of exhibits: the Château de Ramezay with round towers and old cannons, Montgomery's headquarters in the disastrous campaign of 1775 and where that indefatigable propagandist, Ben Franklin, had a printing press in the basement to print tracts that failed to make the Canadians join the Revolution; Notre Dame, with square austere towers; Bonsecours, the sailors' church, first built in 1675, which is almost drowned out now by the rushing tide of new buildings and the clamor of the near-by market; the cathedral of St. James, domed, fat and round like a jolly Frenchman; dozens of other museum pieces. Alas, they are jostled, humiliated, and finally overcome by the skyscraper, the apartment house—not preserved, as in Quebec, with honor in the foreground, but thrust into back alleys and forgotten.

The true flavor of Montreal is to be found not in relics but in the swarming streets, from the spacious, tree-lined boulevards of the West End down to the slums of the East. In the west, on Sherbrooke Street, beside the sleepy campus of McGill—a real street, like a minor "Champs," like a little Vienna Ring, where most of the thoroughfares of America are mere gashes between brick and stone—it is all English. Everywhere there are fine old stone houses, mellow now, a little tired, that used to shelter a life of friendly, slightly stuffy formality in top hats, whiskers, and wide skirts, moving by summer in carriages, by winter in jingling sleighs.

When you cross that formidable boundary, garish, brawling St. Lawrence Street, you have entered another country. Here the inhabitants are all French-Canadian, living in the metropolis and not making a very good job of it. Here the French-Canadian's original genius for communal living in the village is drowned by numbers, by cheap, mean streets and gaudy arcades, by noise and filth, but you can still get a French meal there, as good as in Paris. It is the slum of any great city, our universal vice of accumulation, but the French-Canadian has given it a certain extra barbarity.

If you stroll on down to Bonsecours Market, where the farmers come in from the little farms on the north side of the Island, you find the old habitant spirit, the vigor, thrift, and neighborliness of the landed Frenchman, still living here in the midst of the metropolis. Somehow Montreal clings to the Mountain, to the river, to the woods and fields.

There is a bookstore on a narrow street not far from the Market, where you can buy any book ever printed, and an old man who inhabits it will tell you, if you get him started, how his life was ruined by this process of urbanization, when the city cut down thirty-nine trees in Phillip's Square to make room for a statue of King Edward VII—cut them down at night, mind you, when the residents were asleep and couldn't resist. In the morning nothing but a ruin and a statue of King Edward! Since then the old man has remained in his book-shop, immersed in the classics, refusing to look at this diseased age but ready to argue, at any expenditure of time, that Voltaire was a greater man than Shakespeare.

Near by you walk down St. James Street on tiptoe, for it is the Wall Street of Canada (cursed by every backwoods orator from Gaspé to Okanagan), the headquarters of our great cor-porations, the strong box of our wealth. After listening to the orators in the sticks you expect to see molten gold flowing in the gutters and rich men in carriages running over the children of the poor. It is rather disappointing to find nothing but a few better-dressed gentlemen and the flat dome of the Bank of Montreal.

But there is a rich class here, men of clubs and directorates, of great houses, limousines, and servants, men who control industries from one end of Canada to the other, the survivors of the Great Age, when a few railway builders could shake governments and terrify Parliaments. This caste is powerful still, and in part hereditary, especially among the French, so that, when a rising French-Canadian politician appealed to the party leaders not long ago for a vacant senatorship at Ottawa, one of them retorted: "But, my good friend, you are not a gentleman!" He said it as an obvious fact, with as little thought of insult as you would say: "But you are not English or American, or twenty-one years of age."

Yes, there is something about Montreal, a feeling that we do not have in our other Canadian cities—city manners, the acceptance of the city as a natural home and way of life, where most other cities are only villages trying to ape New York. There is something here which, for lack of a better name, must be called elegance with a touch of wickedness; for beneath all the culture, the refinement, and luxury is not only poverty but an organized underworld of vice and crime, with politics not as bold as in some American cities, but worse than anything Canada has ever known. No one was particularly surprised when that fantastic creature, the mayor of the city, was locked up as dangerous at the beginning of the war.

The kind snow of winter suddenly covers all the ugly memories and sights of Montreal, and it becomes a dream city then, as fine as Budapest or Munich or Brussels, with all its domes, steeples, squares, trees, and crowded bronze statues crusted with white.

In Dominion Square on such a night, with the fat, frosted French dome of St. James on one side, the Gothic, tight-lipped lines of the English church glistening white on the other side, you sense suddenly how men have built here on this island, through the centuries, a complicated structure of luxury, ease, religion, and civilization against the devastation of the Canadian winter—and built it with a sense of the good and the beautiful.

Don't look behind at the skyscrapers crowding the square now, look straight ahead at the snow, the sleigh bells, the glimpse of a beautiful woman in furs, the glitter of lights in the Windsor, the rich people drinking wine in the dining room, the teeming night life of café and club and the encircling cold. This, you think, must be like St. Petersburg before the Revolution—a certain glittering sinfulness and sophistication, which makes us simple western Canadians feel very young, innocent, and gauche.

Montreal! The rolling, thunderous sound of it has always meant for us Canadians life and riches and lovely women, money and power and masterful men. Moréal, the sweeter

French version, has meant for us the city, the metropolis, the gaiety, the splendor that we could never hope to know back home.

The mustard seeds scattered by Maisonneuve on the rich island soil have grown indeed, producing rankest weeds, but some lavish flowers.

The Tower

The Tower of Victory in Ottawa is the most notable symbol in Canada. It is Gothic, in imitation of English design, and yet it belongs wholly to Canada, speaking to Canadians of many things darkly hidden from the stranger, beyond the power of speech.

It grows out of the earth of Canada, and the earth of Canada has made the Tower its own. How grimly it soars up, how cleanly it cuts the sky! The height of our mountains is there and the hardness of our plains and, in many a fretted carving, the richness of our forest growth. More than that. The character of Canada is held in the Tower for all to see. Here is the solid sense of the English, the lean face of the Scotsman, the whimsy of the Irish in wild sculpture, the laughter of the French in delicate tracery of stone.

The Canadian walks up to Parliament Hill and sees the green copper point of the Tower piercing the maple trees or, in winter, rimed with frost and dripping with great icicles among the naked tree branches. He comes closer and finds the Tower growing in size until, as he approaches, it leaves him on the ground no larger than an ant.

He sees its delicate, strong arches, the images of bird and beast hewn into its sides, the grinning shape of gargoyles, the white moon face of the clock, the final upward thrust—all obedient to the first principle of the men who invented this architecture, that you may ornament construction but must not construct ornament. No orament is constructed here. All construction is lavishly ornamented with careful planning of every sun shadow against carved rock, but with no impairment of

77

the complete thing, the symmetry of the clean stone finger pointing to the sky.

The Canadian sees it and he knows that here, imprisoned in the myriad stones, is the deep substance of his country—the immeasurable size, the loneliness, the power, the cruel winds, the prairie blizzard, the warm breezes off the ocean, the hot summer sun, the fertility of the soil, and the mystery of the empty land. He knows that the things best within him are caught somehow in the symbol of the Tower—his strength, his hopes, the yearnings which he cannot convey in words but are spoken aloud here so all may hear.

Under this Tower politicians scheme and argue and make their deals. The Tower is not of them. The politicians, by their compromises, may represent the average and composite will of the people, but the Tower represents something better. It is the symbol of the people's unseen, inward life and secret desire, which they never quite achieve, but must always seek for and hunger for and die for. The Tower is firm and untroubled and secure, as all men would be. It is undefiled, as no man is, and beyond avarice and lust and self-seeking.

It is as pure as our winds, where we are torn by fearful appetites. It is as clean as our forests, where we are grimed by the smoke of too much living. It is as strong as our mountains, where we are frail in temptation. It remains, where we grow old and die and are forgotten. The Tower is the reach that exceeds our grasp, the thing we hope to be.

CHAPTER FIVE

Three o'Clock, Ottawa Time

At three in the afternoon the bells of the Ottawa carillon cease their wild play in the Victory Tower. For an hour or so they have sent hymns, anthems, and old-time airs rolling down the valley of the river. Now they turn to the serious business of sounding the hour, obedient to the moon-faced clock above them.

Three o'clock and Canadian democracy goes to work. Three o'clock and the last cabinet minister (having missed his lunch, as usual) hurries over from the East Block with a worried look. Three o'clock and the Speaker of the Commons, in three-cornered hat, flowing robe and silk knee breeches, parades in dismal procession down the marble corridors with his clerks, his sergeant-at-arms, gold mace on shoulder. Three o'clock and Mr. King, the prime minister, his battered red-leather brief case and its awful secrets clutched under his arm, trots into the House with a cautious, bobbing gait, as if he were walking on eggs.

Three o'clock, the witching hour of Ottawa, and the chamber of gray stone and carved oak is hushed. The Speaker on his richly fretted throne awaits the government's word and the long lines of members at their desks lean forward expectantly. Three o'clock, question time in the House of Commons, when the people, through their representatives, may ask the government anything and generally get an answer.

Today, perhaps, the prime minister, fitting his be-ribboned

glasses over his nose, has nothing to say until he has considered the question. Perhaps he is ready to make an official statement, holding a paper in his small, delicate hands, reading, in ponderous language from well-prepared notes, his eye always on the stenographic record and on history. His statement may have to do with the building of a small wharf in Prince Rupert or it may reveal Canada's decisions on war and peace. So the press gallery is watching this little bald man in black coat and four inches of starched white shirt cuff. His colleagues are watching him, the opposition is watching him, the back benches are watching him, hands cupped over ears not to lose a word. The nation is watching also, and the press wires out to Vancouver, where it is twelve noon, and to Halifax, where it is 4 P.M., have started to tick already. Three o'clock and government answers to the people.

This House of Commons is the true heart of Canada. It reflects every passing mood, sensation, pleasure, and pain in the vast, sprawling body of the nation, and articulates it within a few hours. Yet Parliament, on its green hill, lives strangely aloof, floating in a warm, comfortable vacuum. National politics is a craft apart, and its life is separated from the ordinary life of the nation and even of Ottawa, just outside its stone gates, by a gulf as wide as the sea. It is a separate and wondrous craft unknown to the layman, hidden from the ordinary citizen, who sees only the outward ripples, never the inward movements; a complicated and mysterious process utterly foreign to the life of the people, which it yet manages to reflect, in legislation and government, like a true and clear mirror.

The Canadian citizen is lost in Ottawa. He may admire the architecture, he may meet the agreeable minor politicians and, if he is prominent enough, he may reach the office of a cabinet minister. But he will never know, see, or suspect the deeper flux and flow around him, the conflicts, stresses, deals, compromises, intrigues, rumors, favors, the fear and courage, the power and weakness, the true patriotism and the betrayal, the unpredictable human chemistry by which democracy crystallizes and dissolves, to crystallize in new shape again.

Canada is a political democracy in as full a sense as the world knows. It admits of no hereditary right to rule and its Parliament long ago abolished titles of nobility.

The federal system of the nation, a union of nine provinces which are absolutely sovereign in their own fields of jurisdiction, was copied, of course, from that unique invention of the American Founding Fathers, but the actual machinery of administration, in Ottawa and in the provinces, follows the British pattern, in which the executive is not separated from the legislative wing, but is a part of it.

The government of Canada is a committee of the House of Commons, responsible to it, advising it, and advised by it. The prime minister is the leader of the largest group in the Commons and he is called to office by a governor-general who comes from Britain and represents the King, not the British Government—represents not the King of England but the King of Canada, who happens to live in London. When the new Canadian prime minister accepts the call and recommends a slate of cabinet colleagues to the governor-general, these men are the King's only advisers in Canada. They advise the King, through his representative, directly, not through the British government, and they govern the country as independently of London as if the British government did not exist.

The governor-general has no power, though in theory he is the final custodian of all power, wielding it on the advice of his ministers. The last time a governor-general ventured to exert any serious influence on events, the Canadian people instantly repudiated him, even though they admired him personally, and even though he may have been right in this particular incident, on grounds of common sense. He was wrong on the constitutional ground of refusing the advice of his ministers, who thereupon resigned and were promptly re-elected. The Canadian people would not tolerate counsel from the Crown,

even if it was wise, even if the advice of the cabinet was suspected of self-interest. The people demonstrated in that election of 1926, when Lord Byng refused to dissolve Parliament
on the advice of Mr. King, that their instinct about self-government and national independence was stronger and deeper
than anyone had suspected.

The constitution of Canada created another organ which
seemed to have a useful function but has since all but atrophied.
It is called the Senate, a body of ninety-six members, appointed
by the government for life, and supposed to be so far above
party strife that it can protect the interests of minorities against
the temporary passions of democracy. Actually, it has become
the refuge and reward of old party servants, each party filling
up the vacancies of death with its friends, and rarely on the
basis of ability.

In the Roman and American sense it is not a senate at all,
and though it has absolute power of veto over the legislation
of the House of Commons and must approve it all, those
powers are almost never used. If they were, the Senate would
be emasculated or abolished. As the Senate criticizes but does
not seriously interfere, the Canadian people generally regard it
with amusement, tolerance, or contempt, and while governments have frequently promised to reform it, nothing is done.
The genial old gentlemen who populate the snug red-velvet
chamber at the eastern wing of the Center Block live on, un-
disturbed, meeting for a few weeks in the year, bumbling and
grumbling at the government, making a few good speeches,
and drawing an annual indemnity of $4,000 for less work than
any other citizens of Canada.

This is the constitutional division of power in Canada—a
titular head, advised by a cabinet, a House of Commons making the laws, to be automatically approved by the Senate and
enforced by the cabinet. Behind all this, the real core of Canadian politics, outside of the constitution altogether, is the
party system.

The balance of political parties in Canada is a strange and baffling phenomenon, and the fact that it is now entirely out of date has not seriously inconvenienced the politicians so far. It has its origins in issues that no longer exist, or at least do not dominate. It has not adjusted itself officially to a new age and still asserts for publication that no new age has appeared, but it gets along by marching west with a large banner proclaiming that it is going east, and changing spryly as events require while proclaiming solemnly, hand on heart, that it will never change. It is, in fact, the party system as it exists anywhere.

The two major parties existed before Confederation—the Conservatives and Liberals. They joined together to achieve the Confederation agreement and Sir John A. Macdonald, the Conservative, used to play cards with George Brown, the Liberal, on the Confederation voyage to London, just for the sake of appearances, but they ceased to be on speaking terms as soon as the job was done. From then on the two parties have divided the country and divided office with fair regularity.

They only began to secure an adequate reason for permanent conflict in the last quarter of the nineteenth century, when Sir John devised the National Policy. This had a grand new sound about it, but, in fact, was merely the policy of high protection which was old when the Early Victorians chucked it out in Britain. However, something had to be done. Confederation had not brought prosperity, the reciprocity treaty with the United States had lapsed, and the internal Canadian market seemed to offer Sir John his only hope. So the Conservative Party staked its future on a policy of high tariffs.

This, in turn, provided the Liberal Party with a public appeal by enabling it to sponsor the opposite policy. It became (in name at least) the low-tariff party at a time when the tariff, the movement of goods, the wealth of the nation were important considerations, before ideologies, revolutions, and slogans made people forget that eating, after all, is the basic necessity of men. Thus the Conservative and Liberal Parties roughly compared to their counterparts in Britain, the Conservatives standing for a substantial interference by the state in private business, the Liberals following (a long way behind) the Manchester School, the ideal of laissez-faire and the principles of Gladstone.

Sir John's National Policy was a failure. Prosperity did not occur and the low-tariff Liberals swept into power in 1896 under Sir John's great successor and only other rival in our folklore, Sir Wilfrid Laurier, that unique French-Canadian and very perfect gentleman. The Liberals had advocated a "tariff for revenue only" and they lowered our customs duties substantially enough to help the farmer without damaging the protection of eastern industry too much. They even negotiated the reciprocity treaty with the United States in 1911, which both countries rejected. From then on, while the two great parties of Canada pretended to be divided by their pure aspiration after Protection on one side and Free Trade on the other, actually they were divided by a small difference in the amount of desirable customs duties and by the desire for office.

Elections have been fought between them on many other temporary issues, sometimes religious and racial, when each attempted, by a rare feat of split personality, to appear as the friend of the French Catholics in Quebec and the English Protestants in Ontario; and it was the execution by a Conservative Government of a French-Canadian halfbreed rebel, Louis Riel, that swung Conservative Quebec into the Liberal Party, where it has remained for half a century. That made the Liberal Party, and extracted most of its classical Liberalism. These extraneous accidents of political warfare are a fascinating study, but the continuing issue—not above accidents itself—has been the tariff.

The parties were seldom divided, except by temporary political maneuvers, on foreign policy and British Empire relationships, though the Conservatives have always considered themselves the "loyal" party and the Liberals have credited themselves with Canada's growing independence. Actually, as we shall see later on, both parties, whatever they said at election time, followed a clear and almost unbroken line towards complete Canadian autonomy, balanced by full co-operation with Britain.

On the basic domestic issues of our day—on what you might call, for lack of better definition, the New Deal versus the Old Deal, or Planning versus Individualism—the old parties had been unable to divide even up to the eve of the second World War. They still kept talking about the tariff as if it were the chief concern of the age, in a kind of ritualistic chant, as a Christian may rattle off a creed of words; but of late years they never did much about it.

Finally, as there was no basic issue between them, the Liberals under Mr. King, more ably led and already in office, completely swamped the Conservatives in two elections. It is a question now whether the party of Macdonald is not in the organic and inevitable process of dissolution which seizes all parties if they do not represent an idea; whether, in fact, the Liberal Party has not become the permanent party of the Right, including all those who believe in private initiative, opposed by some new, undiscovered party which believes in the opposite.

Perhaps the Conservatives will find an idea, just before it is too late. The Liberals rather hope so, for when they are finally rejected they do not want something much worse than the Conservatives. They want successors who will stand by the existing system of society. They do not want the C. C. F.

The C. C. F. is the mouth-filling Co-operative Commonwealth Federation, which stands for a moderate socialism but has no immediate hope of achieving it. However, the C. C. F. does have an idea and it does get the votes of thousands of people who do not believe in socialism but are pretty sure there is something wrong with things as they exist. It does represent, as the other parties do not, a definite cleavage on the fundamental domestic issues of our time. Where the old parties both stand for private property and, in terms of basic issues, are identical, the C. C. F. stands for something else entirely. Thus the handful of C. C. F. members who manage to get elected in discontented districts often are more effective in opposition than six times as many Conservatives, who are baffled because they can only attack the government in detail, never on basic principle.

Canada is a two-party nation and the two-party system has been found best for our parliamentary form of government. Third parties have never succeeded for long with us. The Progressive Party, voice of agrarian revolt, swept the prairies clean after the last war, but soon disappeared, absorbed into the Liberal Party by compromises on the tariff. But the C. C. F., or some other party fundamentally opposed to the existing system of society, must develop in Canada, if not to capture the government, at least to provide an alternative to it, to maintain a real criticism of its policy and to enforce reforms.

A political party in Canada can seldom follow a clear line if it is to get elected, for it must represent all the rival racial and economic interests of the whole nation. It must somehow embrace under one policy the isolated Maritimes, the French Catholics of Quebec, the protected manufacturing interests of Ontario, the free-trade aspirations of the prairie farmers, the almost separate economy of British Columbia. It must erect a vast umbrella under which all may take shelter. It must be the best kind of compromise possible while appearing to have a clear-cut plan of its own.

The Liberal Party has succeeded, with one small interruption, ever since the first World War because of its opponents' weakness and because of its leader's genius in achieving the magic compromise. The Liberal omnibus program provides accommodation for all passengers. In the great Liberal bosom is room for almost anyone who cares to enter. In Mr. King's house are many mansions, free to all who vote right when the division bell clangs—deep-dyed Tories from Quebec and Ontario, old-fashioned Liberals from the West, orthodox financiers and prophets of monetary mysticism. But the thing works because, though it satisfies nobody, it is more acceptable to a majority than any visible alternative.

When it comes to the daily practicalities of politics, there are three basic factors to be adjusted, balanced, and reconciled if any party is to succeed, any government retain office, or the nation to be held together. The first is French Canada. By the constitution it is guaranteed 65 members in the House of Commons which, on the basis of our present population, totals 245 members. The French-Canadian members generally vote together, so that a Quebec bloc, if it comes almost entirely out of one party, can usually dominate any government, and a government can hardly be elected without large Quebec support. As French Canada is essentially conservative in society, in economic outlook, and in religion—though it has voted pretty consistently for the Liberal Party since Laurier's time—its influence has been powerful in keeping Canada steady or, as many Canadians feel, in keeping it backward.

The Canadian prime minister must keep his hold on Quebec. His chief job is to maintain unity between the two chief races, and when he fails, the nation faces a racial breach which more than once has threatened to break Confederation at the line of the Ottawa River. Of late years happily the old-time sores of the first World War have healed. But this racial unity is achieved often at the expense of improvisation, evasion, and the long delay of obvious reform. At times it has almost paralyzed Parliament. The deepest question of Canadian politics, and Canadian life, is whether the present unity is permanent, whether the two races, politically at least, can ever be merged; whether Canada must always remain a split personality, at the mercy of a racial or religious incident.

The second basic political factor is the manufacturing interest of central Canada, deeply entrenched behind the tariff.

This must be balanced against the third factor, the exporting raw producer of the country, who must sell in the world's low-price, free markets and buy in the protected, high-price markets at home.

The great pressure groups of Canada, whose lobbies are constantly at work in Ottawa, represent the financial interests, the privately owned railway system, and the manufacturers; and, on the other hand, the basic producers—mixed farmers of the east, grain growers of the prairies, fishermen of the coasts; and back of them labor, which has been guaranteed the right of organization but has never achieved organization as completely as in Britain or the United States, has never been a power in Parliament or sought to be.

To reconcile protection with free trade and capital with labor is difficult enough. To reconcile as well race with race and religion with religion makes government in Canada, as Sir John once remarked, such a difficult business that a new politician needs several years before he learns how to hang up his hat in Ottawa. The successful prime minister must have an uncanny sense of equilibrium, must be an equestrian capable of riding several horses in opposite directions, and, in addition to a deep feeling of destiny, must possess a skill in practical jugglery. National unity is a fine phrase and a lofty ideal. Often it is used for the highest ends. Sometimes it is used as an all-embracing excuse for doing nothing.

Even this does not end the complication of government in Canada. There are always the provinces to consider, and in our version of the American issue of States' Rights, there is seldom peace. The British North America Act was supposed to settle the line where federal government power ended and provincial power began, but it had not been in force long before the line became a blur. A distant Privy Council in London proceeded to interpret the constitution as it saw fit, and as it considered best for the young nation, but it certainly interpreted it out of the recognition of its founders. In great chunks, the power of government was transferred from Ottawa to the provincial capitals, and by the beginning of the second World War the constitution had become so confused, the line between the federal and provincial authority so blurred, that everyone agreed the situation was intolerable.

Yet all efforts to make the constitution workable in the modern world, which the founders had not foreseen, have failed. The constitution is still an act of the British Parliament, which alters it on the petition of Canada and would gladly hand it back to Ottawa if Canada would only ask for it. Canada has not asked for it. Canada has never agreed on a method of transferring it, altering it, or modernizing it, and every thinking Canadian must be humiliated at the spectacle of a nation whose basic law, even in theory, is outside its control.

All this is due, of course, to the suspicion of some provinces and the racial fears of Quebec. They hesitate to open the constitution because, once opened, they do not know what will emerge from it. After a royal commission had labored for years on an acceptable compromise and a redefinition of powers between the federal and provincial governments, a conference called to consider its report broke up at the beginning of 1941 in bitterness and failure. Three provincial governments, putting their own rights above the nation's need, made progress impossible. During wartime the federal government has all the powers it needs, all it asks, but when peace comes Canada must have a constitutional housecleaning. And, in the end, the Supreme Court of Canada, instead of the Privy Council in London, will become the last court of appeal.

We have reached, in fact, a great turning point in our history when only the necessities of war and the unknown character of the postwar world make it possible to postpone longer a realignment of parties and vast changes in the nation's primary domestic and economic policies.

Some of these changes have come already, introduced apologetically as temporary expedients, but many of them will remain. Yet we are still a very conservative nation by the definitions of these times—perhaps the most conservative nation under the democratic system in the world. Beside pre-war Canada Britain was almost socialistic, and the New Deal of the United States was wild radicalism.

The Liberal Party, which has dominated Canada so long, was built originally on the ideal of Manchester Liberalism; and the best Liberals, in their hearts, still believe in free trade, the play of natural economic forces, the sanctity of enterprise, and the evil of monopoly. They behold on all sides precisely the opposite—self-containment, protection, government regulation and enthroned monopoly, but they hope that a better day will dawn, that the world will come to its senses, trade again, reduce government interference, abolish monopoly.

Naturally, therefore, when the New Deal burst upon the world, Canadian Liberals and members of Mr. King's government deplored it as basically unsound, as you can see if you care to read their speeches on the record. They still believe it to be unsound. They still insist that they will not follow it, but step by step they have been following it. The final tragedy of the war compelled a ministry devoted in theory to a minimum of government into complete and detailed control of the nation's economy. This is called emergency policy only, but the fact obvious to all thinking Canadians is that, long before the war, because it lived in that kind of world, Canada was being driven more and more towards statism while insisting that it was moving in its old individualistic groove. These facts and trends will remain whether the King government is still functioning when this is printed or has been succeeded by another.

Still, the reforms—or at least the changes—attempted by other nations, Canada has often resisted. It never went in for large expenditures on public works to relieve unemployment, and never accepted the theory of deficit spending on its own account as a method of priming the pump. Our national budget of half a billion before the war would represent a total United States Government expenditure of only six billions on a per capita basis. Canada never accepted a policy of bonusing agriculture to produce less, until the war forced it to do so by the closing of foreign markets. It is only beginning unemployment insurance now. It has not attempted health insurance. It has done little about public housing.

We Canadians can probably claim the distinction of being the most rugged surviving individualists, but unless the war opens up the world's trade again, unless we return to an age where monopoly is dissolved and needs no regulation, unless the whole course of history in the last forty years is reversed, Canada is now bound headlong into what we may call the New Deal idea. If that is the wish of the people, if that is the ineluctable pull of history, Mr. King will adjust himself to it, if he is still in office. If the negation of Liberalism is necessary, the Liberal Party will call it a new and up-to-date Liberalism. Usually the banners will point in the wrong direction.

When it must operate in such territory it is easy to see why a political party in Canada must be a complicated organism. John W. Dafoe, who knows it better than any man alive, says that the Canadian party is really a commonwealth within the commonwealth, having its own laws, managers, servants, customs, castes. It represents a united front at election time but is almost never at peace within itself. The quarrels between its rival groups and leaders are usually more bitter than those with its avowed enemies. It is in continual process of struggle, tension, compromise adjustment, and ferment.

Its leader, if successful, quickly becomes, as Mr. Dafoe says, an autocrat and an egoist. "The ego and the country soon become interblended in his mind," and "if he comes to office without these characteristics his environment equips him with them as surely as a diet of royal jelly transforms a worker into a queen bee."

Viscount Bryce, an astute observer, once remarked: "Party

(in Canada) seems to exist for its own sake. In Canada ideas are not needed to make parties, for these can live by heredity and, like the Guelfs and Ghibellines of medieval Italy, by memories of past combats; attachment to leaders of such striking gifts and long careers as were Sir John Macdonald and Sir Wilfrid Laurier created a personal loyalty which exposed a man to reproach as a deserter when he voted against his party."

This is true. When the rare Canadian statesman does change his party allegiance he is never quite forgiven in the craft. Only once since Confederation have the two great parties united—to achieve wartime conscription for the army in 1917; and when a few Liberals elected to remain with the Conservative Party after the war, they were suspect forever afterwards.

Among our politicians, we take our politics hard. Yet only a minority of Canadians belongs to any party. Most of us have no interest in party affairs, and they are as much a mystery to us as the lodge meetings of secret societies. Where an American is generally regarded as a Democrat or a Republican and is proud of it, probably more than half the Canadian people have no label and no party loyalty, switching their votes whenever they feel like it. For years now the two major parties have been in somewhat low public esteem because they do not represent any clear-cut alternatives that a man can get hold of. This lack the electors do not yet clearly understand, but they feel an instinctive dissatisfaction.

A small core of expert managers and some public-spirited souls among the populace manage our party machines. They are not weak on that account. Jobs go to the faithful. Contracts go to the men who know that elections are not won with prayers and that campaigns require campaign funds. Yet patronage is not practiced as openly or as widely as in the United States. It is not accepted as a natural and inevitable thing by the public. With a good deal of hypocrisy, it is disguised as far as possible, regarded as something disreputable, which the honest politician knows must exist but seeks to avoid directly. Gradually the public service is being moved more and more away from party appointment, but a man who is looking for preferment had better know a friend in Parliament, in the party machine, or, better still, in the cabinet.

The cabinet is the real ruler of Canada. More and more power centers in it, and during wartime its powers are almost absolute. Parliament must pass the laws, but the cabinet drafts them, and few introduced by anyone else are ever adopted. Indeed, any law proposing to spend a nickel of public money can come into Parliament only on motion of a cabinet minister. Under such rule, members of Parliament break with their party, defy the cabinet, or criticize their leaders much less than in Congress. In Canada the cabinet is sitting opposite you, watching you all the time. And hard and fast are the rules of the game, stern the system of promotion, dismal the future of the rebel who challenges the entrenched oligarchy.

Inside any cabinet there is seldom agreement, though the cabinet, of course, must never display the slightest breach in public. Just as the whole party represents a compromise between many conflicting districts and interests, so does the cabinet divide on geographical and economic lines. According to unwritten rule, each province must have at least one cabinet minister, and often they are struggling against each other because they have no basic point of agreement. Mr. King's cabinets will contain low-tariff men and high-tariff men, leftists and rightists, and yet by some miraculous process of amalgamation they manage to agree on a policy for which every man will fight tenaciously, even if he has fought against it for weeks in the secret cabinet room of the East Block. A queer system, very ancient, long tried, and tested. It works.

The prime minister, the egoist and autocrat as Mr. Dafoe calls him, is not merely the first among equals, not just the chief minister. He is the boss. Theoretically he may be merely the chairman of a committee of parliament, constitutionally he lacks the powers of the American President, and daily his acts are subject to the review and veto of Parliament. But in practice his powers are almost unlimited within the general range of Parliament's will, and finally he carries the terrible right of dissolution. The governor-general must dissolve Parliament on his advice and his alone, as Lord Byng discovered. At a pinch the prime minister can hold out against almost any revolt by threatening dissolution, an election, and a party debacle, which nobody wants. The party will close its ranks, rather than risk destruction.

An able prime minister does not need to make such threats. He rules by acceptance and can remain party leader indefinitely, so long as he can win elections. The rule of Macdonald, Laurier, and King has covered three generations. Such men must have the confidence of Parliament and the approval of their colleagues; but so long as there is general support, they do not have to worry much about detail.

The prime minister will persuade or he will order. He will have his way either by the direct methods of a Bennett or by the kid-glove technique of a King. He will probably allow his great lieutenants to do most of the business, even without reference to him. He will delegate power widely, as King does, but always he has the final say if he wants it. Every line of government policy leads into his hands, and he broods, an unseen presence, a fearful power, over the entire capital. Always he is on top of the pyramid, secure and unchallenged so long as the pyramid itself endures. When it crumbles another party comes in, builds its own pyramid, with another prime minister at the top.

As this is written Rt. Hon. William Lyon Mackenzie King, grandson of a rebel, is prime minister and has been since 1921, with the fortunate interruption of five years during the worst of the depression, when no sensible man would want to be in office. Events move so fast these days that they may conceivably remove Mr. King at any time, though this seems impossible at the moment; but even if that should happen by the time this is read, Mr. King is worth close study, and history will study him closely, as the symbol of an era in our history.

Mr. King is a bachelor in his latter sixties, short, plump, pale, bald, with a single wisp of hair, which is usually sprawling wildly over his forehead, and clear blue eyes that can be as hard as glass or suddenly shy and boyish. He lives alone in the old-fashioned house willed to him by the widow of Laurier, who discovered him. His only companion until recent times was an aged Irish terrier, sleeping by his bed in a basket, covered by a shawl, which Mr. King arranged with his own hands. Now Pat is dead and Mr. King is alone.

He eats in a darkly paneled dining room, usually by candle light, with ghostly oil portraits of Laurier and Lady Laurier on the walls and a discreet butler in the shadows. He works up in the attic, which he has transformed into a study so littered with books, bric-a-brac, the autographed portraits of notables, and other trophies of the political chase as would drive most men to distraction.

This is the real center of the government of Canada. In this immaculate litter Mr. King works alone, at a great desk, and beside him a small table, once the property of George Meredith, to hold his extra papers or a cup of tea and a biscuit (almost never a glass of whisky). Near by, a cozy fire crackles where Mr. King can lounge on a chesterfield and think. On a table beside the fireplace, illuminated always with electric light, like a shrine, is a portrait of his dead mother, whom he adores with a mystical and rather beautiful devotion.

Secretaries come to Laurier House early in the morning and late at night, and quickly wear out under the strain; and it is worse when Mr. King moves for the summer out to his farm in the Gatineau Hills. Seclusion saves his time, however, and he has none to spare, especially when Parliament is in session and he must go to a cabinet meeting at noon and appear in the Commons at three o'clock.

Few people but his colleagues and secretaries see him, but sometimes he will take a notion and invite some obscure fellow up to his study and devote the entire evening to him. Then, while he is generally regarded as fish-cold in public, he can display a sudden charm and intimacy, a surprising shyness, a richly stored mind, and a human touch that the Canadian people never see. He is a highly complicated and finely spun creature, half mystic, reading his Bible, praying daily, believing devoutly in the human soul's immortality; half ruthless and selfish politician, who can slit an enemy's political throat with a single expert motion of the wrist and without changing expression. Altogether the curious combination of politician and prophet, hermit and handshaker.

It is a tough game, and Mr. King is tough enough for it. He is tougher by far than the big, bouncing men of meat and muscle whose feet thud on the stage of events. He has an inner core of toughness, an extra skin of the spirit, made of patience and infinite ability to yield and thrust back at the right moment; more patient than a whole herd of elephants and he remembers better than they, remembers acts of friendship and acts of hate, and keeps them in a mental card-index system commodious and accurate enough for a large business organization. But this cold, calculating and cunning judgment of men and politics is overlaid by a pale cast of thought, a little known layer of sentiment and emotion, and though hardly anybody knows this, at times Mr. King's thoughts, usually so icy and knifelike, can be utterly fuzzy and have no more logic than a pretty wish, a surge of tears to the eyes.

Mr. King is a great man by almost any definition. You may not like him, and many do not, some wasting their entire lives in hatred of him. But you cannot deny him. There he is, on the record.

In Canadian politics his chief accomplishment is not his length of office but the unity he has produced between the two Canadian races, even though it has often been by the method of doing as little as possible about anything. In British Empire politics he has achieved the final independence of Canada, written into statute law the right of Canada to make foreign treaties, declare war or remain neutral in Britain's wars while, at the same time, he has led Canada into the largest measure of co-operation with Britain, the deepest war sacrifices, in its history. Perhaps his greatest work is in bringing together Canada and the United States—militarily at Ogdensburg, economically at Hyde Park. And history will show finally that he was very useful, though very unobtrusive, in bringing together the governments of Britain and the United States in the lease-lend era, interpreting Churchill to Roosevelt and Roosevelt to Churchill. No Canadian statesman has ever exercised so great an effect on the affairs of America as a whole. Yet he is largely unknown publicly to the American people or in his private life to Canadians.

History must decide whether Mr. King was master of the event or merely its reflection, and a contemporary judgment on that point is of very little value. Certainly he has never hurried the event, always let it catch up with him and sometimes push him rudely from behind, but in the end things generally turned out as he desired. He conceives the job of prime minister not as a means of implementing his own views, but as an opportunity to sense all the conflicting views of the nation, reconcile them into the best available compromise, whether he likes it or not, and then to enforce it, until the pressures change.

This does not make for spectacular politics and Mr. King is not spectacular. He carries no torch and makes no great phrases and his governments have no more sex appeal than Donald Duck. But this worshiper of Gladstonian Liberalism has an expanding Gladstone-bag mind, to contain almost any political idea that must somehow be carried on the march. Nothing could be more useful on a march like ours. Mr. King is, in short, a unique paradox, the least typical Canadian of his time and the most sensitive thermometer of Canadianism.

History will study him not for himself alone but as the master and the victim of the last twenty years in Canada— years of hesitation, doubt, confusion, vacillation, growth in part but failure on the whole; an era when not only Canada but all the democratic nations were tired and a little mad; a period which has finally crystallized into something better and stronger in this war.

Under Mr. King and his ministers is the private member of Parliament, who counts individually for little but must not be allowed to suspect it. He is the forgotten man of Ottawa, living a dull and wretched life, which he never willingly surrenders. Usually he is not rich, and the nation pays him only $4,000 a year and railway fares. Yet for six months he must live away from home while his private business goes to ruin, so that at the end of his career he is generally broke, which is a testimony to his honesty, generally higher than that of business life.

All morning he will labor in his office with the correspondence of his constituents, the requests for old-age pensions and jobs, the minutiae of local politics. All afternoon and all evening he will listen to speeches in the House and once or twice every session he will make a speech himself. Nevertheless, in the group he is the final master of the government, and while the government will usually do all its individual acts without consulting him, it will certainly keep aware of his general feelings and alter its general course to suit him.

The politics of such men is not rousing. Canada never sees the solemn and historic drama of Westminster or the passion of the American political convention. No such spectacle of emotion and human upheaval as the Roosevelt-Willkie election was ever witnessed in modern Canada. Where an American statesman can easily rouse a crowd of enthusiastic citizens, the Canadian audience usually sits in the country places and small towns with cold, haddock eyes, fixed grimly on the stranger. Parliament itself is rather stuffy—none of the free and easy conversation of the United States Senate, nor the gentleman's club atmosphere of Westminster, but far more attachment to rule of order and strict punctilio, and a deep aversion to anything as distressing as a "scene." It is only when the Frenchmen speak in their own language (which is as legal as English in the nation's public business) that we get great oratory; or, better still, when we listen to a French master of English like Ernest Lapointe, who could speak nothing but French when he came to Parliament and now, with fascinating variations on the original pronunciation, can make English words sound like the tones of a pipe organ. But if Parliament is not exciting, it is almost never disreputable. While they may quarrel in public, the members generally have been on excellent terms.

Summing it up, Canadian politics for twenty years has been a triumph of mediocrity—competent enough, wise enough, and safe enough, but mediocrity. There has been besides Mr. King no great figure who could hope to hold office for long. A more dynamic person, Lord Bennett, carried the country once but didn't last long and faded sadly into the British nobility. No young man has developed, no successor to Mr. King, no high promise anywhere, or perhaps Mr. King would have faded also.

This blight of pale competence descended upon Canadian politics because politics reflected accurately the baffled mood of the people in the age of disillusionment, and partly because this was Mr. King's method—he wanted no miracles, no trouble and no rivals. We used to produce giants in our country. We had our great flowering of statesmanship at the time of our Confederation, as the United States had at its beginning, but it passed. Another flowering is long overdue and perhaps the war or the aftermath will produce it. Meanwhile our system has not encouraged young men either to enter politics or to progress if they do enter. The hard caste rule of Ottawa has kept the young man down and the old man up. It has been for twenty years a kind of frozen truce, a grand postponement of all decisions while we waited for something to turn up. The war turned up, and in its readjustments much will be swept away in Ottawa, many imposing figures, many old ideas. Out of it will come in men and in policies no one knows what.

Still, looking at the record, there is no reason for Canadians to compare their politics unfavorably with those of Britain, which, in the same twenty years, had sunk to the lowest level since the Georges. And while we lacked the magic of a Roosevelt, our run of politics in Parliament has probably been as sound as that of Congress.

The politics of politicians is only half of Ottawa, the upper half, on the surface. Beneath the surface is the intricate network of the permanent civil service, the servant of the government, but often its unobtrusive master. Year by year Canada has had to hire more experts to run the new processes of government in an age of growing complications, and since the war forced the government to take complete charge of the nation's economy, Ottawa is crawling in boards, committees, controllers, professors and every manner of specialist, until you can hardly find room to sleep in. Generally they have done well, giving the nation a better economic management in wartime than anyone had dared to hope for. To its amazement the country has discovered that, all unknown and unsuspected, it has in its civil service some of the most competent men in the business anywhere.

Such men can often dominate a cabinet minister. He may

speak in the loud voice, make the official announcement, and impress Parliament, but often some unknown fellow, hidden away in the labyrinths of the West Block or the Confederation Building, will have given the minister ideas, policy, and speech, though unfortunately cannot always give him brains. All this is as it should be, for the permanent expert must know his business better than the transient minister.

A brilliant young man like Graham Towers, governor of the Bank of Canada (who is so exquisite under cross-examination by a parliamentary committee that he has been said to suffer from inflammation of the vowels) or Dr. Clifford Clark, deputy minister of finance, or Dr. L. D. Wilgress, on trade or Fraser Elliott on taxation, is likely to have more permanent effect on the course of events than most politicians. These experts would be the last to admit it. They would deny any influence on policy. They would say they merely carried out the government's policy, but to a very great extent they make it.

These men form a caste of their own in Ottawa, which is caste-ridden like any capital. In political caste they rank next to the cabinet itself and above the members of Parliament. The social caste is too complicated for any busy man to remember or care about, but according to rigid rule everyone has his place in society, to be claimed at official functions before the governor-general and his lady, when the finely trained social athletes of Rockcliffe appear with more feathers in their hair than have been seen hereabouts since Dollard fought the Iroquois down the river.

No one who counts in Ottawa has time for this kind of struggle, and the only caste that matters is the real inner circle of government. Many a cabinet minister does not belong to it. The inner circle will depend on the prime minister and his selection of advisers. It will include a group of his most intimate cabinet colleagues, probably a senator or two, battered by elections and life, and a few civil servants who know their jobs. Even Ottawa will hardly know who they are. The nation will never hear of them.

All this weary recital of the nation's business is quite misleading, however, if it suggests a picture of sophistication, drama, and splendid mystery. Ottawa is probably the most unsophisticated capital in the world. It is only Bytown grown up a little—the old lumber village which was selected for a capital because they couldn't agree on any established city. Though a deputy minister's wife may consider herself a trifle above the wife of an assistant deputy and not know the wife of a mere clerk, though the pretensions of a few snobs in Rockcliffe may startle the crude westerner, Ottawa on the whole is neighborly, folksy, essentially simple, a place where you could see the first citizen of the nation strolling with his aged dog, the leader of the opposition getting a shave at the corner, and the governor of the Bank of Canada at a movie. As for mystery, outside of the inner circle itself there is no secret in Ottawa for more than twenty-four hours. The place is a sounding board, a whispering gallery, a natural echoing cave. A rumor started in the parliamentary lobbies at three o'clock will be heard at every dinner table in town by evening. Always Ottawa is drenched in rumor, but not the mighty rumor of London or Washington, just the gossip of the neighbors who happen to live in the capital.

Ottawa is growing slowly but surely into the physical stature of a world capital. Alas, how much better it might have been planned! Here was an almost perfect site—a high, well-treed bank beside a broad river which cascades over a noble waterfall. Budapest was built on almost the identical formation and became a spectacle in fairyland. Instead, Ottawa's falls have been harnessed and lost in dingy power houses, and the north bank of the river is blighted with the industries of Hull, in Quebec, from whose match factory emerges, if the wind is blowing from that quarter, a queer, rather pleasant smell of sulphur. But if you can ignore the industries and look across the river from Hull to the high bank on the Ontario side, you will see a group of Gothic buildings which, in total effect, far surpass those of Westminster itself—the soaring pinnacle of the Center Block, the crazy, windblown turrets of the East and West Blocks, the wondrous flying buttresses of the old library, all mixed together in a lovely tangle, and yet a perfect design of stone and spires, rising out of a green surge of maple trees.

From any direction this is a noble hill. For miles up and down the river you can see the Victory Tower topping the trees like a mirage and hear the music of its bells. From close at hand you can investigate its rich carvings, the strange and feathery lightness of its arched stonework. And it would be a humorless heart which would not rejoice in the wildly improbable towers, turrets, spires, and purely accidental appendages of the West Block, the horrified face, eyes wide, mouth open, which the unwitting stone masons built into the south tower of the East Block.

Or if you want to see how the agony of men's souls went into these stones, go around to the side of the Center Block and over an obscure doorway you will find the word "Vimy" carved deep and true. A humble mason carved that word one day when he knew that his son was fighting with the Canadians on Vimy Ridge in the last war—carved it without instructions or permission, because he had to, and the architect left it there, understanding what it meant. The mason's son was killed next day on Vimy.

Magnificent conceits have burst into stone all over the buildings, inside and out—beavers, frogs, buffaloes, Indians, gargoyles, and, best of all, the sly faces which were suddenly recognized (when they were complete and it was too late to change them) as caricatures of current Canadian statesmen. This carving is not complete yet. Year after year the masons must work on the blank faces of stone which still await their hand. Under the master architects of our future history, they will carve in many curious forms, now unforeseen.

Even now when you enter the front doors and walk through the central circular chamber you find it worthy of any state— the intricate groining and flying arches, like the branches of our Canadian forests, the upswept Gothic arches, the solemn oak and wrought iron. Above, in a chamber within the tower itself, is Canada's memorial to the soldiers of the last war, all their names inscribed in a single book, and the stone walls carved to picture their deeds, with a look as clean as the soil that bore them.

A few paces north and you pass out of the new building into the old parliamentary library, which alone survived the fire of 1916. You pass also into another era, into mid-Victorianism and the age of Confederation. This circular room is crammed with gimcrack wooden galleries, iron railings, and gingerbread carvings, and, lest you fail to realize that you have re-entered Victorian times, the young queen herself stands in the center, with bare feet, sandals, and a classic gown very much like a nightshirt—a medieval saint in pure white marble.

Up the hall to the west is the House of Commons, its gray stone and dark oak marred only by a hideous gold-spangled ceiling, supported by fat and naked cupids; the private smoking lobbies where parliamentarians can be free for once of the electors; and the common room, for interparty conversations, with its jolly flocks of carved black crows. To the east lies the region of the Senate, with its jewel-case chamber in scarlet, richly appointed offices, old and tired residents.

The city of Ottawa clusters around the towered hill of Parliament like a medieval town around its castle. It is an old town as these things are reckoned in Canada, its streets are narrow, and its original buildings drab. They are constantly improving it, however, have built a fine system of driveways and flowering boulevards along the Rideau Canal, carved out grassy parks, started to cut a broad mall from the hill southward, and maintained with jealous care the great trees along its streets.

You can see here in stone how the two races of Canada struggle to blend, to understand, to become one. At the very edge of the English-Gothic hill of Parliament stands the huge mass of the Château Laurier, a hotel which can properly claim that name—pure French like a château in Provence. When its myriad lights shine through the trees of Lovers' Walk on a summer night you would think you were looking at an old French castle across its moat; while just beside it, in a narrow gorge, the stone house of the canal lock keeper, with its tiny garden, a toy beside the Château, has a complete touch of England about it, like a cottage on the Wye. The architects have gone further even than this. In some of the newer buildings, which begin to march in splendid line along the river bank, they seem to have combined the Gothic and the château architecture in a satisfactory Canadian blend of their own.

One usually thinks of Ottawa in the winter when Parliament opens and the Hill is deep in snow and heavy with intrigue. But when Parliament has gone home, Ottawa becomes a leafy Ontario town again, happy beside its river. On a summer evening the sun sinks behind the tangled towers, glints on the populous bronze statues, and makes magic among the carvings of the stone walls. Only a few old men and whispering lovers sit on the benches and the birds are singing their evening song in the elms. Then it is good to be in Ottawa, to meditate on the men who have worked here for Canada, to picture Macdonald climbing these steps beside you, and Laurier strolling these shady streets. It is good to think of the nobler capital which will yet rise here.

Leaves Falling, Dead Men Calling

The leaves at home in Ontario used to turn yellow and then scarlet, and one morning a small boy would wake to see them fluttering down into the backyard. They were big, ragged maple leaves, the best kind for a boy's fire. When they lay thick upon the ground it was a delicious feeling to kick your feet through them as you walked and heard them rustle. If you pushed them with a long motion of the leg they sounded like the swish of a wave on a sandy beach. But the burning was the best of all.

Old William, our man-of-all-work, would rake them up with a wooden rake that he had made himself, and I would help him with a toy rake and a toy wheelbarrow, demanding that we burn right away. But William would squint up at the trees and he would not burn until all the leaves were down. It was unlucky to burn twice, he said. "Leaves fallin', dead men callin'," *William said. I never knew what it meant, but it had a fine sound of doom about it and I would repeat it over and over again—leaves falling, dead men calling. And after a week of raking, after the last leaf had torn itself loose from the naked trees, we would light our fire behind the stable, and now the sweet smoke of maple leaves would go up in the back yards all over town. All eastern Canada would be burning leaves then, an autumn custom, a universal rite.*

Alas, there are no maple leaves where I live now on the western coast. There are oak leaves only—very superior in quality, of much better substance and fertilizing value when rotted down, but they lack the fragrance of the maple leaves and they contain no memories for me. We pile the oak leaves methodically but with none of the old pleasure. We watch them stream off the trees in October like a brown blizzard, while the white gulls beat in from the angry sea. We watch the leaves scampering across the fields, children who have just left their mother. We see them pouring down the rocks in torrents like molten bronze, and piling up in the ditches, imprisoned now, their brief flight over. We stride through them to hear them crackle, but they lack the perfect crisp sound, the whisper and chuckle of the maple leaves.

Slowly the oak leaves rot down, and for two or three years in the great pile they still preserve their shape, closely packed together and thin now as tissue paper. Presently they have turned to dry, powdery compost, the richest soil known, precious, every ounce of it, for growing plants, and the gardener rubs it thoughtfully between his fingers.

We dig down through the stratification of the leaf pile, through the new leaves, through the closely packed leaves of last year, the half-rotten leaves of the previous year, and finally into the black compost of antiquity. Each year has its own vintage. Each layer preserves some little relic of its passage. Near the top a baseball bat belonging to the little boy from next door, buried in the billows of October. Lower down, the wheel of a tricycle which was lost two years ago. In the next layer a toy canoe, with a wooden Indian in it, his feather war bonnet gone. In the last layer a little tin plate, diamond-shaped, which was used to mold cakes in the sand pile. All the history of those years when Robin was growing is written in the stratification of the leaf pile. He will remember oak leaves.

All the memories of Canadian childhood are thus held for most of us in autumn leaves. The sight of them fluttering down from the trees makes us think of the old days in Ontario, in Quebec, and the Maritimes. The maple leaf is Canada's emblem not by any official choice, not for its beauty of scarlet color, but for its memories, its place in our lives. We like to go back to the old provinces in the autumn and smell the leaf smoke and remember when we were young and awoke to see the leaves fluttering down in the back yard, on the village street. Leaves falling, dead men calling.

CHAPTER SIX

Made in Canada

The house where I was born stood at the corner of Dibble and Edward Streets, in Prescott, Ontario. It was a huge, oblong chunk of gray stone, with walls two feet thick. In winter it was warm, in summer cool. Down in the dark basement there was a rich smell of apples in fat barrels and pickles and jam, and the hugely timbered attic was littered with trunks full of ancient clothes, hooped skirts, top hats, useful for dressing up in on rainy days, and discarded bric-a-brac and the musty smell of age. From the upstairs windows you could look through the elms of the garden down to the St. Lawrence and see the smoke of Ogdensburg, New York, on the far side.

In the winter we used to walk across the ice to buy things at the low American price in the stores of Ogdensburg, which seemed to us a city of great splendor. Then we would smuggle our purchases back through the Canadian tariff without serious official interruption. All the women of Prescott had enormous bags suspended from the waist under their skirts to carry this contraband past the sleepy customs officers, and sometimes my grandmothers would waddle up Edward Street from the summer ferry wharf so swathed in bolts of smuggled cloth that they seemed to have doubled their weight since morning and could hardly move—pious women, the salt of the earth, who went to church twice on Sundays and spent most of their lives in charity, but the customs law was fair game. They always brought me a toy from Ogdensburg, stuffed elephants mostly, though they had little money to spare. Nobody objected to this innocent crime and nobody suspected that some day Ogdensburg would be the city of a great historic occasion, when the first military alliance between a British nation and the United States would be signed there in a railway car.

Prescott was the very apotheosis of all Ontario river towns —stone houses, cool, tree-lined streets, large families, a very gentle class system and an unobtrusive neighborliness. When I went to the grocery store of John Newberry he would always give me a stick of candy, and at Christmas time he sent up a case of wine to my grandfather. McCarthy's tobacco store kept a glass tank of newly caught pickerel in the window and in the back room a card game seemed to go on forever. In the autumn the grapes turned purple behind the barn, and a small boy was assured of a worthwhile stomach-ache, and at that season we had vast, pungent fires of scarlet maple leaves. In winter you could slide on your sleigh down Edward Street, and at Christmas there were such boilings, bakings, and fryings in the great kitchen, such a flutter of housemaids, such an assembly of turkeys, geese, ducks, chickens, and sides of beef, all hung up on the back porch to freeze, as no modern housekeeper has ever dreamed of.

In the woodshed, standing there so long that it was hung with cobwebs, was a sentry box, just big enough for one man. It had been used in the Rebellion of 1837. At the time of the Fenian Raids soldiers had been billeted in our house. Not far from the house stood Fort Wellington, out of which the Canadians had slipped in the darkness of winter to burn Ogdensburg in the War of 1812. A piece further down the river loomed the round stone bulk of the windmill, where the Rebels fought it out against the government troops until they had fired the last nail, hinge, and belt buckle from their tiny cannon. Prescott had known events.

But far greater events had passed here than Prescott ever suspected, or suspects to this day. Such towns as Prescott, though they did not know it, were the birthplace of the Ca-

nadian nation; and though they would hardly believe it even
now, were the makers of the present Commonwealth of British
Nations—they, and they alone.

For that purpose they were designed by nature and by history. There was in the stone house where I was born, and in
countless stone houses beside the river, a slightly stuffy gentility of Sunday top hats and tail coats and maidservants, a
proud poverty, but something else, quite unconscious and natural as the breath in their nostrils—a fierce and unquenchable
love of liberty. There was in those ancient horsehair parlors,
with their marble mantel shelves, crystal chandeliers, and silver
candlesticks, a certain rightness, a quiet faith in the individual
and an unspoken belief in God and man.

Out of that, out of those old houses by the river and the
minds of poor men who believed in themselves, came the
nation of Canada, came the British Commonwealth, came the
modern history of the British peoples, but nobody could guess
it at the time. The thing was accomplished, as all great things
are accomplished, without knowledge of the method or foresight of the result—by instinct, by bloodshed, by countless
small daily acts, by men's inarticulate hunger for the right to
govern themselves.

Canadians know the story of the Rebellion, of self-government and Confederation, but there is so much more to be
learned if the past, the present, and the future of Canada are
to be understood; if the British Commonwealth and what it
stands for in the world are to be understood. And here in these
old stone houses, these parlors, amid the trunks of old hooped
skirts, in ancient woodsheds and overgrown gardens—here
you must search for our story. . . .

The United Empire Loyalists are newly come from the victorious United States of America. They move by ship on the
St. Lawrence into Upper Canada. They settle along the shore
and build new shack towns. They hack down the hardwood

forests and chop out narrow roads. They live in log cabins until they can build stone houses; they have brought a few pieces of furniture from the Thirteen Colonies, a grandfather's clock that came out of England long ago, a desk or oak dresser. They are so poor in their cabins among the stumps that often a soup bone is passed from family to family for successive boilings—and many are people who considered themselves the gentry of New England.

They are Tories, they opposed the Revolution, they followed the tattered British flag into this wilderness of Upper Canada, but they are free men, of the New World, who have lived long on this side of the ocean, the sons of men who left Britain because they wanted freedom and elbow room. Here in the British colony of Upper Canada they find no freedom, no elbow room.

At the absurd village capital of York, which will some day become Toronto, the Loyalists find instead a puffed-up imitation of a Georgian court. A governor from England rules there with absolute powers, surrounded by a gang of sycophants, landed gentry, clergy, and hangers-on, knit in such close conspiracy that the poor people call them the Family Compact.

Historians will blandly assume that, having learned its lesson in the United States, Britain eagerly allowed Canada to have whatever freedom it asked. The Loyalists find just the opposite. Britain has decided not to make the old mistake. It will rule Canada so firmly that there can be no rebellion a second time.

Governor John Graves Simcoe looks out from his crude capital on the shore of Lake Ontario, expecting to hear the resounding collapse of the United States at any moment because it is that impossible thing, a democracy; and, to the poor struggling men who murmur among the stumps of their niggard fields, he makes a lofty reply: "The best Security that all just Government has for its Existence is founded on the Morality of the People and such Morality has no true Basis, but when placed on Religious Principles." Francis Gore, a later representative of the King, further pledges himself: "I have had the King's interest only at Heart, and I have and ever will contend against Democratic Principles."

Morality and Religion are not enough for the poor men who have sought freedom under the British flag. They speak out more loudly and insistently from among the stumps. Bartimus Ferguson, of Niagara, dares to criticize Governor Maitland and is put in the stocks daily for a month. Robert Gourlay, a grim Scot, ventures to point out that the Family Compact, founded on Morality and Religious Principles, is making a fortune in land graft, and he is jailed. John Galt, the Scottish poet who is trying to bring British settlers out to Upper Canada, calls York "one of the worst blue-devil haunts on the face of the earth." But a greater Scot is brooding on these evils and will yet fight them in the open, with ball and powder.

William Lyon Mackenzie, who edits the *Colonial Advocate,* calls the Family Compact a "nest of unclean birds," but he is too insignificant for the Compact's attention—a squat man with gigantic head, cadaverous face, a stiff rim of side whiskers, and burning, fanatic eyes. "A tiny creature," says the new governor, Sir Francis Bond Head. A tiny creature and restless as a squirrel in a cage.

Poor Head! "You see, you're such a damned odd fellow," says Lord Melbourne over his shaving mug to the newly appointed governor, who seems to have been appointed by mistake, when the royal messenger confused him with a better man. Poor empty Head, the damned odd fellow, how can he know that the Tiny Creature's grandson will be prime minister of an independent Canada, sign treaties with the United States, declare Canada's right to remain neutral in Britain's wars, and yet—strangest paradox of all, far beyond poor befuddled Head—lead Canada into its greatest war at Britain's side? The damned odd fellow, all the damned odd fellows of York and London, cannot know. Such Tiny Creatures, says

the exquisite and well-barbered Head, can never trouble the
Family Compact, founded on Morality and Religious Principles. Nay, "the people of Canada," he writes home to London, "detest democracy." Damned odd fellow indeed.

The Tiny Creature persists surprisingly. When a gang of
ruffians throws his little hand press into the lake, Mackenzie
sues for damages and recovers them, for the courts must enforce the law in a British country even under the Compact.
But at least the Compact has its revenge. It tears down the
first fourteen stone feet of General Brock's monument at
Queenston Heights because, buried in the cornerstone with
other papers, are copies of the Tiny Creature's newspaper,
the *Colonial Advocate*. Childish gestures, small acts of violence among a few obscure people, lost in their wilderness, and
yet the first stirrings of rebellion. Perhaps Sam Adams and
Ben Franklin and the others looked no more impressive than
this when they began to stir.

Now the Tiny Creature grows bolder. He draws up a Declaration asking that a Congress shape a new system of government for Canada. This, perhaps, is our Canadian Declaration of Independence, though nobody of importance signs it
and the document is soon forgotten. Also, it is treason. Perhaps, thinks the damned odd fellow at York, something must
be done about the restless squirrel in the cage.

Now in the villages along the river, in the backwoods shan-
ties, the Patriots have been organized and scheme by night.
They drill in the forest and practice shooting at wild pigeons.
They have their companies, captains, passwords, and a few
guns. They forge pikes at the village smithy, with their fellows
guarding the door. Everywhere the Tiny Creature is traveling, agitating, orating, conspiring, writing, persuading, threatening. To the French *Patriotes* of Quebec, to Papineau and
Nelson, who are drilling also, he sends word that the time is
at hand.

December fifth is to be the day, the year 1837. A new queen, young Victoria, Kent's daughter, has been awakened in the dawn not many months ago and told that she is the ruler of the British Empire. She has never heard of the Tiny Creature, the desperate men whose fathers were Loyalists and fled into the wilderness to remain under her flag. The Patriots and the *Patriotes* have heard of her. Against Victoria, against her court at York, her Family Compact, they will fight with blunderbuss and new-forged pike, though it be treason, though it may mean death or deportation. They will fight like the patriots of New England, their grandfathers.

December 5, 1837, and meeting of Patriots at Montgomery's Tavern, banners crying "Liberty or Death!", farmers with blunderbuss and pike. But with the meeting confusion and change of plans, argument among leaders, divided counsels, failure of communication, shortage of food. Revolution cannot be fought on biscuits, cheese, and whisky. Yes, but there is no time to lose. Even now in York, four miles down the road, the terrified governor, the damned odd fellow, aroused at last, is armed with sword and three pistols stuffed in belt. The chief justice and other notables of the Compact stand in line, guns on shoulder, drilled by some unknown sergeant.

March on York nevertheless, without breakfast, without ammunition, with pikes and clubs. The Tiny Creature has given the order, cannot draw back, and is mounted now on horseback with a bodyguard, his fanatic eyes burning, his hour come. March on York and capture the Court for liberty, finishing the revolution and accomplishing the new state by nightfall!

At the toll gate the governor's soldiers fire and flee, the front rank of Patriots falls to the ground in terror, and the rear ranks, thinking their comrades all dead and having no arms but pike and club, run for the woods. Both armies of this strange battle in flight from each other—burlesque, indeed, yet much will hang on it, more than anyone can foresee that day.

The Tiny Creature, having no gift of prophecy, having no foresight of his grandson who will bear his name, believes that all is lost. He flees, horse gone, on foot, across the plowed fields and into Hogg's Hollow, wades streams, naked in midwinter, hides in pea stacks and in attics of friendly Patriots. For days Head's soldiers in hot pursuit walk past him, lying in frozen ditches. Once he escapes them disguised in women's clothes—an ugly crone, with growth of gray whisker. From house to house, village to village, hidden by the Patriots, he finally reaches the Niagara River, seizes a boat, and rows across, while Head's soldiers stand cursing him from the Canadian bank. Sanctuary at last for the broken rebel in the United States, but not the end. Not the end by more than a century.

Other Patriots fare differently. Dr. Charles Duncombe hides in bed, dressed as a grandmother, is examined by the soldiers, but not recognized, and they help him cross the river on the ice—the poor old woman who could not make the journey alone. When he reaches the American side he yells back defiantly at them in a man's voice. But eleven Patriots are executed, ninety-two deported to Van Diemen's Land, which is worse. Hundreds flee to the United States, penniless, whence their fathers came as Loyalists.

Meanwhile the *Patriotes* are busy in Quebec also, having there racial as well as economic hatreds. Louis Joseph Papineau has whipped the habitants to fury with his oratory against the governor and his clique at Quebec, and at St. Charles the *Patriotes* plant a tree of liberty, with liberty's cap tied to its top, and they march past, touching it, swearing to be free men or to die, but, defenseless before the well-armed soldiers, they soon flee. At Napierville, near the United States border, they proclaim the Republic of Lower Canada, they fight the soldiers with rusty muskets and pitchforks and they are captured, filling the jails. Liberty, they believe, is finished when it has yet to begin.

Even the Rebellion is not over yet. On the Niagara River (as recounted in detail by Edwin C. Guillet in his great study, *The Lives and Times of the Patriots*), Mackenzie boldly sets up a free government of Upper Canada, issues his own money, raises his own flag with two stars on it. American recruits, more than 400, join him in the cause of freedom and will yet make Canada part of the free United States. Muskets escape mysteriously from the U. S. Government arsenal at Buffalo and a cannon is removed "to shoot wild ducks."

On the Canadian shore the soldiers stand to, for it looks now like the second war with the United States in twenty-five years. In the darkness the Canadians cross the river and seize the American ship *Caroline,* which serves the Rebels, kill her crew, set her afire, and send her drifting down the current, red-hot, until smoldering pieces of her are seen hurtling over the falls. War indeed, but President Van Buren will overlook it, having a depression on his hands and desiring no more trouble.

At Prescott bloodier deeds are afoot. Nils Von Schoultz, a young Pole who loves freedom more than life, has decided to rescue Canada from Britain. With a handful of followers he crosses the St. Lawrence from Ogdensburg, seizes the round stone windmill at the river's bank. Immediately he is outnumbered by the Canadian soldiers, and the people of Prescott do not rise against the tyranny of the Queen, being strangely deaf to liberty. Always the Patriots are outnumbered, poorly armed, hopeless, but desperate with their hatred of the Compact.

Siege of the windmill; cannon balls of the Compact tearing the thick stone wall apart; food short, water gone, no balls for the single cannon, only nails, hinges, and belt buckles; and, at last, surrender. Schoultz, before his hanging, wills money to the new widows of Canadian soldiers and writes a letter to his sister, forgiving the Canadian nation: "My last wish to the Americans is that they may not think of avenging my death. Let no further blood be shed; and believe me, from what I have seen, that all the stories that were told about the suffering of the Canadian people were untrue." Fine young Pole, he does not understand that strange and tolerant organ, the British heart.

Poor deluded Schoultz, who thought that Canadians, however desperate, would join the United States, who did not understand that the cause of the Rebellion itself was a desire for a Canada free of any other nation. And poor Tiny Creature in exile, in an American jail for "breach of neutrality" (just discovered after these many months), melting down his Patriot gold medal to buy food for his family, without even bread in the house on his daughter's birthday—ruined Tiny Creature, who could not know that his daughter's son, William Lyon Mackenzie King, bearing his name, would rise some day in a free Canadian parliament as its master, with fist clenched, to boast of his mother's sufferings, of his Rebel blood. Poor restless squirrel in a cage, but he will yet return to Canada, sit in a free legislature, regretting his violence.

Poor Patriots all, who thought everything lost, who found that most of the Canadians were against them, loyal to the young Queen of England. Loyal, yes, unwilling to rebel, but they would have self-government, none more insistent than those who would not take up the arms of treason. And in London the young Queen and her ministers, terrified by violence in Upper Canada, horrified that Britishers could shed blood again in America within sixty years of Lexington, fearing another American Revolution, bestir themselves. Perhaps it is time to recall that damned odd fellow.

So Governor Head leaves York hurriedly; traveling for safety through the United States, disguised as a valet, he is recognized sitting on a wheelbarrow in an inn yard at Watertown, invited to breakfast by the Canadian refugee Patriots, and sent off with cheers. Even in exile the Canadians do not lose their British sense of humor. Head has gone in valet's clothes, damned odd fellow to the last, and with him the Second British Empire.

The First Empire ended at Yorktown. The Third will begin, all unsuspected, at York. There Lord Durham, hastily dispatched from London to discover what is wrong in the wilderness, recognizes an obvious fact—that Britishers will govern themselves, in metropolis or woods. Thus he reports to the British Government, and the Durham Report, recommending self-government for Canada, is the first charter of the Third Empire.

Upper and Lower Canada are united in a single colony, the governor choosing his ministers out of an elected chamber, but while Durham would limit self-government thus, he has recognized it, London has granted it, and can set no limits to it. Thus planted, the seeds must grow.

In 1800 James Madison has said that the American Revolution was fought because Britain denied "The fundamental principle . . . that the Colonies were co-ordinate members each with the other and with Great Britain of an Empire united by a common executive sovereign." By the Durham Report, Canada has begun to achieve that co-ordinate membership without leaving the Empire. There is much yet to be done, but men like Robert Baldwin, of Upper Canada, the real father of Canadian democracy, will do it.

The whole thing, say the constitutional authorities of London, is constitutionally impossible, for how can an English governor obey the English Crown, which he represents, and accept the advice of Canadian ministers, if Crown and ministers do not agree? Basically unworkable, illogical, sure to break up the Empire. And Baldwin has no answer, except that Canadians must and will govern themselves, logically or otherwise.

Thus throwing logic aside, ignoring the constitutionalists, the new Empire begins to march forward into the dark, hoping for the best. Who can be bold enough to say then, when London thinks its Empire dissolving before its eyes, that it is becoming stronger than ever, with a new and firmer foundation, on the only possible basis of real strength, the willing partnership of its parts?

Thirty years later, when I was a man, I came back to Prescott and found my way without difficulty up Dibble Street to the old house, for no one could mistake that oblong pile of stone, the double door, the green shutters. The elms had been chopped down, the high brick wall around the garden was gone, and the stable and woodshed and sentry box, but the house was little changed.

An old man answered my knock on the door. He had been the son of our washerwoman in Grandfather's time, had saved his money and finally bought our house. We went over it together and he showed it to me with a rather pathetic eagerness —the cavernous parlor and dining room, the sunny room upstairs where all of us were born, and finally up the steep, narrow staircase to the attic. Alas, it was bare now and swept clean, no trunks full of clothes to dress up in, no hooped skirts, no tailor's dummy that could be made conveniently into a bogey man to scare people in a dark hall. An age had passed and a family with it, and the old house, belonging truly to us alone, seemed to sigh a little and wish for its end.

As I was leaving, with the strange feeling of men who have seen suddenly something they have lost and can never recapture, who have grown out of something better than they can ever be again, the owner called me back to the doorstep. He had gone into a cupboard and brought out a little white bust of Sir John A. Macdonald, who was the chief architect and first prime minister of the Dominion of Canada.

The bust stands before me as I write these words—the shock

of curly hair, the tired, wily old eyes, the bulbous caricature of a nose—Sir John, who was my grandfather's friend and idol. The bust, said the old man as he handed it to me, had been left in the attic when our family moved out, left by mistake, no doubt, because he remembered well that Grandfather valued it. He had kept it all these years, thinking that perhaps one of us would turn up. So I took Sir John with me, lugging him in my suit case for months across America and back again, until he finally found repose on my mantel shelf on the Pacific Coast, which he saved for the Canadian Union.

Sir John and his colleagues carried on Baldwin's labor. The constitution of the new colony, formed jointly of English Upper Canada and French Lower Canada, would not work. In the Canadian parliament there was soon deadlock between the two races, but still larger causes impelled a change. Looking across the British territories of North America, Sir John beheld the strong central region surrounded on the east by the colonies of New Brunswick, Nova Scotia, and Prince Edward Island, which had secured a measure of self-government also, but were divided and weak; on the west by an untraveled wilderness of lake and plain; while on the Pacific Coast the colony of British Columbia even then was considering union with the Americans. Assuredly such a disjointed congeries of population would not remain free long. Either it would fall by its own will into the lap of the Americans or they would take it, as indeed many of the Americans intended.

London by now was hardly interested. What use were colonies that wanted to run themselves and might not even fight for England? Gladstone wrote to a friend suggesting that these troublesome Canadian possessions be ceded to the Americans as the price of peace during the strained relations of the Civil War period. John Bright approved this proposal. Canadians were beginning to think they would be invaded from the south again for the third time when the end of the Civil

War gave the Americans time to look around, and apparently no British troops would be on hand to stop them.

In the little Ontario towns, in the villages of Quebec, in the new and untried stuff of Canada, another great idea began to stir. Confederation was the magic word—a federation of all the Canadian colonies in a single nation. Sir John, the Conservative, and George Brown, the Liberal, joined together after long blood feud to make possible the union of the new nation. At Quebec City, on the tenth day of October, 1864, in an old hotel on the cliff, the Fathers of Confederation met. They came from the Canadas, from New Brunswick, Nova Scotia, Prince Edward Island, and Newfoundland; and never was a nation better served, as if the mothers of Canada had recognized the hour of destiny years before and borne men strong enough to carry it.

This was our Canadian version of the Philadelphia Congress, but where the Congress lasted all one weary spring and summer and often was on the verge of going home in despair, and had to recess while General Washington went fishing and the delegates cooled off, the Quebec Conference drafted the pact of Confederation in fourteen working days. It worked in secret, and all its secrets are not known, but we do know that while it encountered difficulties in detail and a few desperate moments, it was agreed to in principle from the start.

The delegates were agreed on the establishment of a new nation, embracing all the British territory of North America, and founded on the federal principle of the United States, with separate and powerful provincial governments, bound to Britain through a representative of the King, and operating generally on the British parliamentary pattern.

Off to England went the Founding Fathers, laid their scheme before Britain, and the British Government, glimpsing for the first time, perhaps, the shape of the Third Empire, approved it. Unable to think of a better name (though Sir John stood out for the Kingdom of Canada), they called the new creation, this doubtful and unheard-of constitutional invention, this second British nation which was to govern itself, the Dominion of Canada.

When the British Parliament passed the British North America Act (Canada's constitution) the Colonial Secretary, Lord Carnarvon, said: "We are laying the foundation of a great state—perhaps one which at a future day may even overshadow this country." Noble lords and gentlemen of Parliament, blink at those words and smile to yourselves. Within seventy years you may think differently.

There were still breakers ahead. Newfoundland rejected the whole scheme. British Columbia had to be persuaded, by a narrow vote, to abandon thought of union with the Americans, on condition that a railway be built to the Pacific Coast —a high price, but Sir John was willing to pay it for a nation stretching from sea to sea. Later, the intervening prairie lands were made into three separate provinces.

For the present Canada had to work still through the darkness, moving no one knew where. The Second Empire was illogical, perhaps impossible, and the shape of the Third, though growing visible in the distance, was not clear. Logic there could be none, and when it was attempted it only made trouble. Sir John began, quietly and with infinite cunning, to resist logic, demurred when Britain asked Canada to send troops overseas automatically and without negotiation. "A British subject I was born, a British subject I will die" is his most memorable saying, but what was a British subject in Canada? Must he fight at the will of a British Government in a purely British war? And how could the King be advised by ministers in London and ministers in Ottawa if the ministers could not agree? Sir John did not know.

Neither did his great French-Canadian successor, Sir Wilfrid Laurier. They could only insist on Canada's rights from day to day, demand this power and that power as seemed necessary, and hope that the end result would work.

The forces of logic rose again in Laurier's time more persistently than ever. When he went to England to consult with the British Government he found a new man there, Joe Chamberlain, father of Neville. The Empire, said Chamberlain and his party, must be welded together, made stronger, made invincible by some form of central government, perhaps by the principle of federation, so successful in the United States and Canada, applied to all the British dominions and colonies.

The pressure on Laurier was well nigh not to be borne. "It is hard," said the tired French-Canadian, "to stand up against the flattery of a gracious duchess. Weak men's minds are turned in an evening and there are few men who can resist long. We were dined and wined by royalty and aristocracy and plutocracy, and always the talk was of empire, empire, empire." It was the age of empire, of a mystical imperialism, hardly of the flesh but a worship of the intangible idea, Race. "That proud, persistent, self-asserting and resolute stock," Chamberlain called it, "which is infallibly destined to be the predominating force in the future history and civilization of the world." (At which Laurier might smile discreetly, belonging to another race entirely.)

It was the last burst of the Second Empire, which was even then dying invisibly, a sudden surge of sentiment which found its outward symbol in the aged Queen Victoria, who would soon die also. In her first year she had seen the Rebellion of 1837. Now, in her last, it was the fervent hope of the Imperialists that she would see the Empire re-consolidated in London.

It was not easy to resist even from the safe distance of Ottawa. All Laurier's long rule of fifteen years he was fighting Empire centralization, fighting an "unrelenting imperialist campaign," as his friend and ablest critic, John W. Dafoe, has shown in a great study of that era. Always Sir Wilfrid resisted, with a smile, with elegance, with postponement, equivocation, delay. What else could he do? He had no real alternative to offer, which the Canadian people would accept. The Third Empire must develop by itself, slowly.

But Laurier would accept no "Great Council of the Empire," as urged by Mr. Chamberlain. No contribution of Canadian money to the British Navy. No Canadian army ready for overseas service. No consultations with Britain on foreign policy even, for that would bind Canada to decisions which must finally be taken by Britain alone. The time was not ripe for Canadian independence, nor Canadian opinion ready. Laurier must fight Chamberlain in London, and at home the Imperialists who saw him breaking up the Empire. He could only hold the fort and wait.

The time came in the first World War. There Canada gave over 600,000 men out of her small population to fight for Britain and the Empire, and left 60,000 of them dead in France. After that sacrifice, that demonstration of full co-operation with Britain, Laurier's successor, Sir Robert Borden, insisted on his country's signing the Treaty of Versailles, becoming a member of the League of Nations. For the first time Canada was a nation and yet still, in theory, inferior in status to Great Britain. The facts, however, had outrun the theory. The Chamberlain idea had failed, the Baldwins, Macdonalds, Lauriers, Bordens had succeeded. A new thing had grown up, little noticed, upon the earth—the British Commonwealth of free nations, though not recognized yet in law.

The Tiny Creature's grandson, William Lyon Mackenzie King, was now prime minister, boasting of his Rebel blood, hating Imperialism, yet destined to back Britain at the final hour. Mr. King held Laurier's fort, being trained by the master himself. In 1922, when Lloyd George wanted to fight Turkey, Mr. King would send no troops without consulting Parliament, a polite way of refusing, and Britain did not fight Turkey. In 1923 Mr. King sent his Ernest Lapointe down to

Washington, unannounced, to sign a treaty between Canada and its neighbor for the protection of halibut fisheries, to the amazement of British and American statesmen and the horror of the *Times*. The Empire was breaking up again, over halibut. Then Mr. King refused to make Canada a part of the ill-fated Locarno Treaty.

These were the facts. The theory could look after itself. The theory was reconciled to the fact in 1926, when a Conservative British statesman, Arthur Balfour, drafted the declaration that the British nations are "equal in status, in no way subordinate to one another in any aspect of their domestic or external affairs, though united by a common allegiance to the Crown and freely associated as members of the British Commonwealth of Nations." That was the birth certificate of the Third Empire, which no longer was an empire by any recognizable parallel in history.

In 1931 the Balfour Declaration was written into the Statute of Westminster and became the constitution of the Commonwealth, or perhaps it would be better to say the acknowledged lack of constitution, the defiance of constitution, and the complete reliance on free will and free co-operation.

Britain, says the press of Mr. W. R. Hearst, has never surrendered "any valuable territory, any strategic harbor" and would never think of giving up "the great gold lands of the Rand." Britain by 1926 had surrendered all the best and richest of its Empire, had lost all control of the gold lands of the Rand, and the Irish harbors belonged to the Irish people, who would not permit them to be used by the desperate fleets of Britain in its death struggle with Germany.

The Empire indeed was given away, as a heartbroken Disraeli had long ago predicted. Chamberlain's dream had ended. There remained only to write the obituary.

Instead of an obituary Canada wrote a declaration of war on Germany in September, 1939, staked everything on a British victory, sent its sons overseas again, raised its national budget six times and loaned Britain enormous sums. Yet in that very act Canada saw to it that its final right of independence was conceded. It advised the King on its own behalf, its own King direct, not the British Government, to declare a state of war. Thus was Canada's right to remain neutral in any war also declared in the same breath by which Canada resolved to stand by Britain in this just war, win or lose.

The restless spirit of the Tiny Creature must have been in the House of Commons, beside his grandson that day, and the spirits of Baldwin, Macdonald, Laurier, and Borden, the men who had known that Canadians could be persuaded by a good cause but not pushed by a British government.

This is the story which begins in little stone houses, like the one at the corner of Dibble and Edward Streets, the story of a people slow to anger, seeking change by evolution and rather slowly, conservative of mind, expecting no miracles but strangely persistent underneath it all, with a hard streak seldom seen, a deep hunger for a liberty. That passion lacked orators, lacked a Jefferson or a Henry, but could not be stifled.

Such is the story that comes out of the houses along the river and such today is the British Commonwealth which the men of those houses wrung from history. For it was they and no other who compelled the formation of the Third Empire; they who could not foresee its form nor draw its plans but built it day by day through improvisation and blind hope.

If you would look for the birthplace of that Commonwealth, which at this writing is fighting for its life, look not in Downing Street, in Westminster, or the Palace. Look in the little towns of the St. Lawrence, the bleak stone houses where our grandfathers lived and believed in themselves and each other.

The Ready Way to Canada

The statesmen made a treaty. They signed it in the gloomy East Block of Ottawa on a cold spring morning. In the silence of an historic moment the cameras clicked and the pens scratched. They would tame the River to men's uses.

Did the River hear the faint scratching of the pens? Was the sound of cameras perceptible beside the falls of Niagara, in the whirlpools, eddies, and rapids? No, the River only smiled that morning and went about its spring business of breaking the winter's ice, for it knew men would never tame it. They might use it, grasp a little of its power for themselves, build cities at its sides, and launch their ships upon its current, but nothing could alter by more than a few yards the irresistible current of the St. Lawrence or curb its yearning towards the sea.

How often the River had seen men calculate its future and measure its value! "And the said men did, moreover, certify unto us," wrote Cartier, "that there was the way and beginning of the great river of Hochelaga, and ready way to Canada, which river the farther it went the narrower it came, even unto Canada, and that then there was fresh water which went so far upwards that they had never heard of any man who had gone to the head of it."

So Cartier, sailing into a bay at the River's mouth on August 10, 1535, the feast day of St. Lawrence, named the ready way to Canada after that holy man. Poor Lawrence, who died on a red-hot gridiron by order of the Emperor Valerian because he would not surrender the treasures of the Christian church—

holy man, he could not foresee that his name would dominate a new world beyond the ocean.

The ready way indeed, for Indian scalping party, for singing voyageur, for black-robed Jesuit missionary eager to die in the Indian fires, for French noble in silks, satin, and saber. The ready way which, held by the Iroquois, could force the white man to go inland by the Ottawa and the long portages, until Frontenac, with his navy of 120 canoes, his banners, muskets and swords, thrust back the Indians, seized the Lakes and saw, with sure soldier's eye, that whoever held them held the West and the whole heart of the continent.

Thence the exploration of the Mississippi, the line of French forts to the Gulf, which New France might have held, but for the betrayals of the court in Versailles. Thence Etienne Brulé, first white man to see Lake Superior, only to be boiled and eaten by the Hurons. Thence also the wanderers on foot across the prairies—La Verendrye of Three Rivers, whose sons saw the Rockies from the Mandan country.

To all travelers the River was the ready way, to all communities the road, to all industry the source of life. To all invaders the ready way as well. Wolfe came up the river. Montgomery crossed it and was shot down in Lower Town. The Americans of 1812 crossed it again and Brock died beside it. On the river and its lakes the little warships fired their tiny guns, and as his brig Simcoe *sank beneath him Jim Richardson climbed into the shrouds and aimed his musket at the Yankees.*

Sea battles on the River current, soldiers fighting on its banks because they knew the River controlled the land and the boundaries of nations, but peaceful men remembering it not as a war path but as the ready way of commerce. Absurd, said the British Admiralty, to talk of taking ships up to Montreal. Dredge the channel, said the Admiralty, and the silt will slip back again. But the habitant, fishing through the ice, knew of a deep channel gouged by the current and easily widened. By the fifties the ships were going up the river and soon the first shallow canals were dug around the rapids.

Sir John A. Macdonald, a lad fresh out of Scotland, saw the blue water over the side of the ship—wee lad, did he hope then to rule this land beside the river and make it a nation? Laurier, his successor, saw the gray Ottawa join the blue St. Lawrence and both flow in bands of separate color like the two races of Canada, their difference clearly marked, but in perfect unity.

The ready way to Canada, and the statesmen sign their treaty, the engineers dream their dreams, and the St. Lawrence rolls on, draining the interior of the continent, bearing outward the loaded ships as easily as it bears the fine earth, the silt, the rain, the ice—rolls on, knowing that it will bear races of men yet unborn and still roll after all races of men have gone. Will roll as long as rain falls in America and water seeks the ocean.

CHAPTER SEVEN

The Wedge

Between Lake Huron on the west, Lakes Erie and Ontario on the south, and the Ottawa River system on the north, a ragged Canadian wedge juts southward, across the forty-ninth parallel of latitude, deep into the United States.

It is physically almost an island, surrounded by lake and river. Economically it is still more insular behind a Chinese wall of tariffs. Spiritually it is isolated from the rest of Canada. Yet it is the very core and hub of Canada.

Here beats its great industrial heart, with the steady beat of forges, factories, and arsenals. Here breathes steadily its lung, sucking commerce through river and canal. Here also is the stomach, absorbing nourishment from the rest of the country with ravenous appetite. Here is the chief nerve ganglion of electrical power. At the top of the wedge is the nation's brain in Ottawa.

To this vital organic region, you might almost say, the rest of Canada forms but the extremities, supplying the food, digesting the products. Cut the wedge out of Canada, run the boundary straight along the forty-ninth parallel, and Canada's heart stops beating, it suffocates and collapses.

In economic power, in money, in politics, in population, the wedge of Ontario is the true center of Canada. Yet in some ways it is the least typical part of the country. Most of us in the west came from there originally and scattered everywhere, but we can never return. Our birthplace is forever a stranger to us and its people not of our ways. Why, we do not rightly

understand. We only know that these eastern people are different from us so that a westerner—or a French-Canadian or
a Maritimer for that matter—does not feel at home here.

This is more than envy of Ontario's power and prosperity,
or jealousy of its tariff, which costs us so dear. Urban Quebec
around Montreal is economically part of the same wedge, and
shares its fortunes, but in outlook is far removed from it. No,
it is the life of industrial Ontario which baffles us, the feeling,
the attitude. We take our goods from there, we take our politics largely from there, our business management, but we do
not take our ideas. We feel, we who have gone from there and
spread across the nation, like the son returning in middle age
to his father's house, which he loves and sighs for, but cannot
live in any more.

To any Canadian from a distance, Toronto, Ontario's capital and metropolis, is almost an alien city. He may well feel
more at home in Boston or San Francisco. "One of the worst
blue-devil haunts on the face of the earth!" cried John Galt,
the Scottish immigrant poet, in the days of the Family Compact. "The City of Toronto has more grasping, greedy, unc-
tuous people in it than any other city in the world!" shouts
Ralph Maybank, of Winnipeg, in the Parliament of Canada
today. These are fearful words out of desperate mouths—too
fearful, too desperate.

Toronto is a great and gracious city, second only to Montreal in size (getting on for a million people) ; and the remains
of York, except for a few earthworks, barracks, and rusty
cannons, have been engulfed in stone and mortar. By the lake
shore the streets are old and narrow but they turn to noble
avenues as the city marches ever northward. There Toronto
has spacious parks, fine homes, modern skyscrapers, an illustrious university. If there is a Canadian culture in the strict
sense, this probably is its center. Here books are published,
and national magazines. Here writers and artists work. Here
Banting made insulin. Here, too, the financial headquarters of

Canada are fast centering, in place of their old capital at Montreal. In Toronto most of the larger commercial organizations of the country maintain their central offices.

Still, to many Canadians it retains the old name given to it by jealous neighbors long ago. It is Hog Town—Hog Town one supposes, because it fattened on the rest of the surrounding country through a protective tariff, at the expense of other towns and whole provinces. An unfair name for any city, but Toronto is certainly a queer place, an exhibit which no student of Canada can afford to overlook.

It comes out of our deep past and uncertain present. It is the United Empire Loyalist town of York grown up and, perhaps, the Family Compact in a twentieth-century incarnation. That fine old Loyalist stock is the foundation of modern Toronto and one of the three great influences which merge in its strange character.

That part of Toronto which comes of this stout breed often remains more British than Britain, more loyal than the King. It brought with it from the revolting Thirteen Colonies, a prejudice against the United States and this, among some natives, has never died. There is still a hard kernel of people here who have not outgrown the War of 1812 or the Rebellion of 1837. It is not without significance that not until a few years ago was a statue raised in Toronto to William Lyon Mackenzie, the Rebel, and then only at the side of the legislative buildings, as if Toronto were rather ashamed of him.

Here the Colonial Mind, that curious vestigial organ which no longer functions but often can ache, still manages to exist without nourishment and without reason or use. Out of Toronto occasionally comes such a bleat of colonialism and inferiority complex, such a desire to be in chains again, such a moan for the world that has gone, as no other North American can understand. This is sometimes miscalled Imperialism. Actually, it is pure nostalgia. But it is not to be confused with something better which makes the young men of Toronto rush to the colors whenever war breaks out—a considered belief in the British Commonwealth of Nations. In the wails of a few people who are afraid to grow up, this finer sentiment is often misunderstood among Canadians, which is a pity.

It should not be forgotten either that out of Toronto has come some bold Canadian national thinking and more influence towards co-operation with the United States than the public yet knows. Still, Toryism, old-fashioned nineteenth-century Imperialism, and Family Compactism still form one of the three basic strains in this Toronto character.

The second is Ontario's attitude towards Quebec. To the French race, its aspirations, character, and religion, Ontario considers itself the necessary counterbalance. At times this feeling becomes plain race prejudice, blue-devil worship in the worst form. Orange Lodges parading down the streets with King William on a white horse, clerics screeching against the Pope in obscure Toronto churches, frenzied editorial howls in the *Telegram* have been the outward manifestations of this anti-French feeling, which ebbs and flows perpetually.

The third factor in this character is purely economic. Central Ontario, the great wedge, with Toronto in the middle of it, has been built on the principle of isolation, on the basis of economic self-containment, in the shelter of a high tariff. It cannot conceive of life without this protection. It cannot imagine how its great industries could survive if they had to compete on equal terms with the richer, more economical industries of the United States. Ontario has to cling to what it owns, to fight down all attempts to remove its tariff wall, to drive its wedge ever deeper into the economy of Canada, if necessary to bonus its poor neighbors so that they will accept the high price of Ontario goods.

That is why the wedge is a separate community of its own, far more than a physical island. It is an economic and spiritual island. That is why Toronto must be the most insular city of its size anywhere, the largest small town in the world. That, too, is part of the old prejudice against Americans—a secret fear of American goods. But the final paradox lies in the fact that of all Canadian cities Toronto is the most American in appearance, in organization, and in daily habits.

I do not pretend to understand Toronto. All students of Canada have tried to plumb these depths, but all, so far as I know, have failed. The views of outsiders must be weighed against their prejudice, distance from the place, and envy. The fact remains, however, that Toronto is a city apart, and the Canadian from other places stifles here. He finds Toronto people busy with their own local affairs and not interested in his, and much of the content of the newspapers, the largest in Canada, are a mystery to him.

He finds an odd stuffiness and exaggerated respectability (or so it seems to him), a strait-jacket regularity of behavior, a deep-blue conventionalism, and not merely the lack of the free and easy life as we know it out West but, worse, the lack of a desire for it, the knowledge of its possibility. He finds also a piety here which annoys him (perhaps because he is not so virtuous himself) and in every Canadian's mind the symbol of Toronto, the accepted caricature, is a gentleman in a top hat walking to church on Sunday with a Bible under his arm, and frowning at the neighbor who is cutting the grass. Few cut the grass in Toronto on Sunday. Toronto the Good, we call it, and that is the sneer of the tough boy who doesn't like Sunday school.

Something deep is stirring here. The old values are in flux. You cannot mistake that from the current character of Ontario politics. As this is written there presides at Queen's Park, in the wrinkled old legislative buildings, an important phenomenon of Canadian life, Mr. Mitchell Hepburn, whose memory, if not his person, will long outlast these present stirrings. That the Family Compact, within a century, could have heaved up such a successor must surely puzzle historians.

In these buildings great men have ruled. Government has been in the hands generally of a caste not hereditary but at least genteel. Now this young farm boy, powerfully supported by the newly rich mining and other big interests, has utterly shattered the old crust, has introduced a shrill scream and a glib wisecrack into Canadian politics, has conducted a perpetual blood feud with the prime minister of Canada, the leader of his own party, has appeared on one hand as the dirt farmer, on the other, as the friend of the rich industrialist, and altogether as a creature impossible to classify in the traditions of this country.

He looks like a country boy who has come to town and got a good job and slick clothes, and now comes back to the village store to sit on a cracker barrel telling jokes. He looks like the original of all the traveling-salesmen stories. And he has always looked as if he wouldn't last another election. But, by native shrewdness and a breezy friendliness which makes men cling to him, he remains in power, and remains a danger to any national government because he represents the wedge, and because he knows how to appeal to the mob.

That is Hepburn's only importance—as a symptom of a changing Ontario, the end of something and the beginning of something else which nobody yet understands. You can call him merely the cracker-barrel prophet of Hog Town, but this old conservative province, this province of gentility and of aristocratic tradition, of imperialism and, above all, of respectability, elects and re-elects the brawling antithesis of its supposed character.

That character must be in ferment. The ferment is deep indeed and more hopeful than we had thought, when Wendell Willkie, an American, is mobbed by cheering crowds in the Toronto streets and the Stars and Stripes flies in the legislature. Perhaps the wedge has changed far more than we have suspected. Perhaps it was never quite what we thought. Perhaps all we have been saying of it, all our painful analyses, are out of date, are shadows only of a thing which is quietly disappearing.

So much for speculation, which never can reach any goal. Toronto is not Ontario any more than New York is the United States, and you feel that as soon as you drive out of the city into the pleasant Ontario countryside.

Here you are in the region of the little towns again, with their remaining flavor of the old days, the smell of quiet and contentment—the old farms and the old roads where soldiers and rebels used to march. No other part of Canada is like this. It is the only part with sufficient population and density of towns, villages and industries to be compared with the industrial regions of the United States. Here—a spectacle unknown in most parts of our country—you may see furnace flame against the darkness at night and smoke against the daylight sky. Here you may feel the regular pulse of industry, which is strange to most of us. Yet a garden, outside the factory gate, and the only district of Canada so well tilled, tended, and beloved that you can see in it a touch of the English countryside, which has taken ten centuries to make—orchards in the Niagara Peninsula; clusters of apple and peach trees and long fields of grapes; old brick farmhouses under immemorial elms; fat barns reeling drunkenly homeward over the hills; cool lanes and rambling country roads; and always behind them the hard and glittering sheet of Lake Ontario.

I wanted to go to Niagara again as I had first gone, long ago, on a little steamer from Toronto. I still remembered the trees along the river, the fluid and ever changing flow of green down the steep hillsides, the trilliums in May so thick that you could not put your foot between them. I want to go on the absurd trolley which used to run in endless rattle up and down the river canyon between the autumn smolder of red maple leaves. But the Man from Toronto said we must drive this time by the new highways. He was a kindly man, but with a hard tongue, logical brain, and a face of native flint, and he wanted to show me that the old turnpikes of Ontario had been made as broad and smooth as the superhighways of the United States. I saw that they were, but it didn't interest me.

Like any Canadian from the outlands I could not keep my eyes off the great estates, mansions, gardens, and wealth of the homes along the lake shore. We do not have them in other parts of Canada—a few estates, maybe, the odd country home of the rich man, but never the concentrated, heaped-up riches of the Toronto suburbs, palace after palace, in broad grounds, too perfectly tended.

"Wrung," I said, "out of the toil of millions of farmers, lumberjacks, and fishermen you never heard of." And Jean complained at the tariff-swollen price of her washing machine and electric egg beater compared with the American price. "Still," said Jean, westerner from Vancouver, "if this is Canada, I rather like it. I think I'll take out my Canadian papers."

"Nonsense," said the Man from Toronto. "The whole country lives and fattens on us. Who makes the goods? Who pays the taxes? Who foots the bills? Who mans the armies?"

That I could not take time to answer. All around were the homes of the men in the upper income brackets, the heads of corporations, the directors of companies, the captains of industry, the men who paid the bills. They seemed to be standing it pretty well.

What surprises the outlander most is the stone house of Ontario. We are largely a nation of wood houses or, at best, of brick. Few Canadians ever live behind stone walls, but here in Ontario they have stone, some of the best in the world, and they know how to use it out of long experience. Still, as I said to my hard Toronto friend, we have no house architecture in Canada. We have originated nothing, unless it be the Quebec farm house, low and clinging to the soil, with deep eaves and vast chimneys at each end, a clean, simple, and good design. But it came in the first place out of Europe. Perhaps the old Ontario house, the oblong stone house with green shutters, is our best Canadian attempt, if a pretty literal copy of the Georgian can be called ours.

Alas, I said, as we raced along the superhighway down into the Niagara country, what they have done to these earlier and uncorrupted models! The brick house of the nineties, with its tortured gingerbread ornament of wood, its ghastly porches, stuck to its side with mucilage, its monstrous and glaring ugliness, has littered our older cities and now, in its feeble old age and poverty, becomes an evil slum. Or the square, grisly clapboard house in our wooded country, a perversion of all architectural line, a bastard Georgian in the wrong materials —what right has it to live when wood can be burned so easily?

"It's functional," said my Toronto friend. "That's the reason for its existence. It's functional."

"Yes," said Jean, with a sudden burst of understanding, "but so is an elephant functional, the most perfectly functional thing I ever saw, but who wants to be an elephant?"

"You would want to be one if you had to live like an elephant," my friend grumbled.

"But why must we live like elephants?" Jean demanded. "And why must we live like savages when we have all the materials at hand to build beautiful homes?"

"Men," said he, "don't require much beauty if they can keep warm."

That dismal theory the houses of America generally confirm. Why, even on our Pacific Coast, where grows the finest building wood out of doors, we have never yet invented a form to capture and use it, a Canadian design natural to our Canadian materials, as the cuckoo-clock houses are to Switzerland, the white colonial houses to New England; and though I could see along the Niagara road how much the modern architect has improved on the red-brick era, it is theft only, of English designs mostly, and occasionally out of American modernism.

"Too busy," said the Man from Toronto, who was a man of few words.

Yes, too busy. Too busy tilling the land, building the factories. Here in this Ontario country you could see what appeared to be the perfect balance between land and machine—the finely tilled farms with their walls of field stones, gathered through the years out of the soil, and then, a few miles apart, the pleasant little towns built around their factories. Lively towns, streets crammed with cars, stores crowded, indistinguishable from the main streets of any manufacturing town in America. Perfect balance, yes, but so vulnerable.

How many of these people in the little towns understood, I asked, that they lived not on their own resources but on the resources of the sprawling, empty nation around them—on the ability of the prairie farmer to sell his wheat in the world and buy his machinery, tools, binder twine, clothes, shoes, automobile, breakfast food here in Ontario? Too busy, my friend repeated. Too busy indeed. Never realizing that this great wedge of industry is an artificial creation largely, made by the tariff which forces Canada to buy Canadian-made products even at a high price.

What marvelous growth in this wedge, despite all natural obstacles! The wedge has no iron of its own and can buy its supplies more cheaply from the Mesabi Range of Minnesota than from any source in Canada, though new iron deposits are being opened up now along the north shore of Lake Superior. Yet, bringing its raw materials so far, the wedge makes most of Canada's steel products, all its automobiles, nearly all its machinery.

The wedge also lacks that other basic ingredient, coal. This must come from the United States, or, in smaller quantities, from Nova Scotia or Alberta, at artificial cost and government subsidy to cover the long haul, or from Britain. Oil was discovered in the wedge more than eighty years ago, but it is a small trickle now and present supplies must come from the

United States or overseas. Yet so strategic is the location of the wedge, by geography and by tariff arrangement, that it can take these outside ingredients and mold them into more than half of all Canada's industrial output.

If Canada lacks iron, coal, and oil where they are most needed, it can buy them with exports of other minerals, for it produces a tenth of the world's gold, most of it in Ontario, 90 per cent of the nickel, 12 per cent of the copper and lead, 10 per cent of the zinc, half of the platinum metals, and more asbestos than any other country. Specialization is the secret of Canadian industry—concentrating on the things we have and trading them for what we lack. That is why we are vulnerable. Let our outside markets fail and we cannot import the lacking essentials.

The wedge of Ontario has advantages possessed by no other part of the country. It is the center of population and domestic markets, but, more than that, it is really a huge inland port, a thousand miles from the sea. Men made it a port with the work of their hands. Perhaps when Father Hennepin, the first white man to see them, looked down on the vortex of the rapids of the Onghiaras, and then at the appalling barrier of the falls above, he dreamed of the day when they would be circumvented and be made into the long-sought route to China. De La Moths, one of Louis XIV's engineers, thought he could do it in 1710, but his superiors said the idea of a canal was preposterous. For a long time yet—its Indian name perverted into Niagara—the great obstruction was to be passed only by the long and weary portage of canoe. Boats built on the lakes above were locked there.

Now, as we drove down to Niagara, we could see, littering the land, the remains of men's attempts to end the portage. Four canals have been built to join Lake Ontario and Lake Erie, to carry ships up and down the single great step of Niagara Falls. As long ago as 1829 they built the first canal here with four crude wooden locks, using every little local stream to save digging, but only boats of eight-foot draft could use this channel. Sixteen years later they built again, and still again in 1887 with twenty-five locks. We could see some of them now, with walls of field stone, weathered, overgrown, like the locks of England, and the lazy channels, which only needed a bulbous barge boat, with pots of red geraniums and a stout woman knitting at the tiller, to look like the canals of France. Now we could see the fourth channel—the Welland Canal, which has revolutionized the geography, economics, transportation, and defense of the whole continent.

To me its engineering was all figures and mystery, but my Toronto friend knew it in fantastic detail. The digging of this canal, he said, was equivalent to digging a seven-foot hole from Montreal to Australia. Where the Panama Canal lifted ships 85 feet, the Welland heaved them up 326 feet with seven gigantic locks. I could believe it. Even now, across the fields, we saw the weird stage spectacle of a lake freighter climbing a hill, far above the surrounding country. The locks were carrying it up with the ease of an animated cartoon, lifting it bodily with the tide of water flowing from the south. When we got to the locks, the ship had disappeared on her way. She had climbed up Niagara Falls in defiance of all the laws of gravity and the geographical arrangements of nature.

We gazed at the concrete lock, stark and enormous, rising sheer out of the earth, and above it lay the canal, smooth and placid, the water high above the road where we stood. From another point we could see the channel below the lock, the gaping ditch that men have carved deep enough and wide enough to carry the ocean freighters of the world. The man from Toronto said with a sudden note of triumph: "That's functional! And it's beautiful. And we live by it."

Yes, live by it. This is indeed the breathing lung of Canada. Without its first beginnings we could not have built our country. Without the larger ditch and the giant mechanism of locks, we could not exist in our present form. Steadily the lung breathes, carrying commerce into our arteries and remote veins, far into the inner regions of Canada, expelling our goods, our wheat, our minerals, taking cheap freight in and out of our inland seas, making the wedge an ocean port.

De La Moths' vision is not yet complete. It had to wait more than two centuries until the St. Lawrence Seaway was projected jointly by Canada and the United States. This scheme will circumvent the rapids that lie in the river system below the Welland Canal, so that the great freighters may come up, uninterrupted from the sea. Canada contributed to this inland route the channel between Lake Ontario and Lake Erie and built it to carry these ocean vessels, for Canada was looking ahead. At present the larger grain ships can only move from the Lake Head down to Lake Ontario and transfer their cargoes to smaller craft, which move by the smaller lower canals to the ocean, but the completed Seaway will make this transfer unnecessary.

The Great Lakes system will carry cheap freight into the middle of the continent, create naval shipbuilding yards far from possible attack, alter the whole economic balance of America. Of that project the Welland Canal, the product of Canadian engineering, Canadian money, and Canadian imagination, is the key. It is the route around the most difficult barrier of all, the portage of the Onghiaras.

The Seaway is only one of a series of titanic changes in a region always selected for events. Once, said the Man from Toronto, Lake Huron emptied into Lake Ontario east of Toronto by rivers now dry, and the lakes emptied southward through what is now New York State. Lake Ontario rested then at a far higher level, he said, and he pointed to the horseshoe of low hills around the lake's western end. Once this escarpment held the lake but when the St. Lawrence finally broke into its present course, the lake level dropped and created Niagara Falls, the downward step between Erie and Ontario. Also created was the Niagara Peninsula, once the bottom of the lake, now a rich shelf of red land, a vineyard and an orchard.

But my friend would not pause to gaze at the remains of this upheaval, when the land of North America trembled in the cold agony of the ice ages. He wanted to show me the fragile works of men. So we found ourselves presently, after careful examination by the soldier guards, in the power house of Queenston. Here they have utilized the entire height of Niagara Falls and the rapids below it to develop electrical power in a swarming den of dynamos that used to be the largest in the world before the Americans built their new western dams.

From a roaring inferno, where the dynamos sit like spinning tops, fat and solemn in their long line, the power goes out to serve the industries of the Ontario wedge. In a control room like a movie set a couple of young engineers, by watching the red and green lights flash, can direct this energy all over the country, to city and remote hamlet. Now we could see why the wedge had become the heart of Canada. It has the power. The falls of the Onghiaras, which used to be the chief obstacle to Canada's development, have become one of its chief servants and, with the canal, have formed a combination of energy and transportation which keeps the heart beating.

Hundreds of thousands of people, Americans and Canadians, pass this way, catching a glimpse of the canal or the wires of the power lines, but never pausing to think that the whole economy of this country, the living of its people, depend on them. Block the canal, cut the wires, blow up the power plants, and you have a new Canada of poverty, privation, and peasantry. If you wanted to take a map and thrust a pin into the most vital point in Canada, I suppose you could do no better than to place it at Queenston, where all the ganglia of the national body meet in final concentration of energy.

This is the creation of man through government. This is the prodigious child of the Ontario Hydro, owned by the taxpayers, a huge experiment in socialism in a territory which would be horrified at the world. Call it public ownership and it is accepted as a natural and reasonable scheme. Call it socialism and people will not understand you. The name does not matter. The Hydro, a public undertaking, the obvious assumption of an inevitable monopoly by the state, has been a complete success, has provided cheap power to the factories, cheap electricity to the homes. The housewife of this region, like the industrialists, is the envy of all others throughout the nation.

This Queenston power house may be taken by the thoughtful man as a symbol of Canada's industrial development. We call ourselves a purely capitalistic society, but a considerable part of our capital is owned directly by the state, half of the Canadian railways, for instance. In a second economic territory normal competition has disappeared in the monolithic monopolies, the centralized business organizations which dominate Canadian production. On the Maritime coast, fishing companies; in central Ontario and Quebec, manufacturers; on the prairies, grain companies; on the Pacific Coast, timber and mining industries—these have been organized by the technique of consolidation and merger, by price agreement, and by the process of giantism, probably with less interference from the state than in any civilized country. Also, with less labor trouble and less organization of labor, 85 per cent of the workers being unorganized and the rival union groups unable to get together.

Nowhere among modern nations, perhaps, has labor been so class-unconscious. Up to the beginning of the second World War there was no national minimum wage standard in Canada, and, at this writing, there is merely the federal government's suggestion to arbitration boards that the 1926-29 wage level should be enforced in new wage agreements with a bonus to cover war prices. But the war produces a new stirring, the penetration of the C.I.O., the frantic alarm of the giant industries, and what else, no one can foresee.

We drove up to the falls by the road which follows the ragged lip of the canyon. I always like the falls best when they are bearded in winter, with white whiskers of icicle, and the rocks beside them are frosted with a lace of solid foam, and down below lies a gigantic pile of whipped cream. The falls look rather small at first, until you see the black ant-spots of people walking on the ice below them. Now the ice was gone and the falls ran freely again, with the fury and beauty which no man has yet put into words.

They are being ruined. Their water supply is protected against the demands of industry, but the skyline of New York state, the grimy factories and hideous hotel tower, the Neon signs and small skyscrapers must spoil the whole picture as surely as a single garbage can would ruin the design of the largest and finest room. In time, they tell me, you can look at the falls without noticing the background. You become immune to it, as to any disease. If you are not a native, however, you must shade your eyes and block out the view at the level of the canyon top and concentrate your mind deliberately on the foreground. They have done their best to repair this first fatal mistake of industry. Parks have been laid out, with driveways and flowers, and nature itself has larger plans. In the end the falls will fool the engineers and the industrialists.

I met a frail old man strolling on the boulevard, blinking at the spectacle through dark glasses. He pointed to the deepening circle of the Horseshoe Falls and observed that every year some more rock fell down there, carved away by the force of the water beneath. The falls were marching steadily towards Lake Erie, several feet a year, he thought. He calculated that in a mere 15,000 years there would be no more falls at all, Lake Erie would drop in sudden cataclysm to the level of Lake Ontario, there would be hell to pay further up the Great Lakes, and the Welland Canal would be high and dry. Yes, a mere parvenu in geological time, these falls, but an energetic thruster which started miles down the river at Lake Ontario and still gallops fast towards Erie.

"About fifteen thousand years I've figured it," the old man

said and then sighed. "I'm eighty in November," he added. He would hardly live to see it.

Move but a mile from the river and you are out of the reach of industry and in an ancient land. That is what charms the person from the city or from the raw country of the West—the loving care of these fields, the contented smile of old brick houses, the stone walls overgrown with creepers, the venerable orchards, the little rivers, and the bridges of field stone. Every bridge should be built of field stone, in a single arch, with a lazy stream beneath it and a barefoot boy fishing, a can of worms beside him. And preferably, as you may find them in Ontario, beside the remains of an old flour mill, with quiet mill pond and mossy dam. Yes, and near by a clump of hard maples, the family sugar bush, where the trees will be tapped in the spring, the slow, oozing sap collected and boiled endlessly in iron pot and kettle until it is sugar or syrup.

Sugar time and kettles boiling! Pause a moment on the road to recall the memories of your boyhood, when you bored your own trees, collected your own sap and boiled it in kerosene can or stolen kettle over a pungent fire in the bush, and spread the syrup on the clean snow to harden, and wound it on a twig to form the king of all-day suckers. Most precious time of the year, when sap was running and snow beginning to melt and the first smell of thaw coming out of the earth, and the sound of a wheel creaking on the country road, and the city folks managing, by sheer accident, to arrive out at the farm with convenient jars to carry home some liquid treasure! Syrup time, forever lost, like your first love.

The healthy, earthy, and always beautifying touch of England is strong on this Ontario land, surviving those long years in the Thirteen English Colonies, those Loyalist days and the Family Compact. The villages snuggle by the streams, hidden and modest, under their plume of elm trees, and always a church spire pierces the highest leaves. Why, you could stand a mile away, almost anywhere in this little pocket of cultivation and, looking across at spire and old house, at stone bridge and gnarled tree, swear that you were in the Cotswolds. Only centuries of labor and living can produce this feeling, and this precious garden of Ontario is but a spot on the map of Canada of less than postage-stamp size, a tiny morsel of land which has given itself and yielded fully to man. A few miles away stretches forever and forever the solemn wilderness, or the raw lands which men have tortured, raped, and butchered.

English, yes, pure English, with England's care and cultivation and sure instinct of soil and growth. Most of Dundas Street, the old road into Toronto, where Rebels fled and soldiers marched in the War of 1812, and the Tiny Creature hid in frozen ditches, could be transported and set down in Warwickshire or Kent, and no one would suspect the fraud. The same elms, the same little streams, grassy banks, rolling valleys, and the same fat and rubicund houses, built by virtuous Loyalists but looking now, in old age, like port-red Early Victorians, who would kiss the parlor maid behind the door on the way to church.

Then the green abyss of the Dundas Valley, flowing in huge, bubbling tide of green out to Lake Ontario, with villages, church spires, roads drowned in its greenery, as if it had been specially designed by nature and improved by man, according to cunning plan, to form the perfect picture for the mail-order calendar, or for the *Saturday Evening Post* advertisement of the ideal North American habitation. It is too perfect to be real, a picture on a calendar, an ad in the *Post*.

Some of the little towns are almost as perfect, with picture-book streets arched by trees, with dozing stone houses and old men sleeping in the sun. But come near the ganglia of commerce and once more you are plunged into ugliness. For miles we followed the Canal, with its black towers of steel that lift its highway bridges when the boats come through. Again the Man from Toronto excused them on the ground that they were functional and so, apparently, must have some hidden and mystical beauty of their own. To me they were grisly steel girders against the sky. But at Port Colborne, the beginning of the Canal, there was something rather charming about the ugliness of the whaleback grain ships, tied up for the winter and now making ready to start their weary shuttle upon the lakes. They were too comical to be entirely disagreeable— round, cigar-shaped tanks of steel, bottoms rusty, with pilot houses stuck to them at odd places as if by an afterthought, like waddling, fat women gathered here at the dock for an hour of gossip.

Strange to think that the whole prairies, from the Lakes to the Mountains, depend upon these absurd creatures to move their grain—these tiny corpuscles in the main artery of Canada and essential to its life. They contain a life of their own here on the lakes, unknown and mysterious to Canadians, a desperate life sometimes, when the winds blow, tilting Lake Erie so that the flow of water into the Queenston power plant actually diminishes. A lonely life with legends of shipwreck and rescue and drowning that go far back into our history, back to the days of Indian war parties and birchbark, the days when Frontenac moved in splendor with a fleet of a hundred canoes, flags flying, wine flowing; back to the days of sail when ships were built here to fight the American ships from the opposite shore, and the days of the first grain boom, when the wheat tide started to flow. Now, in a different age, when the first grain boat moves through the rotten ice of the spring, it is as if the organs of Canada had started to pulsate again after long sleep.

We spent some time in Port Colborne because the Man from Toronto had some vivid childhood memories that he desired to renew. He said he had once eaten some bad sardines here, the gift of a neighbor, when he was seven years old, and he wanted to rediscover the scene of his agony. We humored him, searching up and down the tree-lined streets and even exploring the moving sand dunes of Lake Erie for the missing neighbor's house, because we were delighted to see so much sentiment coming from such an unsuspected quarter. Alas, we never found the house of the poisoned sardines and our friend drove off, depressed.

Through many a nursery-rhyme town we drove that day and through the suppurating sores of modern industry, the slums growing like rank water weeds beside the canal, the horrid factory towns that mean wealth for the nation and poverty for the inhabitants. All of them were heralded on the highway as usual by a rash of billboards, those painted whores of the written word that should be kept where they belong, in restricted areas.

Intolerable evils of industry Canada has endured and faithfully investigated before royal commission and parliamentary committee, and generally done little to correct. The famous Price Spreads report, showing what monopoly does to poor worker and poor farmer, lies limp and apparently dead in the archives, but in time will be found still alive. For here in this wedge Canada is piling up today not only enormous accumulation of wealth, not only fierce hives of energy, output, labor, but deep problems as well. Here, because there is power and transportation and proximity to materials, Canada is concentrating the industry of the second World War, building up a vested interest of capital and labor in output which must cease when the war is over. It is building up new towns, new labor unions, new proletariat, which will insist on the right to eat even if the world is at peace; which will declare, over all the warnings of economist and politician, that if the nation can find work and prosper while making unconsumable guns it can prosper while making goods which men can use.

Therein lies the basic fact of Canadian politics, casting long shadows into the future—the discovery of Canada's productive power, the discovery that all men may work in war time at good wages by state mobilization of industry. Out of that discovery will come a demand for continual employment in peacetime. It is unescapable but here, on the ground, men do not think of these things now. They are too busy. The factories beat in steady pulse, the Canal breathes, the ganglia of power strain under full load, and the wedge rumbles and heaves and drives ever deeper into the living stuff of the Canadian nation.

Meanwhile, in general, the Ontario town is that perfect balance of size, of industry and agriculture, of small men and neighborliness, which most of the world has lost. And always the merciful Ontario countryside is just around the bend in the road, unblighted, tilled, and pampered and beloved.

A final touch of nostalgia we discovered that day—a village of toylike houses with embroidered wooden balconies by the shore of Lake Ontario. This was the faded summer resort of the gay nineties, where pious people met on Sunday in a hall of prayer shaped like a beehive. The Man from Toronto admitted that he used to come here as a boy and he sighed again for the days of his poverty, and quickly changed the gears of his handsome car.

All this is only a blurred glance at the industrial wedge of Ontario, a breakneck journey which hardly touches the out-lines of the wedge itself. Towns innumerable swarm here along the lakes and in the interior, each with local industry, steady payroll, and high skills: some, like shady old Kingston, with long history—Frontenac's western fortress, where even today the thick walls of Fort Henry are still at war, imprisoning German sailors; some crowded and retching with the industry of the second World War, with blast furnaces glaring against the night sky, with powder works, airplane factories and auto-mobile assembly lines that turn out trucks and gun carriers for use in the Mediterranean deserts; and some with friendly local legends like Windsor.

That industrial city is forever fixed in my mind by the story of the small boy who was discovered, lost, with head firmly wedged in one of those iron bedroom receptacles now generally obsolete. The tale of it traveled throughout the nation, gathering ornament from editorial writers and columnists until it became a Canadian saga. It started wide technical speculation as to cause and effect. It prompted deep historical research into the origin of the receptacle and inquiry as to whether, perhaps, it was an heirloom of Loyalist times, with a fine record of service in the Family Compact. Ah, those were the days when the tale of a pot could charm a nation, before the war blotted out all of these simple, familiar things. Whatever happened to the boy and his monstrous prison I have never been able to discover. I like to think he still wanders somewhere, with strange headgear, through the dark and boundless folklore of Ontario.

Even if you knew every town and road in the wedge you would still not know Ontario. Up to Hudson's Bay it sweeps and to the edge of the prairies, an empty land of rocks and woods and so much water, so many lakes and rivers, that you could almost paddle a canoe from one end of it to the other. Parks, camping places, resorts are strewn lavishly over it and I judge by the local press that every citizen of the province at one time or another has caught a twenty-pound fish and held it before a camera.

Thousand Islands sprinkled black upon the river, Bay of Quinte, lush Ottawa Valley, clean Georgian Bay, Stratford on a local Avon, in loyal imitation of the poet's birthplace, even to swans (kept in a barn in winter), Dionne Quintuplets, the prolific lakes of Haliburton and Muskoka, Algonquin Park, the little canals and locks where a dozing lock keeper will let your boat through, endless leagues of glittering water, rounded rocks and twisted pine, hot and pungent under the sun—even this is only the beginning of Ontario.

These are pleasant lands, made for men's homes and holidays, but to the west glooms the dark, somber shore of Lake Superior, the pinched, cold towns at its ragged edge, the steel mills of the Soo, and those ghastly, eyeless monuments of concrete, the round grain elevators of Fort William, where the prairie wheat is loaded on the lake boats. Farther north again, on into wilderness as wild as when the Frenchmen first saw it, where Indians yet travel by canoe and carry their young on papoose boards—even here the industry of Ontario does not pause. In the fabulous horseshoe of the Precambrian Shield, left by a fortunate convulsion when the earth crust was liquid, men have found minerals, built towns, piled up fortunes, bred millionaires, enriched distant cities, bought newspapers, sucked up the immigration of Europe, merged races, ravened through the wilderness with their lonely railways and drawn riches even from these endless barrens of glacial rocks and tiny trees.

Wild country and beautiful, but never home again to the westerner. Once he has seen the Rockies, once he has lived among the deep canyons and shattered peaks, the sheer size and savage roughness of British Columbia, all this seems lovely but never wild enough. Where are the mountains? Always in his subconscious he is searching for them, expecting to see them over the next hill, but there are more hills only, and the growth of hardwoods, which he does not know at home. No stark, parched beauty here, of dry belt and fearful cliff shape and open range, no seashore and salt smell.

The transplanted native of Ontario may sigh, but he knows that he can never go back again.

Mrs. Noggins

My good neighbor, Mrs. Alfred Noggins, who came out to Canada from London before the war, has recently returned from a visit to her distant cousin in Seattle. While Mrs. Noggins' views are hardly official, they may serve to introduce by easy stages the rather formidable subject of the next chapter.

"Well," said Mrs. Noggins, boarding my car at the end of the road and depositing her usual basket of eggs and two dead ducks on the front seat beside me, "Well, you know, the 'ole thing is a complete surprise. The Americans, I mean. Why, bless you, I'd 'eard such stories about them! Uncle 'Erbert at 'ome—and 'im an alderman in Liverpool—used to say the Americans were a very queer lot because they 'ad up and left the family, along of George the third, you know. Poor Uncle 'Erbert drunk 'imself to death, worryin' about the sewers in Liverpool, and I will say that if the Americans was leavin' 'is family they didn't make any mistake, but I never said that to 'im.

"From wot I'd seen of the Americans in the movies, I must say I was a bit afraid of 'em, goin' across the border for the first time. I really 'ad 'alf an idear they shot each other up all the time, with revolvers 'idden in every drawer and be'ind the radio. And besides, the luxury of 'em! Enough to turn a poor body's 'ead! Why, you'd think to see 'em in the movies they lived in tiled bathrooms and took a barth every mornin'. Not that I'm against it, and since we got the barth tub hinstalled —it'd bin layin' in the basement for three years and our bull-dog, 'Orace, sleepin' in it—well, since then, I do like to 'ave

155

a good 'ot soak once in a while, after cleanin' out the 'en
'ouse. But the Americans carried it too far in the movies.
Besides, the size of their 'ouses and the furnichure and everybody drinkin' cocktails at the bar, you know!

"Why, I 'alf thought all the women would look like Greta
Garbo or 'Edy Lamarr and dressed all up in jools, and the
men excitin' and devilish like that Gable. That's the trouble
with the movies, they do give a body such ideàrs. A man will
come 'ome from the movies and beat 'is wife because she don't
look like an oomph gel, which isn't likely, after she's bin
standin' over the stove all day cookin' 'is dinner.

"Well, you might say I didn't know much about the Americans, only wot I read in the newspapers that Mrs. Boggs used
to wrap the garbage up in when she sent it over for my 'ens
—and Mrs. Boggs expectin' 'er fourth any day now, and this
wartime, too. I can't understand some people.

"Well, you would 'ave bin surprised if you 'ad seen me in
Seattle at Bertha's place. I felt at 'ome! There we was, all together, and everybody as nice as could be. George—that's
Bertha's man—didn't look any more like the movies than I
did and the gels looked the same as they do 'ere. No better
lookin' and talkin' the same, too. That's wot surprised me.
You'd 'ardly know you'd walked across the street. And they
were that kind to me! Breakfast in bed even, such a fine
wicked feelin'!

"Mindju, there are some people in the Old Country and
'ere, too, as wouldn't let the Americans be themselves if they
could 'elp it. They think the Americans ort to be exactly like
us in every partic'lar, and they get vexed with 'em if they're
not. The only way to treat 'em is to let 'em be theirselves, and
soon you get used to it. Why, I found Canada very strange at
first, with everybody speakin' so queer, but I got used to it
and now I got the barth hinstalled, you couldn't budge me,
with dynamite.

"The trouble with the Americans is, nobody knows wot

they're like. Everybody judges 'em by the movies and the radio, and you'd think they spent their lives makin' jokes or fallin' in love or shootin' somebody's wife, but when you get there, they're jest ordinary folks like us. So you could of knocked me over with a feather.

"It seems like no matter 'ow clever we get with radios and all like that, we can never get a real idear across, only a popular song or a wisecrack. No, you got to see 'em to know 'em," said Mrs. Noggins as she backed massively out of my car, the heads of her ducks trailing from the basket. "When you see 'em, you like 'em. Wot's more, they like you. 'Erbert was wrong, as usual, but it's too late to tell 'im now. Poor fella, 'e drunk 'imself to death jest worryin' about the sewers."

CHAPTER EIGHT

General Brock's Bloody Hill

On the Heights of Queenston, beside the canyon of Niagara, stands a vast and grisly monument. Mark it well. If the spirit of a nation can be said to have a birthplace, this is it. If the relations of Canada and the United States are important, this is the place to understand them. If the two neighbors have seldom behaved as well as we like to imagine, here, on this hill, we can see why. If Canada is the curious joint product of Britain and the United States, acting and reacting upon one another, the hill of Queenston is the crucible of this chemistry.

The monument at Queenston marks far more than its builders ever dreamed of, and perhaps that excuses their fearful design. In shape this erection is like Nelson's monument in Trafalgar Square. The stark single column soars up as in London on the foundation of four carved lions, but at Queenston they are poor emaciated creatures, hardly better than snarling cats. The figure at the top of the column is bulbous, ill-shaped, in absurd cocked hat, hand out in stupid gesture. It wears, as a final insult, a web of steel lightning rods (without which, perhaps, a merciful nature would shatter it in a single flash and make way for a worthier memorial).

Still, despite its ugliness, we love it. This is our monument to a great Canadian soldier, General Isaac Brock. He won his battle here, on this wooded hill. He died a few feet away, torn by an American bullet. But not before he had showed the Canadian people, in a single hour, that they could make an independent nation.

What a perfect spot is this for a great passage of history! The hill flows in waves of foliage down to the edge of the canyon, and you can see the green zigzag of the river clear to the glitter of Lake Ontario. All around the fat farm lands lie in a checkerboard, dotted with villages and friendly steeples. It would be a noble sweep of country even if it lacked noble memories.

From this hill the invading Americans of 1812 watched, far below, a tiny figure in red, riding hard along the river road on a white horse. That was Brock, galloping up from Fort George, his followers far behind. If the Americans could hold bloody Queenston Heights, they might win the whole war that day, for then, as now, the Niagara Peninsula was the key to Canada. No one knew that better than Brock. The Heights must be retaken.

Up the hill swarmed Brock and his Canadians, a handful of men battling here among the maple trees for half a continent. Near the top Brock went down, seeing in his last moment the retreat of his men. So he died, thinking Canada lost. Had he lived half an hour longer he would have seen the Canadians charge up the hill again, with Indians whooping on their flanks, drive the Americans down to the canyon, and capture 900 of them at the river's edge, while their friends watched, helpless, from the other shore.

This, with its handful of men and half dozen little guns, was one of the decisive battles of history. From it grew a Canadian nation which realized in that single hour at Queenston that it could fight for its existence, even against the American Republic. From it came the present division of North America. From it came also that phenomenon unique in all the world and in all history—two neighboring nations living at peace, without envy and without hate.

The War of 1812 was a crazy thing. Crazy in origin, crazy in execution, crazy in results. "How pleasing," said Andrew Jackson, "the prospect that would open up to the young volunteer while performing a military promenade into a distant country!" A promenade which was to be a profitable incident in the wars of Napoleon, a calculated plan, as we think in Canada, to conquer our country and make it part of the Union.

No doubt it would have succeeded, with six million Americans facing half a million Canadians, but for the bungling of American politicians, the undoubted fact that the heart of the American people was not in it, and the desperate courage of a few men fighting for their homes. For Canada, the war was a great victory against such odds, though it seemed to end in a draw, with boundaries unchanged. A victory because Canadians had learned to fight, not as British colonists but as citizens of Canada. For the first time they felt the surge of nationhood in their veins and from that everything else followed —self-government, Confederation, nationhood.

Laura Secord, driving her cow to graze past the unsuspecting American sentries, and warning the British of the attack at Beaver Dam; tiny sailing ships blowing each other into wooden splinters on the lakes; exhausted men fighting all night in Lundy's Lane until they dropped down to sleep on the battlefield; York parliament buildings rifled and burned by the Americans (as the British would later burn the White House in Washington); down the river, at Chateauguay, three hundred French-Canadian habitants routing an American expedition which was to take Montreal—these obscure struggles in the wilderness tested the quality of Canadians and settled the question of the French people's place in Canada. The British and French would fight together for Canada against any odds. The American people saw that for some curious reason these neighbors of two separate races wanted to be their own men and not part of any other nation.

It had taken the Americans some time to learn this. In the midst of their own Revolution they had invaded Canada, assuming that the French would be eager to escape British rule, and the British glad to join the new and free Republic. The gallant Montgomery, lying dead in the snow, in a dark Quebec street, had found the answer. The misled American militia, blundering into the ambushes of Niagara, found the same answer again. And still again in 1837, the Americans who fought beside the Patriots to deliver Canada from the Family Compact discovered that the Canadian people wanted to settle their own troubles without the help of the neighbors.

Today on Queenston Heights there is nothing but Brock's monument to remind us of these old follies—the raised shaft of stone and, hard by, a few old earthworks and gun pits, in the center of a peaceful park, where the children play. Along the river some stone cairns mark the minor battlefields of 1812, and old Fort Erie has been restored, complete with wooden drawbridge and powder magazine, which blew the attacking Canadians to pieces. But the old scars are gone and we imagine, listening to our after-dinner speakers and visiting politicians, that all has been sweetness and light on our international border in the last century and a quarter.

That, of course, is not true, but we have generally thought it best to assume the truth of it, even if we knew better. It is a serious mistake to forget or distort history. Better by far to recognize that Canada and the United States have been, up to recent times, fretful and fitful neighbors, and to seek out the causes of their difficulties, so that they may be removed; for though we are the only example of real neighborliness in the record of modern times, much remains to be settled between us, much depends on us, for our own welfare and the welfare of mankind. Many more difficulties lie ahead of us.

If we face the facts of history, then, we shall find that the War of 1812 settled for Canadians their future as a nation, but it did not settle that question for Americans. The minor interference in the Rebellion of '37 and the later raids of the American Fenians across the Canadian border were easily repelled. A more serious danger developed out of the American

Civil War. Having confirmed its own nationhood in that struggle, the United States looked around and wondered whether it should stop there. Britain had favored the South, relations between Washington and London were strained thin, General Grant had a large army which could move northward easily enough, and against it Canada was defenseless. For a moment the Republic had a slight attack of imperialism.

In 1867 the American House of Representatives even protested that the Confederation of Canada was a violation of the Monroe Doctrine when, of course, it strengthened the Doctrine by assuring Canada of ultimate independence from Europe. In 1869 Seward suggested the "cession" of Canada by Britain in payment of the *Alabama* claims, and the British ambassador was sounded out on this plan. A senator from Minnesota proposed a treaty by which western Canada only (a remarkable concession) would be handed over to satisfy the claims. "It is quite evident to me," wrote Sir John A. Macdonald, the Canadian prime minister, "that the United States Government are resolved to do all they can short of war to get possession of the western territory and we must take immediate and vigorous steps to counteract them."

The Americans had discovered a new thing which they called Manifest Destiny. To Canadians it seemed only a fancy phrase to cover the absorption of Canada. The Americans, for their part, never construed absorption as conquest, as violence, as imperialistic. They still regarded Canada as a natural part of their own country and union ultimately inevitable.

This drive for union had long been foreseen in Canada. In his report which gave Canada responsible government, Durham had realized that, without freedom, Canadians would be attracted to the free institutions of their neighbors while, on the other hand, "the maintenance of an absolute form of government on any part of the North American Continent can never continue for any long time without exciting a general feeling in the United States against a power of which the existence is secured by means so odious to the people." A profound truth, hidden away in the musty pages of the Durham Report.

It was Manifest Destiny, the threat of outside interference, that forced the Canadian colonies to build Confederation. Instead of weakening Canada, as some Americans hoped, Manifest Destiny made it strong. Once again, as in United Empire Loyalist times, the United States had deeply influenced the destiny of Canada, but not in the way the Americans had expected.

To the amazement of the British government and prophets of Manifest Destiny, Canadians showed no inclination towards union with their neighbors. Much is made of a manifesto in favor of annexation, signed mostly by the merchants of Montreal in 1849, but this was only the cry of men who had lost their old tariff preference in the British market and had lost as well their control of Canadian affairs. In the Pacific Coast colony of British Columbia there was a strong minority agitation for union, and during the Cariboo gold rush a few American adventurers thought they could take over the country, until Governor Douglas sent a steamboat up to Fort Yale, with a cannon mounted on its bow. These incidents only served to strengthen the great majority of Canadians, who had first decided in the streets of Quebec that they wanted to remain Canadian, had demonstrated it again at Queenston Heights, and established it in the act of Confederation.

But by far the most remarkable fact in all this is that the United States, unlike the other great powers of history, never seriously attempted after 1812 to interfere directly in this small nation's affairs, never attempted an easy conquest at its doors, and its advocates of such a course were never more than an insignificant minority. In an age of anarchy Canadians are just now beginning to appreciate what kind of a friend they have beside them, a power content to remain at home, the best neighbor in the world.

Still, while it lasted, Manifest Destiny was a dangerous, if only a passing phase. At one time a quarrel over the boundary in the Gulf of Georgia almost brought war, Canadian and American garrisons facing each other on the disputed island of San Juan, until an arbitration settled (as usual) in favor of the Americans. More serious and greater in consequence was the Alaska boundary trouble.

The details of it, and the proper location of the boundary are of no concern to us here, but the method of settlement is. President Theodore Roosevelt demonstrated beyond all doubt to Canadians as late as 1903 that he intended to have his way about the size of Alaska, even if he had to achieve it by force. The establishment of a joint commission of "impartial jurists" to settle the trouble was an elaborate fiction, for Roosevelt had decided that, if he could not secure the boundary he desired "I shall move troops into the territory"—a direct quotation set down by the American historian, James Ford Rhodes, after a conversation with the President. Not only did Manifest Destiny bob up again in 1903, but something else, and that is the only reason for mentioning an old argument here.

The Canadians found in the boundary dispute that a British Government was letting them down. That, for Canada, was the important thing, far more important in its results than the location of the boundary.

The two Canadians who sat on the boundary commission would not accept the final award, but the third member, a Britisher, accepted it, voting with the Americans, simply to avoid trouble between the British Empire and the United States. Roosevelt had told Justice Holmes to tip the British Government off as to his true intentions. The British Government could not risk the consequences of a boundary award unsatisfactory to the President. But Canadians could not be expected to like it.

These facts are no longer in dispute. As Canadians realized them in the first heat of discovery, the movement towards Canadian independence took another great stride further. Whether Canada's views on the boundary were sound or not, it was clear that Canada could never trust its own affairs again entirely to a British government. In the measured and moderate words of Premier Laurier: "The difficulty . . . is that so long as Canada remains a dependency of the British Crown, the present powers that we have are not sufficient for the maintenance of our rights."

Within twenty years Canada had sent a representative to Washington to sign a treaty on its own account, scandalizing the British Government. Canada soon insisted also on sending its own ambassadors abroad to maintain its own rights. Canada had learned a deep lesson on the inlets of the Alaskan Panhandle and would never forget it. Still again the United States, unknowingly, had contributed a new stone to the arch of Canadian nationhood.

Altogether it is not a story of unbroken bliss between the two neighbors. Canada has had to fight off two invasions from the United States and two series of raids. These things are good to remember because they show the extent of our accomplishment in keeping the peace for five generations and reaching our present point of co-operation, where war is utterly unthinkable to both.

We have come a long way even since our fathers' time, when Canadian elections were fought on the ridiculous proposition that we would have "no truck nor trade with the Yankees." Many a Canadian politician has been damned because his sympathy with Americans was taken as a sign of disloyalty to Britain. Even in Mr. King's early days his long American associations were a serious liability among some of the Colonial Minds of Canada, whereas today his recognized and most popular achievement is in his treaties with the United States.

Even a man as wise as Carlyle, within living memory, was guilty of this outburst: "So you are an American? Ah, that's a wretched nation! It's all wrong, has been wrong from the beginning! That great man of yours, George, was a monstrous bore and wants taking down a few hundred pegs . . . an Oliver Cromwell with all the juice squeezed out." And William Kirby, a respectable Canadian historian of the last century, could write and publish such stuff as this: "Jefferson hired the renegade Englishman, Paine, to write up the Declaration of Independence and to write down religion and the sacred Scriptures," and he could call Washington "the prince of land jobbers," who had violated a flag of truce at Fort Necessity, murdering the French commander and escaping himself the same fate only through French generosity.

It is good to remember these quaint and preposterous things because they show how much we have learned. The International Joint Commission—an unexampled achievement of statecraft—which has settled all disputes between us by unanimous agreement, is the legal evidence of this relationship, but beneath it lies that deeper thing, the feelings of the ordinary man, a foundation of genuine friendship. Canadians and Americans simply like one another, and statecraft, legal documents, treaties, negotiations are mere reflections of that fact.

Yet how blind, how stupid, how hesitant we have been about some things!

It happened, by the merest chance, that I discovered in Washington in 1938 that Canada was secretly exchanging military information and plans of fortifications on the Pacific Coast with the United States. Anyone could have discovered it in this friendly, wide-open capital, simply by asking. When I wrote the story for my papers, at once the opposition was on its feet in Parliament to demand whether this was true, and Premier King, nervously and in guarded language, admitted that it was. The sacred politicians of Canada evidently expected a fierce protest from the surviving Colonials of the country, who wanted no truck, trade, nor military understanding with the Yankees. Instead the government's common-sense action met with unanimous approval throughout the nation. It could have been taken long before, it should have been taken long before, if the Canadian politicians had not lacked faith in the public intelligence.

It was not until August 17, 1940—after a year of war, after the fall of France, the siege of Britain, the peril of this continent—that President Roosevelt and Premier King met on a railway car in Ogdensburg and signed a permanent agreement of joint defense and set up a joint board to plan it. Even then the timid Canadian Government tried to tell Parliament that there were "no commitments," as if nature, history, geography, necessity, and men's hearts had not long ago committed both countries to fight for the protection of the other. The Ogdensburg agreement should have been signed long before. Joint defense should have been planned and executed long before, but in the days of appeasement, North America seemed safe enough. However, a Canadian is bound to say, if he knows Washington, that in all this Canada has been the hesitant party. The United States has been extraordinarily forbearing, to the point of joint danger, in pressing for any deal which might embarrass Canada and its government. This after-you-Alphonse attitude dominated us until we were actually at war and left us without any plan for fighting an invader.

When the agreement came at last the unanimous acceptance of it in Canada showed how rapidly this country had traveled in its thinking in the last few years. We saw now, in the light of Europe's flames, that we and the Americans were necessary to one another—inhabiting the same continent, menaced jointly, defensible only by joint action, militarily inseparable.

Finally, when the United States found itself arrayed against Germany for the second time, it was not, as the Lindberghs had feared, because the United States had to defend a British nation in America, already involved in the war, but because the United States had to defend itself.

That is the political record. The economic record is equally checkered and much less satisfactory. Politically Canada and the United States have learned to live together and have implemented that knowledge by many peaceful treaties and by stern military agreement. Economically they have not learned to live together. On the contrary, more and more, until very recently, they have learned to live further apart.

While the Thirteen Colonies of America were in separate, watertight compartments, each with its own tariff and trade restrictions, progress was impossible and poverty inevitable. It was when they were joined together to form a single trading unit, when the United States became the greatest free-trade area in the world, that the world's largest economic system and highest living standard suddenly emerged. But neither the United States nor Canada has ever recognized that if this principle could apply successfully south of an imaginary line called the forty-ninth parallel of latitude, it could apply with equal purpose north of it also.

Obviously, by specialization of output, by economy of labor, by the simple, businesslike process of producing at the lowest possible cost, in the most advantageous place, Canada and the United States could both prosper best if they traded freely. Once they sensed this fact, but not for long. The Elgin-Marcy reciprocity treaty was abrogated, after only ten years' service, in 1866; the tariff rose out of the invisible boundary with a surging, toadstool growth; and from then on economic lunacy has been pursued with unswerving persistence, with fabulous outpouring of energy, money, and labor to the impoverishment of both nations. The smaller, of course, felt this process most.

Partly the trouble was natural greed—the hope that some local advantage could be built up under the lee of a tariff wall even if the nation as a whole suffered from it. Partly it was the stupidity of men unable to perceive the insanity of producing goods at high expenditure of time, labor, and money when they could be bought cheaply from a neighbor, who would buy cheap goods in return. Partly it was the delusion that if foreign goods were kept out, a country must be richer, even though, as a result, it could not export its own goods. But very largely the economic mismanagement of this continent is due to political suspicion, genuine and synthetic.

In the last century Manifest Destiny had made Canada so fearful of the Yankees that reciprocity was called the first step towards annexation. The Liberal Party lost the election of 1891 when somebody stole the proofs of an editorial written for the *Toronto Globe* by Edward Farrer, a distinguished Liberal journalist, to advocate political union with the United States. In 1911 the real test came.

That year the Laurier Government negotiated with the administration of President Taft a reciprocity treaty, after years of effort. It was an obvious step, but it was obstructed by Manifest Destiny, or rather the ghost of that long-dead slogan. The Laurier Government's enemies saw a chance to win an election by conjuring up the ancient phantom of annexation, and they found their chief allies among the mistaken politicians of the United States. The Speaker of the House of Representatives repeatedly advocated the reciprocity treaty because it would hasten political union, a United States Senator called annexation "the logical conclusion of reciprocity," and even the President said that Canada had come to "the parting of the ways." Canada was scared by annexation and by the false patriotism of its own industrialists, who wanted to hang on to tariff protection. The Laurier Government was defeated at the polls, reciprocity rejected.

From then on the record is melancholy. The incredible Fordney and Smoot-Hawley tariffs of the postwar period— attempting to collect American debts while refusing to accept goods—demoralized Canada's foreign trade and were one of the chief causes of the Ottawa Conference of 1932. That conference attempted, by preferential tariffs, to create something like a self-contained trading area within the British Empire —another rigidity in the world's tortured economy which helped along the second world war.

Yet the evidence of this lunacy in North American trade was always perfectly clear. Whenever the tariff was reduced (which was seldom) trade between the two neighbors burst across the border, as if the top layer had been taken off a dam, multiplying fifteen times in three years under the old reciprocity treaty. Even despite the tariff, this trade has been the greatest single movement of commerce in the world, and in normal times Canada has been the United States' best customer, while the United States has bought more Canadian goods than any other nation. How much greater the trade would be, the production and wealth of both nations, if the original tariff blunder, powerfully aided by politics and suspicion, had not intervened!

By 1937 the two nations, or at least their governments, were beginning to realize this, faintly. One recalls the day when Mr. King bounded into the Common Room of Parliament to tell the press gallery that he was going to Washington to talk with Mr. Roosevelt, and how he showed us the President's invitation, written by hand, but he quickly thrust it into his inner pocket when we grew curious about its full contents. Its contents, I have always suspected, were rather cosmic in their sweep. The story goes in Ottawa that Messrs.

Roosevelt and King, sitting on a chesterfield in the White House, laid down the architect's drawing of a new heaven and a new earth.

Anyway, after Washington, Mr. King went to London and took with him Mr. Roosevelt's views, and in London the British Empire agreed to retrace its steps. The British preferential tariff system was modified, the bars taken down a peg or two, and new individual trade treaties were negotiated between the British nations and the United States. This was to be the beginning of the world's deliverance, the retreat from autarchy and totalitarianism, the opening of trade which would forestall another world war. It came too late.

The need of it remained, however, and finally grew desperate. By 1941, to secure war materials, Canada found that it was buying from the United States about $400,000,000 more per year than it was selling there. In a world which could no longer buy Canadian goods, Canada simply could not find that many American dollars to pay for these imports. Before the war, when it had an unfavorable balance in the United States, this could easily be covered by the favorable balance in Britain and the conversion of sterling into American funds, but now Canada was shipping to Britain on credit.

Once again the old pals, Messrs. Roosevelt and King, executed one of their splendid informalities. After a brief luncheon at Hyde Park they announced a deal by which the United States would buy enough extra Canadian products to cover the United States' exports to Canada. While this Hyde Park Declaration was called a war-emergency plan only, and was quickly forgotten in the rush of other events, it was, in fact, the obvious, natural thing, which both nations had avoided so long. It was now possible because both had learned to trust the other completely. At Hyde Park the ghost of Manifest Destiny was finally laid.

From this record certain things are now clear. Sitting here

at the base of Brock's monument, on the grass of Queenston Heights, we can contemplate them dispassionately, our wars long behind us, brave Brock and his soldiers long dead.

It is clear, first, that Canada is as much a product of the United States as of Britain. The story of our origins in the Thirteen Colonies has been told already, but long after that, American influence has flowed northward—the influence of journalism, of the movies, and the radio, which daily make Canadians think the same thoughts as their neighbors, adopt the same manners, copy the same fashions, eat the same food. Besides these, there has been the other influence of old quarrels that forced Canada to stand on its own feet, that gave birth to the Canadian spirit here on Queenston Heights, that compelled responsible government and Confederation itself. Without knowing it, and sometimes hoping to prevent it, the Americans have been the joint architects in the construction of our Canadian nation.

It is clear, second, that the relations between Canada and the United States have vastly improved of late years. As this is written, it is only thirty years since Canada rejected reciprocity in fear of American imperialism, only thirty-eight years since Theodore Roosevelt was ready to use force on the Alaska boundary. And today we have a joint defense agreement which no one dared to propose before 1940. We have the Hyde Park declaration which is something very like reciprocity. We have, for the war anyway, a meshing of the two national economies.

There is more to this than mere official compliments and legal agreements. There is in Canada a deep and universal change in feeling towards Americans. One would hardly know that our neighbors are the same people who lived beside us in my youth.

The Americans, for their part, seem to understand us better. Until a year or two ago you found even in Washington an unbelievable ignorance about Canada at peace and Canada at war. You heard the very opposite of the known facts and figures solemnly proclaimed in the United States Senate. You found well-informed men imagining, for example, that Britain dragged us into the second world war and that we were making Britain pay cash for the war goods bought here.

This was due in part to the folly of the Canadian Government in refusing to give its neighbor any information, for fear of offending it and incurring the suspicion of propaganda. In part it was due to a large nation's natural lack of interest in the affairs of a small one. Canadians inevitably know the United States, through its movies, radio, and magazines, better than Americans know Canada, but the present war is helping to right the balance by dramatizing the fact that any danger to Canada is a danger to the United States. Ogdensburg and Hyde Park turned the eyes of Americans northward.

It is none too soon, for the interdependence of these countries has long needed recognition. It is merely our stupidity on both sides, our vice of insularity, our selfishness that has kept us minding our own business too much and neglecting the common business of both. Long ago, if we had listened, we would have realized the danger of halting our thoughts at the forty-ninth parallel.

When the beaten British Government was negotiating peace with the victorious United States after the Revolutionary War, David Hartley, an English representative, laid before the American peace commissioners "an awful and important truth" in these words:

Our respective territories are in vicinity and, therefore, we must be inseparable. Great Britain, with the British power in America, is the only nation with whom, by absolute necessity, you must have the most intimate concerns, either of friendship or hostility. All other nations are three thousand miles distant from you. You may have political connections with any of these distant nations, but with regard to Britain, it must be so. Political intercourse and interests will obtrude themselves between our two countries, because they are the two great powers dividing the Continent of North America.

This remains as true today as it was when uttered, though Canada has become a nation in its own right. More true in this shrunken world.

It is clear, third, that the co-operative process between Canada and the United States has only started, that our long-range economic problems have not been solved. We have made the Hyde Park bargain for the war period, but we have made no permanent bargain. When the war is over, the old tariff difficulty will return, the old pressures for local advantage, the old vested interests that depend upon the tariffs—and new ones built up for armament production during the war.

Have we learned enough to meet this issue squarely at last? Have we learned enough to make temporary sacrifices in some industries and some areas in the sure knowledge that larger trade flowing across the border in the end will benefit both countries? Or can a few industrialists and a few farmers hold up forever the natural movement of goods, denying the evident facts of nature and geography?

In Washington I hear much big talk about the future— about a new North American hemispheric economy, in which all our trade will be rationalized, allocated by agreement and perfectly organized by New Deal methods. I have heard New Dealers outline a brave new world over an old-fashioned at the Carlton bar on many a hot Washington afternoon, but I have looked out the window, past the busy street, out across the grain fields of Canada, the protected industries of Ontario, the factories of the United States, the ranches which fear Canadian beef, the lumber mills that oppose even a trickle of Canadian lumber, and I have wondered.

The most important fact which emerges from all this, however—and it is well worth repeating—is that a big nation can live beside a small, defenseless one and not absorb it; that the small nation will not envy enough the prosperity of the large to desire union; that the large nation will not covet enough the resources of the small to steal them. It is, in our time, a unique spectacle to amaze the earth. It is a recognition, after all, of a very simple fact long known in all families—that relatives can often live best and most amicably apart, in separate houses, shaped to fit their different tastes, sizes, and temperaments.

Political union with the United States ceased long ago to be practical politics in Canada, and Canadians can see no evidence of a desire for it in the United States; on the contrary, only sympathy in the American government for a neighbor which is now fighting for its life.

No one can foretell what changes the future may bring in a fluid world of this sort. Disaster to the British Empire might well compel a closer relationship between Canada and the United States, but, short of that, nothing at the moment suggests it, and no considerable body of opinion on either side seems to want it. Yet it is never forgotten as a remote possibility in the far future. There is in both countries, among some people, a subconscious feeling that political union may come some day, perhaps not in this century or in the next, but in the end by the force of geography. Unless the United States changes its whole habit of thought, union will only come when both countries want it, and then there will be no serious argument. Meanwhile the old trouble is forgotten, and General Brock, from his ugly pinnacle, smiles across the border.

Some strange men—a very few—do not smile back at General Brock. In some quarters—very small—Canada is represented as one of America's chief liabilities, a kind of chronic headache extending over 3,000 painful miles of frontier. This view annoys Canadians and would worry them, if it were widely held by Americans. Most Americans, as I have observed them in a fairly wide contact, do not hold it. They remember that Canada is their best customer, a producer of needed materials, a safe field for investment, making no trouble in peacetime and, in war, arming itself to defend this continent jointly with its neighbor. They see in Canada the only warlike, fighting nation besides their own in the western hemisphere, its ability to fight proved in two world wars.

This is no easy corridor for an invader to follow into the United States. It is a barrier, an armed outpost, a place where invasion, if not stopped, at least can be held up until the United States can concentrate its own power at the danger point. Likewise, if the safety of Britain is important to the United States, as its President has said, Canada has helped its neighbor through its contributions to Britain's defense. More important than all this, Canadians and Americans understand one another better than any people in the world. If America is attacked, they will fight together like brothers.

These few facts, without elaboration, have long convinced most Americans, I believe, that they would not be richer, safer, happier if Canada disappeared suddenly into the ocean, leaving the United States with the waves lapping the forty-ninth parallel of latitude and no Canada to defend. To the suggestion of men like Mr. Lindbergh that Canada is a serious difficulty because it fights in Britain's war, the Canadian would make this simple reply: "If you had your choice of neighbors, who among all the races of the world would you place in Canada instead of the Canadians?" This may seem to contain an element of self-flattery, but it is a fair question to ask those few Americans who raise the issue. We Canadians are content to leave the answer to the American people.

This is the rough story of our dealings with each other from the beginning. It is not the story generally told at international conventions and official banquets. It is a better and more satisfactory story. We are not children who have grown up sheltered from life, and weak from lack of experience at the moment of crisis. We have struggled against each other. We have learned to know each other on battlefield and at conference table, with bloodshed, with trade, with travel, with common language. We have passed the danger stages. We have learned the lesson and understood the facts, not by theory but often by violence and always by the daily, humble talk of men gossiping across a friendly fence. The understanding we have today, which goes so far beyond treaties and the speeches of statesmen, could not be built except on such a human foundation. We are old friends who are closer because we have quarreled, have seen the folly of quarreling, and have recognized each other's failings and virtues alike. We have yet a long way to travel together, many bridges to cross.

Winter

Yesterday the last leaves tugged at the branches, and soon all the branches were bare. The wind was from the north.

They looked up from the stable yard on the prairies, saw the slate-gray sky, and knew that it had come. The cattle wandered dolefully, picking at the dried grass, and the long autumn hair of the horses was ruffled in the wind. The fishermen along the Nova Scotia coast battened down their boats and ran for shore. In the Hope Mountains of British Columbia, Bill Robinson denned up in his cabin, twenty-five miles from other human life, hoping his radio battery would keep going until spring.

Today it came, the Canadian winter. Snow eddying across the prairies until a woman peering through the windows could not see the neighbor's house and knew she was a prisoner until April. Snow sifting through the streets of Winnipeg and everyone hurrying to get anti-freeze in his radiator, a heater on the windshield; and the vacant lots flooded for the kids' skating rinks. Winter marching eastward over the badlands, placing a puff of snow carefully on every tiny Christmas tree. Winter tiptoeing into an Ontario village by night and all the children awaking with a whoop to get out sleighs and skis and hockey sticks, and the black squirrel in the garden taking one look and disappearing for good.

In Ottawa the prime minister and other distinguished statesmen taking their fur caps out of moth balls and coming forth suddenly, like an invasion of Russian Cossacks on the Hill, the policeman at the Senate Entrance sheathed in buffalo coat like an aged bison, members of Parliament hurrying from the Château to the Buildings, diving into the warmth of steam heat

179

and never leaving until midnight, rubbers and overshoes piled high in the washroom of the Rideau Club.

In Quebec the big stoves crammed with wood and the habitant out in the back yard with axe and saw, eyeing the wood pile with careful calculation. In the kitchen the pot bubbling with pea soup. In the silent woods, the sleighs brought out, with jingle of bells, to carry logs to the river.

In the Maritimes the fisherman hauls up his boat. Snow smudges out the harbor of Halifax and ships move through it vaguely. The liners come into port from the North Atlantic, their shapes distorted with ice, like layers of glass, rigging turned solid, sailors' faces pinched and blue.

Now Winter turns westward at his leisure. The valleys of the Rockies can be filled up quickly with snow, and more slides off the hills, carrying trees and rocks with it. Every drip and trickle of water has long since seized up, the rivers drop, and over them grows the winter skin, save where the water breaks it with fierce bubbling and then plunges again under the dumb ice. On the untouched smoothness of the snow there is a single track of moose, or the light touch of weasel or rabbit, or perhaps the smooth path of a ski. Every spruce tree and cedar bears an incredible burden, all the branches borne down, and the snow lies on the bare twigs of tamarack like cotton carefully glued there.

It is time now for Winter to make his annual holiday trip to the Pacific Coast. By December he has settled down in Vancouver, in a cottage by the sea, but he is a changed man. He puffs out a few billows of fog, ties up the traffic for a day or two, forces the coastwise captains to navigate entirely by the echoes of their whistles against the shore and then, after turning on the shower bath, Winter forgets to turn it off. Apart from that, he is a considerate guest. Even the last weary roses escape his touch until January when, as a matter of form, he makes a brief show of anger. Then the Victoria golfers are outraged to miss their eighteen holes even for a day and sadly the gardener cuts down the last frozen chrysanthemum. But the snowdrops are out already, and the first crocus opens its brave cup of gold to show the drop of sunshine inside, the first faint wink of Spring.

CHAPTER NINE

Wood, Wind, Water

Evé Gaudet squinted up at the schooner's four thin masts and intricate rigging. He was a big man, with a long, unshaven face of leather, and gnarled, craftsman's hands. He still held his chisel and mallet as we stood there on the beach, looking at the wounded hulk of the *Reine Marie Stewart*. The bad news had just come from Halifax.

"A cot-damn shame!" Gaudet muttered. The schooner could be repaired for twenty or thirty thousand dollars, he said, hauled off the beach, replanked and rigged again, and she would earn the cost in two or three trips with lumber down to the West Indies. But the owners were going to wreck her here on the Nova Scotia shore, one of the last handful of great sailing ships.

To Gaudet it was not the loss of a job. He had plenty of work in his little shipbuilding shop at the beach edge. At present he was working on a fifty-foot fishing boat, to be powered with an automobile engine, but what is such a craft to a man who has built Bluenose schooners and seen them set out, full sail, against the dawn?

When Gaudet was ten years old his father gave him some old tools and lumber and let him explore wood. He had been working with tools and wood ever since, like his father, his grandfather, his great-grandfather, and several generations before that. Always the Gaudets have built ships here on the North Shore. And here was the last of them that Gaudet expected to see, the beautiful, clean-lined *Reine Marie Stewart*, listed deeply into the sand of Belliveau's Cove, with holes bored into her sides to let the water balance her.

They had used the antique spelling for the name of the *Reine Marie Stewart,* in memory of a beautiful Stuart queen, but there was nothing wrong with the ship's construction and she was worthy, by her beauty, of the name. For miles around you could see her tall masts, her mass of rigging, etched in tangled pattern against the blue, cold April sky. The waves slapped the motionless hulk as we watched, and day by day the sand was piling up around her.

"Cot-damn shame," Gaudet grumbled again. He turned to the wretched little rowboat beside him and started to chisel out a broken plank in the stern—Gaudet, the son of shipbuilders, who had built ships in sail. Men like him had known how to build ships in sail for nearly two hundred years, on this beach, but would build no more.

This has always been shipbuilding country, Acadian country, along the North Shore of Nova Scotia, beside the Bay of Fundy. This is where the French Acadians and their apocryphal daughter, Evangeline, came back and settled after the Expulsion. But these French people at Belliveau's Cove, speaking their own language, form a small pocket only. Nova Scotia is British, the second part of Canada after Quebec, the place where the British started to become Canadian. It is the sanctuary of the United Empire Loyalists, the first refuge of the Tories, who refused to join the American Revolution, preferring to come up here and struggle for a living on this niggard coast.

The stern character of these people is plainly written on their peninsula. It is written in glistening little towns beside every cove, in white houses shining on every windy rock, in men's tight, grooved faces. On the basic rock stratum of the country is laid a gritty deposit out of Scotland, and over it, weathering it, furrowing it, blows the clean sea wind, and every house, every man and woman is encrusted with sea salt.

Poor country, and proud, with the fierce pride of the Scot. Once it knew wealth, in the days of sail, when its fleets sailed every sea, entered every port, and were the fourth of the world's merchant carriers—the great age of wood, wind, and water, alas, all too short. Since that age died, poverty has never left here for long, but Nova Scotia has not surrendered to poverty. It has not sunk down, hopeless and apathetic, like the slums of cities and the sad ruins of farming towns out West. The shore accepts poverty as a natural state and has learned to live with it, decently and unashamed. It keeps its clothes patched, its shoes shined, its plain, square houses painted, and every face glistens with soap and water.

They are a long way from the rest of Canada, all the three Maritime Provinces of Nova Scotia, New Brunswick, and Prince Edward Island. Gaudet asked me if I came from Upper Canada—Ontario's old colonial name, forgotten by its own people these fifty years. Upper Canada is almost like another country to these folk, separated from them by a thousand miles of wilderness.

What a strange and brittle structure it is, the economy of Canada, when you come to see its distant extremity thus, at first hand! This eastern region has no fundamental economic connection with Canada at all. It is, as nature and geography laid it out, much more a part of New England than of Canada, but the Loyalists, fleeing from the Revolution, made it British. This was not easy. To get the steel, coal, and fish of this eastern shore into the central, populated areas of Canada, the nation must pay bonuses and subventions and favorable freight rates, or the Maritimes, shut off by tariffs from their natural market in New England, could not live at all.

This region is but one of four great compartments that make up Canada. The second is the central area of Ontario and Quebec, where Canada has concentrated its manufacturers behind a tariff wall, and the people living there, guaranteed the internal market, battening on the rural parts of the country through

high, protected prices, must support their poor relations like
the Maritimes by sharing a small part of their artificial earn-
ings. In bad times the central area also must bonus the third
compartment, the plains that lie from the Great Lakes to the
Rockies, that live on one export crop, wheat, and cannot be
protected by the tariff; but the bonus is never enough to keep
the prairies much above the starvation line when the world
wheat market is closed by tariffs or wars. The fourth compartment lies west of the Rockies, in a region which also lives on
foreign markets but has resources varied enough to survive,
so far, any national tariff policy or any world collapse.

Standing here on this Atlantic Coast, amid clean, proud poverty, you can see how delicate is the balance between these four
regions, how unnatural and precarious the economic organization of Canada—an attempt to make goods move across mountain barriers, leagues of lonely plains and empty forests. No
economic rhyme or reason in it, or in the economic organization of the continent at large, when an imaginary forty-ninth
parallel of latitude can stop the goods traveling as nature and
geography intended, northward and southward. No economic
reason for the economy of Canada, but an overpowering political reason—the construction of a nation. That project has succeeded in defiance of geography and economics. All politics in
Canada, all the unconscious toil of its people, the sectional differences, tariff elections, struggles between provincial governments, have been nothing but an attempt to maintain some
kind of compromise and balance between the four rival economic regions, between those that want tariff protection, the
home market, and those that want world markets for raw
products, and cheap manufactured goods for themselves.

Against all the natural tugs of trade, all the stresses of
financial interest, the thing has worked; has made Canada,
with less than 1 per cent of the world's population, the fourth
exporter, the sixth nation in total trade, eighth in industry
though thirtieth in number of inhabitants; has given Canada,

next to the United States, the highest living standard and per capita income.

More than any other important nation, Canada is built on the world market, earns 30 per cent of its income from exports, prospers on its ability to specialize in the production of its special products like wheat, newsprint, lumber, minerals, fish and their sale mostly to the United States and Britain. The slightest loss in these sales produces a devastating effect on what is probably the most vulnerable economy in the world; and in a world permanently consigned to self-containment and trade restriction, Canada would have to adopt an unthinkably low standard of living.

For all its outward resemblance, the economy of Canada is far different from that of its neighbor, which depends for over 90 per cent of its business on its own market. Canada, as a royal commission reported, with a graphic touch never before achieved by such a body, is like a small man sitting in a big poker game among rich men—if he wins, his profits in relation to his capital are large, but if he loses he may be cleaned out.

So our Canadian economy has grown, not by considered plan but day by day, with constant shifts and changes, into a roughly balanced whole which works surprisingly well in a sane, trading world—an economy in which, incidentally, the United States has risked nearly four billion dollars, about a third of its total foreign investments. Now we look at the thing which grew by itself, by the urgent, human needs of men who wanted to live together as an independent nation, in their own way, and we speak of it as our economic system, as if we had created it by deliberate design.

In such a compromise no equality of wealth as between the four compartments has been possible. This eastern seaboard has generally received the smallest share. A trading world, with sailing ships, brought the Maritimes their only real era of prosperity, when their ports were crammed, their fleets ranged the world, and every cove echoed to the sound of the ship-builder's hammer. Since the American market was almost closed by tariffs, the Maritimes' chief export, so the saying goes, has been its young men, seeking jobs in the United States or in other parts of Canada that have profited more under the great Canadian compromise. The *Reine Marie Stewart,* sunk deep in the sand, with the old shipbuilder looking at her sadly, was the symbol of deep economic, as well as human, change— and the symbol also of men's mismanagement of their affairs in North America.

I strolled back toward Belliveau's Cove with Louis Belliveau himself, descendant of an Acadian exile who founded the original village in 1760. M. Belliveau, a dark, wiry little man, who speaks excellent English, is the postmaster, but he hires a girl to run the office and this morning was carting lumber, to be loaded on a little freighter. He walked beside his two sleek oxen. They pulled his rough wagon by curious yokes fitted not on their necks but bound around their horns and broad foreheads in Breton style—Herefords, with a sailor's rolling gait, well kept and well fed like pets, and wearing little brass knobs on the ends of their horns for decoration.

When M. Belliveau wanted them to turn right or left he would say: "Haw, back!" or "Gee, back!" but I never did discover what he said when he wanted them to back up. They were five years old, Mr. Belliveau said, and when they were eight he would sell them to the butcher for $200, as much as he paid for them in their youth. There is no depreciation in an ox team—no spirit or dash either, but deep wisdom and enormous strength.

All along this shore you see no horses, only the innumerable Herefords, with yokes on their foreheads, hauling the little logs out of the woods to the three-man sawmills, hauling the rough lumber to the wharves. The ox team is the greatest pride of the owner's life, to be pampered, to be decorated with brass ornament and tooled leather, to be entered in the annual fair

so that it may prove it can haul a heavier load of rocks on a
sleigh than the oxen from the next farm. An Acadian farmer,
it is said, will take longer and use more care in choosing an ox
whip than a wife, and on an ox the whip is mostly used as a
gesture only.

Beyond the village—bare of trees, squarely in the wind, but
each little house along the road shining with white paint—I
walked on down the beach, where the breakers were pounding
in, and trudged along the wet sand out to a lonely point. There,
among a few wind-tortured pines and in small, bare fields,
stood some of the original yellow houses built by the Acadians
when they landed from their ships, coming back after their
exile, sneaking in here where the English would not see them
—a gallant little band, homesick for this lean land.

Looking across the bay from the point, I could see the masts
of the *Reine Marie Stewart* upthrust above the intervening hill,
and back of her the immense and grisly towers of a gray stone
church, preposterously large for the little white houses creeping
about it. In the wind blowing up from Fundy it was difficult
to stand here, and the wind never seems to drop along this
shore. Always the sound of surf is in your ears and the taste of
sea salt on your tongue, and the peculiar clarity and utter cleanliness of sea air. Now I could understand better why the Acadians came back.

They had dinner ready for me at the Inn—hot lobsters,
caught an hour before—and I ate them in state alone, for there
were no travelers on the spring roads yet. I was glad of that,
for I could revel by myself, as dusk gathered, among the ghosts
of the old Inn. It was freshly painted, it was well managed by
a charming lady from Boston (a kind of delayed Loyalist, a
century or so late), and it was bright and comfortable; yes,
but it was a pirates' haunt beyond question.

It was the kind of *Treasure Island* inn that used to thrive
along the south coast of England, where Captain John Silver
would sit by the fire drinking rum. Rum? Why, this whole

coast is beautifully steeped and preserved in it, richly colored with it, perfumed by it—kegs of rum that rolled in here from the bootlegging boats during American Prohibition, a second golden age for this coast; rum smuggled at night in fishing craft and dories; rum hauled by oxen under loads of wood; rum hidden in dark cellars and woodsheds and in the forest; rum selling for $5 a full gallon; rum bound from the French islands of St. Pierre and Miquelon to the U. S. market. But no more rum now, none of the real essence, the undiluted contraband, only the expensive, weak, and spurious stuff sold by the government liquor stores, which no pirate would touch.

It was a pirates' inn all right, worth visiting merely to hear the ghostly singing in the night above the sea wind, the sound of hoarse voices roaring, "Fifteen men on a dead man's chest!" and then, in a sudden burst of rain on the window, "Yo ho, and a bottle of rum!" In my snug room just below the roof I hid under the covers and listened to them while the Inn shook and creaked in the wind (though it was built long ago with all the strength and finish of a ship), and all night long I could hear them whispering in the attic, at the window, at the door, and the wooden leg of Captain Silver stumped up and down the stairs.

My landlubber's imagination, I suppose, had been overwhelmed by the stories they had told me before the fire that evening as the storm blew up. An old man, very stout and short of breath, recounted the legends of the coast, gasping out half a sentence and then pausing to catch his wind. He told me of the great ships built here, of wrecks and drownings, of the rum runners, and of Jerome.

There was a tale to set your hair on end in that old inn, as the gale whistled through the village and the rain hammered on the window, and the fire rose and fell in sudden gusts! There was a tale more grisly than Stevenson could invent for his *Treasure Island,* a tale that Kipling would have traveled across the world to hear and write, giving it just the little distortion needed for the perfection of a masterpiece. I can only give the bare facts.

Long ago, perhaps in the eighties of the last century, or maybe before (the stout old gentleman paused and gasped for breath, his cheeks turning purple) the fisherman along the coast here saw a sailing ship of great size come up the long inlet from the Bay of Fundy. For two days she stood off the far side of the inlet, and they could see through a telescope that boards had been nailed over the letters of her name at bow and stern. (The wind blew the front door open with a sudden bang and I cowered closer to the guttering fire.)

Next morning the ship had disappeared. But when a fisherman went to lift his lobster pots on the far shore that day, he heard a shriek of agony, and on the beach he found a young man, both legs gone. The stumps were carefully bandaged by the hands of a skilled surgeon, who had performed the amputation, evidently a few hours before. (The boards of the inn creaked and the rain beat with sudden gusts on the windows.) They took the unfortunate stranger into an Acadian home, they saw by his smooth hands that he was a man of breeding, and they waited for him to speak.

He never spoke. Doctors examined his throat and found he was not dumb. Linguists were brought to speak with him in many languages. But he never spoke—never a word, only a few muttered curses now and then when he felt himself unobserved, and in some strange tongue. Once it sounded like "Jerome," and they called him by that name.

Jerome became the wonder and the mystery of Nova Scotia. Sometimes he would write on a child's slate, but he would rub the writing off if anyone approached, and he would never write on paper. The government paid a cottager to care for him, and old people still living can remember him well, sitting on his chair, legless, silent. Sitting there on the porch, looking at the sea, he grew to a great age and never spoke. What he knew, what he had learned on that unknown sailing ship, why they had skillfully amputated his legs and cast him ashore, what terrible secret he was hiding—of piracy, perhaps, and murder and pillage—no one ever knew and no one ever will know. Jerome died here after a lifetime of silence and of terror, watching the sea, waiting, they say, for his enemies to come and get him.

Next morning I bought a ticket for the bus in the store of P. A. Theriault et Cie. The Theriaults and Belliveaus have been the leading families of the Cove for a hundred and eighty-one years. Now Madame Theriault has a fine business selling groceries, lanterns, ox whips, crockery with roses on it, biscuits, brooms, socks, dresses, threads, needles, and drugs, all of which give off the immemorial smell of the real country store, which is the very essence of North America.

Two ladies of the village, dressed neatly like all French women, were sitting on the stools by the counter, doing more talking than buying (although one of them, as I learned, had drawn seventy-five cents from the bank for her purchases) and they told me that things were very dull about the Cove these days.

A strict curé would not permit dancing and the young people were in smoldering revolt. So they proposed to hold a dance anyway, which a war charity would make respectable, and the curé would fail to observe it. The only fun they had, they said, was on a feast day, the name of which I could not pronounce or spell, when the young folks dressed up in masks made of old stockings, talked in squeaky voices, went from house to house, played games, and had the very devil of a time. In the lusty rum-running days people behaved better, merely drinking rum. Now they were buying soft drinks, fortifying them with some commercial perversion of Jamaica ginger, and creating a deadly drink called Jakie, which set them crazy. Rum, the ladies said, was much healthier.

Madame Theriault turned on a red light at the front door and stopped the northbound bus for me. In it sat an aged woman, wearing a kind of pointed white night cap, trimmed with red, and, after one glance at that fearful face, I knew her to be a witch, whose broomstick was temporarily out of repair. But when she started to converse with her neighbors, in a high, cackling voice, I saw that she was harmless enough —perhaps only Mother Goose out on a holiday.

Beside her was the Old Woman Who Lived in a Shoe, with a beflowered hat and a string bag full of parcels for her brood, and she fluttered and fussed and complained like a setting hen. The third passenger was an old man with thick glasses that gave his face a look as blank as a plate. He had a gigantic gold watch chain, a home-made walking stick, and a stiff, out-thrust leg, which kept getting in everybody's way. These were English-speaking people, true Nova Scotians, offspring, no doubt, of the Loyalists. To one who has lived in the smoothed-off conformity of cities, they were so fantastic and yet so perfectly natural and childlike that I could have been sitting on that railway coach in Wonderland, where Alice found herself between a gentleman dressed in white paper, a talkative goat, and a friendly beetle.

All the way up to Digby this curious trio argued about the price of eggs. "I only get twenty-seven cents," Mother Goose said in her sharp cackle, which must have been acquired, by long association, from her chickens. "But my pullets lay as big as any hen."

"Plymouth Rocks are best," said the old man, gazing blankly through his glasses. "Such fine brown eggs."

"Leghorns," said the Old Woman Who Lived in a Shoe with a sudden fierce defiance. "Leghorns! They lay."

"But not brown eggs," said the old man, hitching his stiff leg around angrily. "Not brown eggs."

"Taste just as good, Leghorns," said the Woman from the Shoe.

"But what have you got to eat when they're finished layin'?" Stiff Leg demanded. "Might as well eat a crow."

"Plymouth Rocks are good, but they do get spiteful," said Mother Goose. "My rooster has turned cranky on me. He gathered up his spurs at me and I had to cut a switch and hit him. I didn't keep him long after that, you might be sure! But twenty-seven cents for eggs! It's a scandal."

"I get thirty," Stiff Leg grunted sourly. "But they're brown."

"He's crotchety," Mother Goose whispered to the Old Woman from the Shoe. "They get that way, livin' alone. Sometimes he talks like a Commune-ist." And then, as if to pacify Stiff Leg, Mother Goose added: "Well, we'll get more snow yet. But I heerd the gulls ahollerin'. The smelts is comin' in."

A little mollified, Stiff Leg confessed: "I'm longin' for some smelts, a mess of smelts, after a winter of salt stuff."

"I like smelts about twice," said the Old Woman from the Shoe. "Twice and you're sick of them."

"Cod," said Stiff Leg. "Yes, cod, but nobody knows how to cook cod any more."

For the next ten miles they argued about the virtues of smelts and cod, but always returned to the great issue of Leg-horns versus Plymouth Rocks. And all along the road you could see the kind of houses and tiny postage-stamp farms these people came from—narrow fields cleared from among the dark whisker of pine woods, meadows running down to the rocks of the shore, and everywhere little houses standing defiantly in the wind, hard by the beach, and villages snuggling into every little cove at the mouth of a friendly river. Nowhere else in Canada quite the same feeling, quite the same architecture of white wooden houses, such a feel of the sea, and such proud poverty, which is accepted not as a hardship but as the normal way of life. Smelts and Plymouth Rocks and Leghorns—these are the things to worry over.

To a Canadian who has not seen it before it is, indeed, another country. You feel it the moment you enter Digby for the first time—preferably not by bus from the south, but by ferry steamer out of St. John, across the Bay of Fundy. From the heaving bay you slide suddenly into Digby Gut, a long narrow channel with bare walls of rock on either side, where the tattered fishermen's houses cling like barnacles, and a few pitiful fields are carved out of the naked cliffs. The Gut opens suddenly into a kind of inland lake, placid and comfortable, ringed with forest. No wonder Champlain and his companions, amazed at this friendly haven, decided to make Canada's first settlement here along this pleasant shore. But it was a false beginning and they moved to Quebec.

Now Digby looks pure Scottish. You see it from the boat at first like a picture cunningly arranged, according to the laws of design, a Hollywood set for a fishing village, with a perfection of white houses scattered like dice on the hillside, among puffs of green foliage, and a long church spire in precisely the right spot. As the boat eases into the wharf, the picture falls apart, and there are only houses, a few brick buildings, and an old church. The composition, so complete at a distance, has broken up, like many other of life's anticipations.

But there is a fine, fish-smelling Scottish activity about Digby, the busy wharves, the cargoes of dried cod ready for shipment, the well-scrubbed people, the clean little town, the scallop boats starting out for Fundy, the tangle of rigging and masts by the shore, the swoop and dart of the white gulls everywhere and a sea vigor in the air, making you feel all at once a pleasure in living—making you forget what sort of world lies beyond the Gut, where the big ships are loading in St. John for the Battle of the Atlantic.

Looking at Digby for the first time, I thought of fishing villages on the Cornish coast behind their stone moles, of herring towns on the shore of Scotland, when the fleet is in after the night's catch, and the burly men in oilskins gossip on the quay. Digby lacks the old Norman church, the ancient inn, but it is our nearest approach to the historic fishing ports of Britain, and it is filled with precisely the same people, who have brought their habits, instincts, and very looks with them. Even now, as I watched from the decks, the little boats were setting out through the Gut to wallow on the vast sweep of Fundy, dragging up scallops with steel nets from the bottom of the sea and risking destruction with every voyage.

An old soldier with a battered taxi and a wooden leg, which marked his honorable service to his country, drove me up the shore of Annapolis Basin through the pleasant farm lands and tiny hamlets, past coves where men painted fishing boats while a few sheep watched them curiously from the shore, over clean little rivers, past apple orchards and stretches of squat spruce. At the head of the long Basin is the village of Annapolis, a few stores and fine old houses and a graceful church among the elm trees. It is, I suppose, if you reckon it by the sheer number of events, the most historic spot in North America.

Here, or a few miles around the corner of the bay, De Monts, Champlain, and de Poutrincourt established the first Canadian settlement of white men in 1605, calling it Port Royal. Here they whiled away the long winter by founding their Order of Good Cheer, each man providing a feast and entertainment one day a week, and in this wilderness, snowbound, thousands of miles from home, they would march in to the dinner table, bearing platters of game and pastry, with all the ceremony of a French court.

From then on the vicissitudes, the sieges, battles, captures, transfers from England to France and from France to England, the surrenders, occupations, burnings, destructions, and reconstructions of Port Royal—or Annapolis Royal as the English named it after Queen Anne—take three and a half pages merely to list in Morris Longstreth's lovely book, *To Nova Scotia,* which I bought down the street, and proceeded to plunder for its store of historic dates. Of this teeming record and fierce life nothing is left but the earthworks of the old fort, and a little museum of antiquities, across the green from the village.

You can wander now about the grassy ditches where men once died for France or England (who cared nothing for them) and through the deep gun emplacements where a few old cannon still doze in the sun. From the ramparts you can look down the glistening channel and remember the commanders who looked thus at the approaching sails of the enemy. And so careless is history of its heroes that you may find a clothes line strung across a trench in which soldiers went down fighting, and on the line will hang the washing of the present caretaker's family, featuring some pink silk underclothes.

For a long time I stood there on the grassy earthworks, trying to conjure up a picture of the old fort, the battles and hand-to-hand fighting, the bursting cannon, the square-rigged ships in the Basin, belching their broadsides; and then the genteel colonial life in later days, when the Duke of Wellington's lady friend, Gregoria Remona Autonia, lived here in banishment with her French poodles, and Lieutenant Walker beat his cow for eating Methodist grass. The picture would not emerge—only the long channel, the overgrown earthworks, the sunny little town. So I nodded respectfully to the bronze bust of Port Royal's founder and trudged across the street, feeling low and unworthy.

My old soldier was waiting for me in a restaurant. Looking over the varied bill of fare with this opportunity of a free lunch, price unlimited, he finally ordered fried cod, which undoubtedly he had eaten every day for twenty years. This country fishes cod, sells cod, and eats cod, and smells it, drying in the wind, day and night.

This is the Acadians' first country, spied out by Champlain, settled by French peasants, and then seized by the English. Up the coast not far is Grand Pré, where Evangeline was

AN OLD BOAT BUILDER,
CAPE BRETON, NOVA SCOTIA

AN OLD SPINNER, CAPE
BRETON, NOVA SCOTIA

OLD CLOCK TOWER, HALIFAX, NOVA SCOTIA

THE BIG WASH, NEAR PRESQUE ILE, NOVA SCOTIA

OX CART, GREENFIELD, NOVA SCOTIA

WINDMILL, GASPÉ, P.Q.

HOPEWELL ROCKS, NEAR MONCTON, NEW BRUNSWICK

IN CHARLOTTETOWN HARBOR, PRINCE EDWARD ISLAND

PERCE ROCK AND ETERNAL CROSS, GASPÉ, QUEBEC

FISHING BOATS AT CAPE COVE, GASPÉ

OUTDOOR BAKE OVEN, GASPÉ

MANOIR MAUVIDE GENEST, ISLAND OF ORLEANS, QUEBEC

INSIDE THE CHAPEL AT **MANOIR**

QUEBEC CITY OVERLOOKING THE ST. LAWRENCE

QUEBEC CITY FROM THE ST. LAWRENCE RIVER

THE LOWER TOWN IN QUEBEC

ST. ANNE DE BEAUPRÉ, QUEBEC

LA CONCEPTION, LAURENTIANS, QUEBEC

MONTREAL AND THE ST. LAWRENCE FROM MOUNT ROYAL

PARLIAMENT BUILDINGS, OTTAWA, ONTARIO

FORT WILLIAM, ONTARIO

OUR LADY ST. MARY, MIDLAND, ONTARIO

WATERFRONT AT TORONTO, ONTARIO

FORT YORK, TORONTO, ONTARIO

PROVINCIAL PARLIAMENT BUILDINGS, REGINA, SASKATCHEWAN

CALGARY, ALBERTA

MALIGNE LAKE, ALBERTA

THRESHING ON A FARM IN CALGARY, ALBERTA

TIMBER CUTTING, VANCOUVER, BRITISH COLUMBIA

THE FRASER RIVER VALLEY NEAR YALE, BRITISH COLUMBIA

THE WATERFRONT, VANCOUVER, BRITISH COLUMBIA
PARLIAMENT BUILDINGS, VICTORIA, BRITISH COLUMBIA

born out of the virgin mind of Henry Wadsworth Longfellow
—an immaculate conception which has deeply moved the
world.

There was no Evangeline in Grand Pré, and Longfellow
never even bothered to come and look over his locale, or he
would have avoided a few mistakes in local color, but the fiction
told the story better than the historical facts—the ignorant
peasants refusing for forty years to take the British oath of
allegiance, the scheming priest, Le Loutre, agitating them to
hopeless resistance, the exasperated New England authorities, the British and colonial soldiery herding the settlers into
their church at Grand Pré, burning their homes, loading them
into ships, and scattering six thousand of them down the coast
of America. One of the crimes of our race and of the New
World, demanded by New Englanders, carried out on the
orders of the English King by officers from Boston, immortalized by a Cambridge poet.

Even though New Englanders seized their well-dyked
farms, the Acadians came back. They slipped into lonely,
barren spots like Belliveau's Cove. They walked north from
New England through eight hundred miles of wilderness.
Nothing could keep them away from this land and nothing
has moved them for nearly two centuries. Up and down the
Annapolis Valley the orchards still surge into a foam of blossom every spring, where Pierre Martin planted the first apple
seed in 1633, and the old dykes still hold back the sea, and,
except in history books, the old crime is forgotten.

The fates had decided that Acadia would be British. Not
even Louisbourg could hold it for France—the greatest fortress ever built in the New World, heaved up on the cliffs of
Cape Breton Island, bearing the Sun King's name, filled with
cannons, replete with bastions, barracks, ballrooms, châteaux,
and rotten with French graft. Impregnable they called it at
Versailles—and some raw New Englanders under a merchant
named Pepperell captured it in six weeks. It was France's first

Maginot Line and a portent of greater disaster which history did not note at the time.

Accustomed to trading nations and continents among his fellow monarchs, the King of England gave back the wondrous toy to Louis. When the English began the serious job of conquering North America, Amherst had to take Louisbourg all over again in 1758 after a siege of forty-eight days—young Wolfe leaping ashore first out of the boats and just saving his scalp from the Indians, or the story of Quebec a few months later might have been different. The great fortress, the impregnable citadel of French politics, was torn apart, stone by stone, to build farmers' barns, until nothing is left but a few green mounds and ditches, high above the lonely sea.

The New Englanders took to Acadia. It was something like their own New England, but harder. Before the Revolution some of them came north and afterwards the men called Tories in the United States and Loyalists in Canada swarmed up to this barren coast in every ship they could lay hands on, 35,000 of them between Nova Scotia and New Brunswick, 15,000 more going inland to Upper Canada.

Basically, therefore, like Quebec, this is part of the New World, its first people North American, as is the foundation stock of all Canada. But the Scots claim it for their own by right of peaceful penetration and sheer numbers, and they have fixed their name on it—New Scotland—as they have fixed on it their ways, their outlook, their houses, habits, and their very cast of features. Bluenoses these Nova Scotia people are called. It is the blue nose of the Scot, the finely weathered nose that comes out of Scotland, out of sea winds and a hard codfish diet, and an undying will to live.

A Scottish nobleman, Sir William Alexander, was the first Britisher to see that this was land fit for Scotsmen. He persuaded the British Government to sponsor the settlement of a country which was given a Scottish name. By Alexander's invention—a pleasant fiction, unctuously performed—the king established the Baronets of Nova Scotia, and in Edinburgh a stretch of parade ground was declared part of Nova Scotia so that the baronets could receive their titles without the inconvenience of crossing the ocean. No sooner were these noble fellows ready to send their retainers to settle Nova Scotia than England, having newly won it by the capture of Louisbourg, made a grand gesture of restitution to France. Alexander died bankrupt, and the Baronets of Nova Scotia, with their unhappy order of nobility, died also.

That did not discourage the Scots. In 1773 the good ship *Hector* sailed into Pictou Harbor, on the northern elbow of Nova Scotia, her hold crammed with Scottish crofters. They walked ashore led by a piper (who had stowed away and paid for his passage by piping the passengers across the Atlantic), and when the Indians heard the wild wail of the white man's music, they fled. Having listened to the pipes at the siege of Quebec, they knew what kind of men marched to them in skirts.

Also on the *Hector*—that *Mayflower* of Canadian history—was a school teacher. From the first these Scottish people insisted on educating their children, and as ship after ship came over, bearing more immigrants, they built schools and then universities. As in Scotland, families who had barely enough to eat would manage somehow to send their sons to college.

They were free men now, owning their land, no longer tenants to be ejected at will from rich men's estates. A fierce hunger for liberty they brought with them and the seeds of democracy which throve, as always, in a poor land. At Pictou Academy Dr. McCulloch's lectures—frowned upon by some of the aristocrats of the day—were the first faint stirrings of responsible government, to be followed by the struggle of Joseph Howe, Nova Scotia's greatest son, and by the final creation of an independent country.

The Scottish accent is gone from most of Nova Scotia now, but everywhere are Scottish names—enough Macdonalds,

McDonalds, and MacDonalds to found a city of their own (and even in the eastern townships of Quebec there are other Macdonalds, descendants of Scottish soldiers and French wives, who speak only French). Up on Cape Breton Island the old folks still speak Gaelic. Middle-aged Nova Scotians can remember when, in some villages, Gaelic was the usual tongue in their boyhood, some people knowing no English. In those days the Scottish farmers, too poor to buy shoes, wore "shanks" or galligaskins, made of the skin of a cow's leg, crudely sewn. Even today the chief public figure of Nova Scotia, Angus Macdonald, loves to speak Gaelic in hours of relaxation, although he is an accomplished orator in English.

Such men from Nova Scotia pushed out across all Canada and into the United States. There are as many of them in New England as there are left in Nova Scotia. They are always adaptable, generally competent, invariably thrifty. In the national politics of Canada, in the big business of Montreal, in the cities of the west, they have always been leaders and usually bosses.

Such people gave Nova Scotia more character, more variation, more local differences than any part of English-speaking Canada. You would have to write a large book merely to list the different towns of Nova Scotia and their special characteristics, their ideas, prejudices, and mores. These things can grow only in a country where settlement was early and far apart, where men of one village seldom saw those of another, and these things disappear in the newer country of the west where settlement came suddenly in an age of communication and uniformity.

Nova Scotia thus is the most storied, the most deeply grooved part of British Canada and the greatest respecter of family, clan, and local tradition. An old Nova Scotian can tell you the history of every family for miles around and, in an almost pathetic fashion, he will take pride in the local celebrity. The Nova Scotian statesman, even though politics here is hard, bitter, and often ruthless, invariably is surrounded by a certain aura of distinction, whereas the cabinet minister from Winnipeg or Saskatoon will hardly get his name into the newspapers.

These people, like the French-Canadians, have lived long in this land, but more important, they expect to remain here all their lives, while most Canadians, like most Americans, live only in the hope of moving as soon as possible to a better street, a better apartment, a larger town. Run-down, they call the Maritimes, a little gone-to-seed, some of its best blood lost through the continual emigration of its strongest sons. There is, no doubt, some truth in this rather glib diagnosis, but the real wonder is that in a country so poor, cut off from all its natural markets in New England, isolated from the markets of its own nation, people still have been able to live, to support good homes, to maintain some of the best universities in America, to preserve a true culture and a living way of their own choice.

To explain Nova Scotia would take many volumes longer than this one, written by a native and not a westerner as I am. Some formidable attempts have been made to interpret this peculiar life, but few people read them now-a-days. The first, *An Historical and Statistical Account of Nova Scotia* was written at Annapolis by Judge Thomas Chandler Haliburton to deny the reputation given to Nova Scotia by Burke, who had called it in the British Parliament "that ill-thriven, hard-visaged and ill-favored brat." Haliburton's book almost broke its publisher, Howe, and the author would be annoyed now if he knew that his Sam Slick, almost the first notable humorous character in North American literature, was better known than his history. Haliburton, the grim judge, used to joke brutally at prisoners in his court. History has paid him back by remembering his jokes far better than the chief work of his life.

Mr. Longstreth's book, *To Nova Scotia*, is easier to read,

and worth reading if only for his detailed instructions on the
pronunciation of Antigonish, in which "one is supposed to
put all the accent on the *An,* allowing the rest of the word to
unfold glitteringly, like a serpent disappearing under a stone,
but be sure and wave the tail once at the *ish.*" Antigonish—
its lavish syllables inevitably prompt a digression—is the most
famous of Nova Scotia place names for its sheer sibilance
and Scottish flavor. It will fool you. It is pure Indian—Micmac
for "The Place Where Branches Are Torn off the Trees by
Bears Gathering Beechnuts," quite a neat feat of condensation,
when you come to analyze it. Personally, I prefer Mr. Longstreth's dragon tail to the Micmac beechnuts, but in either
version Antigonish is a rare gem of language and a rare old
town by the sea.

Haliburton, Longstreth, Archibald MacMechan (in a schol-
arly work), Clara Dennis, and many others have pictured
Nova Scotia and in part they have succeeded. It is not my
section of the country, and I do not claim to know it except as
a fleeting traveler, but I cannot feel that any of the books has
entirely caught its flavor, the pull of an ancient land where
every man knows his ancestors, their struggles, and triumphs
and battles long ago. Bliss Carman's poetry, Charles G. D.
Roberts' fiction, the younger Roberts' little sketches perhaps
have better captured the land's essence. "The Sweetheart of
the Sea," Carman called it, and the name will do.

Who save the painter can capture the toylike, almost too
perfect picture of Peggy's Cove, of stilted houses and littered
wharves, and sea shadows and little boats and the smell of low
tide? Who can put into words the sight of schooners setting
out in the evening, under full sail? Or the battered lines of
pine trees on the rocks, the little lonely farms hewn out of the
timber, the autumn meadows deep in the fire of scarlet foliage,
the secret rivers and lonely lakes and the stain of spruce forests
down to the sea edge?

Each town has its story and its special beauty. Lunenburg,

where they put the German immigrants because their numbers threatened to swamp the new village of Halifax—Lunenburg, which is still German by blood today but stanch British by conviction, the home of fishermen and the fastest Bluenose schooners afloat.

Shelburne, which was to be the great Loyalist metropolis, a new Philadelphia, where 10,000 Tories and their retainers cut down trees, built log houses on well-planned streets, established their slaves, and moved away in despair from such a hard land—Shelburne more ancient, perhaps, than any town in America, for here, they say, Leif the Norseman fought the Indians.

Yarmouth, settled not by aristocrats but by poor Massachusetts fishermen, who were horrified at wicked Shelburne and riotous Halifax and, strangers to pleasure or ease, built the wooden ships that sailed the world's oceans—Yarmouth, perhaps as ancient as Shelburne, for they have found a Punic stone there which may record the landing of the Norsemen and at least encourages the landing of many tourists from Boston.

Antigonish, with its serpent sound, the town of Scottish Catholics, whose university of St. Francis Xavier has started a co-operative movement among fishermen and farmers, notable among social experiments of our time in Canada.

For contrast, the grim town of Sydney, up on Cape Breton Island, where the miners go under the sea for coal to be used in smelting the iron ores of Newfoundland. And countless other villages of long legend and old harbors, and rocks where the ships of the Atlantic have laid their bones.

The chief city, Halifax, I had to see again, but before I went there I felt a longing for one more look at the coast. So I found myself one bleak afternoon at Meteghan, amid the litter of a little shipyard. No more sailing ships are built here by the Acadian craftsmen, but the clean ribs of a minesweeper stood out against the sky, a small but useful contribution to the British Empire's war, hewed out by the hands of Frenchmen, who had once been exiled by the British from this land.

Near by, the fishing boats were hauled up on crude ways and men were calking them, swinging their long-headed hammers in a clattering chorus, each man grunting as the hammer hit home, while the oakum streamed in the wind. It was an accidental but perfect composition in rich color—the fishing boats in reds, blues, and greens, the brightly painted lobster buoys, a busy flock of white chickens, behind them the little bay of rough water, and at its edge the sprawling village with a rusty old church and jagged spire.

At the wharf the first of the lobster boats had come in and I stood watching the fishermen take the lobsters out of the wet barrels. A blue-nosed Scotsman, with cold, sea-pebble eyes, measured the smaller lobsters expertly to a sixteenth of an inch with a brass gauge, and threw the illegal ones into a separate barrel for return to the sea tomorrow. Another fellow, a swarthy, squat Acadian, took each lobster as the Bluenose handed it to him and, in a single motion, inserted a little wooden peg into the creature's claws, wedging them closed so that it could not fight with its companions on the journey down to Boston.

There were 161 lobsters altogether in the catch—a good day. The fishermen relaxed, lit cigarettes, and looked out at the bay where a few boats were still tending their lobster pots, standing on beam ends in the afternoon blow. It was hard work, they said, in cold weather, and the Scotsman held up his hand for me to see. It was as blue as his nose and wrinkled from the sea water. A man might make forty or fifty dollars on a big day, he said, and then make nothing worth while for a whole week. Later would come the cod season. By the beach of every fishing village the fish would lie on the "flakes," curing in the sun, with a rich and universal smell, pleasant only to the seasoned Bluenose.

I walked up the bay to the single street of the town. The children, just out of school, followed me shyly, curious to see a stranger and not quite daring to speak to him, but squealing among themselves in mixed French and English. Behind them, an old, tired sheep brought up the end of this interesting procession. A woman eyed me through cracks in the window blind and an old man, sitting on a porch, allowed it was a windy day. That was true. The wind was making sport of the tattered laundry on the clothes lines and flapping many a hooked rug of brilliant pattern which would be a collector's piece almost anywhere else in America.

It was getting dusk now and cold in these first days of a feeble spring and I had an hour to wait before the bus came along. There was no place to go for warmth but the general store halfway along the main street, and there, to provide an excuse for staying, I drank pop with the proprietor, a young Frenchman with a sharp eye for trade. In the corner an old man with gigantic whiskers lolled in a chair, alternately sleeping and starting suddenly awake. Presently half a dozen of the townsmen came in to make small purchases but mostly, I suspected, for company and the warmth of the fat-bellied stove. They talked in French among themselves but answered my questions in good English. Eagerly they told me about the better days of Rum, when there was money to be made, quite honestly, as they thought, in handling a few "kaigs" in their ox carts, for the mysterious gentlemen who used to come here in fancy cars from the States.

The talk turned to ships and wrecks—the fragmentary, inarticulate talk of ignorant men, but richer than fiction in real color and authentic incident. They had seen ships pile up on the rocks along this coast and fished up the corpses next morning, for this must have been the port from which the Three Fishers went sailing out into the west. Even now, in the dusk, I could look out on the bay and see the little boats dancing wildly on the waves, balancing on their bows and sterns, almost threatening to turn somersaults, for a few lobsters, a few dollars.

Now I remembered all the stories I had read of shipwreck in Nova Scotia, and of the old pirates and privateersmen who sailed out of here for the Spanish Main. I remembered Alex Godfrey and his invincible ship *Rover,* as recounted by Longstreth, and Colonel Simeon Perkins, who wrote in his famous diary that Godfrey had just landed with Spanish plunder and added: "We must esteem it a Wonderful Interposition of Divine Providence. O! That men would praise the Lord for His Goodness and for His wonderful works to the Children of Men!" Only 160 Spanish sailormen had been killed in the battle and Colonel Perkins' prosperity was assured.

The wind rose higher and drove the last lobster boat scurrying from the bay. The proprietor lit a lamp, but it hardly touched the darkness of the store. The little building, clinging desperately to its rock, swayed and shook and threatened to roll away. The men muttered to each other in a corner. The old man dozed and awakened suddenly, his huge whiskers bristling, mumbled a few words in French, and went to sleep again.

To these men it was just an ordinary country store on a stormy evening, a few moments of companionship, a little spot of light in the darkness and the wind and cold of this coast, but to the stranger it was ten thousand miles from Canada, another country and another age.

As the store creaked and shook in the wind and the flames leaped in the stove, and the lamp cast dark shadows on the faces of the men in the corner, I could believe any ghost story or pirate tale. Any moment, I felt sure, the legless spirit of Jerome would crawl up the steps on its bleeding stumps, burst into the store, and reveal, at last, its awful secret.

Jerome did not come, only the bus, and I left, full of legends and soft drinks. One day Jerome will come, you may be sure, and the pirates of the Spanish Main, and the drowned skippers of tall sailing ships. Perhaps they have come already. Perhaps, when the stranger has gone, and only the townsmen are gathered around the stove on a stormy night, with the sea growling at the door, the dead men will assemble here and drink their rum again.

I took one last look at the old man in the corner. He had roused himself and now peered at me with cold, cruel, cunning eyes. I knew then. He had seen them. He had been one of them in his time.

The Names of Canada

Strange, haunting, and full of exciting sound are the names of Canada. Noble names, like the roll of an organ, are Saguenay, Miramichi, Okanagan, Lachine, Anse-à-Valleau, and Forillon. The surge of the tide and the sound of waves on the rocks are in the name of Fundy, and the shape of naked cliff in Blomidon. But there is soft music, for lovers made, in Trois Rivières, in the Grand and Petit Chlorydorme and Verchères, and there is the smell of spring flowers in Cap-des-Rosiers, Champlain's cape of wild roses, where the great Irish immigrant ship went down.

Who cannot hear the tinkle of evening bells in Similkameen, in Chaudière (the falls where Champlain saw the Indians empty tobacco to placate their gods), in Wallasheen, though they foolishly spell it Wallachin? Nipigon is the beat of a drum and Yoho the call of a trumpet echoing in the hills, and there is the piping of a far-off flute in Rainy River as your lips form the words.

Hard, manly names for daily use are here also—the Shick-shocks, the Gatineau, Jasper and Rimouski ("the retreat of dogs") and Chippewa (a windy fellow). Plain English names brought across the sea by homesick immigrants—Halifax, Edmonton, Stratford, Grimsby, Guildford, Windsor, Victoria, Lytton, and that loveliest of all names, Windermere, and the Scottish Glengarry. Each with its great story in another land.

Can you not hear the splash of the mountain river in the name of Illecillewaet? Or the sound of mountain thunder in the names of Kootenay and Cariboo, and the bubble of river rapids in the Ottawa? Who does not sense the happy shout of *wonderment in Montreal? Or the dark terror of Rivière du Loup, the river of wolves? Or the gush of wind in the name Assiniboine? Well might Whittier be fascinated by the sound of that word, though he had never seen the river, and his "Smoke of the hunting lodges of the wild Assiniboine" fixes the picture of the Indians forever in the mind of childhood.*

Or Huron, Nipissing, Temiskaming—have they lost their Indian smell and the memories of massacre? There are soft Indian names as well, like a sigh of contentment. There are Saanich, Cowichan, Squamish, Nanoose, Koksilah, and suddenly the sound of foaming water on the Pacific shores, in Uchucklesit and Qualicum.

There are strange, ugly names like Spuzzum, Saskatoon, Sarnia, Schreiber, Scugog, and Scubenacadie; lost exile names like Dauphin, on the distant prairies, which was chosen by the French explorers to honor a little prince in Versailles; and the curious name of Medicine Hat, where the Cree medicine man lost his professional headdress in a fight with a Blackfoot.

The name of Canada itself is strange enough, like the cry of some wild sea bird. Some say it came from the Iroquois kanata, a cabin, or lodge, some from the Algonquin odanah, a settlement. There is also the legend of the Spanish sailors who, failing to find gold mines, cried: "Aca nada!"—there is nothing of value here.

Names full of our history, our achievements, our failures, our memories, the lost dreams of our youth, the splendid hope of our future.

CHAPTER TEN

Sailors' Town

The Duke of Kent, fourth son of King George III, was an urgent, stubborn, and prolific young man. He lived for years with a lady of his choice and without any legal recognition of his household. He married, and begat Queen Victoria. He scattered fortresses and defense works from Quebec to Gibraltar like a farmer sowing seed. But his most notable job of work, the thing he enjoyed best, was the city of Halifax. It looks, somehow, exactly like its godfather.

He did not build Halifax, of course, but this last of the great Georgians seemed to leave not only his own image, but the stout, dingy, and genial image of a whole age upon this Canadian city, so far from home. It has a Georgian look of square old brown stone houses and fanlight windows, and narrow Georgian streets, and neat little squares and parks laid out with the stiff precision of a Georgian nosegay, and fine old churches, where eminent worshipers used to sit in long coats and skin-tight pants, graciously accepting God into the very best society.

Halifax looks like a Georgian countess living in reduced circumstances in a run-down mansion, still fond of a touch of gin and a pinch of snuff. It looks like the spirit of Madame Julie de St. Laurent, Kent's faithful paramour (long dead of heartbreak), brooding there on the shore, waiting for the royal lover to come back to her.

But that is Halifax only in its domestic life, in its overstuffed parlor beside the white china figures of its mantel shelf. Halifax in its outdoor setting is one of the most beautiful cities of men, and in business hours, one of the world's busiest ports. In the broad shelter of Bedford Basin the great convoys of war ride at anchor, waiting to slip through the narrow sea gates into the Atlantic—more ships than you have ever seen in one place before, with crews of almost every language. Among the merchantmen move the lean little Canadian destroyers, herding them, barking at them like sheep dogs.

When the St. Lawrence freezes, and Quebec and Montreal are closed with ice, Halifax, with its neighbor, St. John, must handle Canada's Atlantic exports, and winter is always a rushing time down here. When war came in 1939 Halifax found itself the most vital shipping port in the British Commonwealth. Into Halifax, by rail and ship, poured the goods of war from all over America, on their way to the siege of Britain. The streets were soon crowded with soldiers, ready to embark for overseas. Every barrack, every shed and hall they could find was crammed with Canadian sailors in training for a new navy, started after the war began. In Admiralty House, that spacious Georgian mansion, set in its little park, you found in the mess the young officers who, next morning, would take the convoys out to sea, and a good many of them would not come back again. So crowded was Halifax with the bustle, the goods, and the litter of war that you could hardly find a vacant room to sleep in.

Of a sudden the old Georgian has awakened from her doze beside the sea and perhaps she will never find time to sleep again.

The British knew what they were doing when they sent young Edward Cornwallis out in 1749 to found a city which would counter the supposedly impregnable French fortress of Louisbourg to the northward. Cornwallis beheld one of the best harbors on any seashore of the new world, lying between low wooded hills, with a gate so narrow that a few guns could defend it. Still today the long fingers of the sea reach into the very heart of the city, clutching it in jealous grip.

Cornwallis did a better job than his cousin at Yorktown. On the site of the Indian Chebucto (even the natives recognized it as the Mighty Haven) he coaxed, ordered, and drove a band of lazy settlers while they cut down the forest, squared logs, built stockades, and laid out the first English city of importance in Canada. The Indians murdered the settlers if they ventured outside the walls at night (the French paying a fixed rate per English scalp), there was the usual trouble with stupid home governments, and Cornwallis wore out his health trying to get work out of "the English rabble, generally tumultuous, refractory, full of discontent and murmuring."

It was not Cornwallis, however, who fixed the character of Halifax, but rather the Prince Edward Augustus, whose royal father had cut him off in his youth with an allowance of a guinea and a half a week, and made sure that he would be forever in debt. He arrived with his Julie in 1794—exiled, not yet a duke, a king's son but a mere military commander, on a continent which King George by this time had abandoned to its fate.

The Prince had been in other places. He had lived in a gracious white mansion above the falls of Montmorency and tampered with the defenses of Quebec. He had traveled penuriously in Europe. He had governed Gibraltar until his attempt to introduce temperance among the soldiery caused a rebellion. But it was in Halifax that he found just what he was looking for—a city which needed the hand of an architect.

It was a substantial place by now as towns went in the new world, and it was filled with Loyalists from New England who had come northward in the great post-revolutionary trek, but though they were sternly British they lacked the elegance to which the Prince was accustomed. He applied the architect's hand firmly and lavishly. It was not a delicate hand, to be sure, and the results were not always beautiful, but there was a kind of stodgy elegance about them which, in time, with a moss growth of age and use, weathered down into a peculiar loveliness and acquired the nostalgia of buckles, lace, and lavender.

The Prince plunged with delight into the job of making Halifax into a vast Georgian folly, and fortunately he failed. He built himself a fantastic residence with paths in the shapes of all the letters of the alphabet, with grottos, towers, and arbors, and a heart-shaped lily pond for his lady. Halifax fortunately was too large to be ruined altogether.

However, the people of the town danced at the Prince's balls, made love in his arbors, basked in his swollen Georgian court, ate his Gargantuan feasts, and overlooked the technical fact that his companion was not his wife according to the strict letter of the law.

These were merely the Prince's hobbies. His serious work was fortification. He could not see a hill, from Quebec to Gibraltar, without erecting a fort upon it. He could not see a stone wall without tearing it down and building it up again. When his eye lit on the hill in the center of Halifax, a fort from the earliest days, he could hardly wait to rebuild it. Ravenously he removed seventy feet of height from its top, built new walls, and reared up the Citadel, which is still there and has a kind of friendly pomposity and stout virtue, like its builder.

Clocks, chronometers, and watches were his passion. He had them everywhere, marking every minute of his day in an age when there was practically nothing but superfluous time, and his crowning plan was a great clock on the citadel. Alas, he never saw the clock. As the story is so charmingly told by Clara Dennis in her *Down in Nova Scotia,* the works for the clock arrived from England after the Prince had gone home, and they lay in a junk yard because no one knew how to make them tick. Finally they found a soldier who could fix them, and they went for a century and a quarter without serious trouble, except that the numerals wore off the dial in the sea gales. A

public subscription was taken up to replace them as a memorial
to the illustrious architect, a motive which "should be suffi-
ciently powerful in a boastingly enlightened and loyal community to prevent from crumbling to dust an edifice which
stood as a monument to the revered and cherished memory of
His Royal Highness, the Duke of Kent." There spoke the
spirit of Halifax.

The Citadel still marks the Duke's memory, and its ugly,
ornate, but agreeable old tower, like the decorations of a battered wedding cake, seems to set the style of the city. From
the Citadel you can look out over the city, the open sea, the
crawling islands, the ragged Northwest Arm reaching among
the streets and buildings.

The Duke, alas, never saw his monument here in final form,
with the white face of the clock smiling a royal and indulgent
smile upon Halifax. He had heard England's demand for a
royal heir, he had cast aside his Julie, become a duke, married
the Princess Saxe-Coburg. He had fathered a daughter who
was to become Queen of England and was to pay his debts.
To complete this wildly improbable version of the *Student
Prince* plot, Julie pined away in a convent and soon died—a
curious love story, tender and moving even under the hoop
skirts and parasols. That the Prince's Citadel should have been
for a brief space the prison of Leon Trotsky seems to add a
final touch of tragedy to the tale.

The gentry of the Great Age used to drive through Halifax
in open carriages with outriders. In St. Paul's, opened in 1750
and still in perfect health—a dear old relic like an English
cathedral, full of fine memories—they sat in their private pews
with all the grandeur of wigs and bonnets. Now, though the
port has surged up all around, though the streets are filled with
commerce, there is yet that old flavor in out-of-the-way streets,
in Georgian houses and high garden walls, in public gardens
laid out before there was a city to surround them.

Some parts of Halifax are run-down and dingy, after years

of genteel poverty, but the gentility does remain. None of the blaring crudity of our western cities is there, none of the push and salesmanship, but a kind of sober, trim, cheerful life which, though it is essentially North American out of New England, makes you think of life in a faded mansion on the coast of old England. That, I suppose, is only fancy, and the merchant of Halifax would not know what you were talking about; nor the modern politician, though he makes his laws in the weathered grandeur of Province House, which certainly does not belong to this age.

Most Canadian cities spread a blight across their outskirts, but the country around Halifax is strangely unspoiled. The shoreline of bare rock still clutches somehow the lop-sided pine trees. The little boats ride at anchor in the bays and inlets. Heather grows in a wild park from seed out of the heather-stuffed mattresses of Scottish soldiers. One of the Prince's fat Martello Towers (poor Corsican traveler) has lost its way in the forest. Over everything hangs the salt rime and briny taste of the sea.

Always the sea has been the central fact of the city's life. Always the ships of sail, of steam, and of war have sailed in and out of Bedford Basin, and the Citadel has smiled down at them impartially. Fleets beyond number have anchored there from the beginning—friends mostly and sometimes enemies, among them the French fleet which had come out to burn Boston and rested there while the New England Pilgrims were uttering their canny prayer:

> *Oh, Lord, we would not advise,*
> *But if in thy Providence*
> *A tempest should arise*
> *To drive the French fleet hence,*
> *And scatter it far and wide,*
> *Or sink it in the sea,*
> *We shall be satisfied*
> *And Thine the Glory Be.*

The prayer was answered. Storm scattered the fleet, its commander died, his successor killed himself, and for years the natives saw his ghost walking on the shore of the Basin, where his crew had perished among the Indians.

The great British fleet was there before the expedition to Quebec, Wolfe with it. Privateers have sailed out of here and smugglers and rum runners. Into Halifax came the *Shannon* with the beaten *Chesapeake* in tow. Into Halifax were brought the survivors of the *Titanic* and 150 of them were buried here. In the last war the Norwegian ship *Imo,* ready to sail with food for the starving Belgians, plowed into the French munitions ship *Mont Blanc,* which, floating along for a few minutes in a hideous blue flame, blew up and took a large part of the city with it, killing 2,000 people, wounding 6,000, making 10,000 homeless. As the tidal wave of the explosion receded, it sucked the shipping down to the harbor bottom.

Always Halifax has lived with the sea. It is a sailors' town with the air of the navy about it. The Canadian Navy is yet small, but has been growing at an astonishing rate, and most of it is in Halifax. Its young officers give the society of the town a certain breeziness, as the sailors keep the streets gay and the girls a-flutter. These boys came from inland prairies, from landlocked interior towns, but they have taken to the sea as naturally as sea fowl, discovering suddenly that they have the ancient blood of Norse sea rovers in their veins. To go out to sea with them in their destroyers, to see a twenty-five-year-old lad from Winnipeg or Calgary bossing a great convoy of British merchantmen is to see how the tradition of the British Navy has been blended with the free initiative of Canada. Having found its sea legs, Canada will never be without a navy again. Halifax will always be a sailors' town.

It is a students' town also. On May 22, 1820—which is a long time ago as education is reckoned in America—they laid the foundation of a university, calling it Dalhousie, after the governor. The money to pay for the building had been acquired in a shrewd Scottish fashion which suited the governor and the community. In the War of 1812 a Halifax expedition had taken over the American town of Castine, Maine, and, by the peaceful collection of customs duties, had returned with £11,500. Never were customs duties put to better use, for Dalhousie, among its noble trees, hard by the sea inlet, is so beloved and such a breeder of learned men that you will find its students in every part of Canada, and all eager to talk of their old college.

Out of Halifax come grim men and grim, thin-lipped politics. Halifax gave Joe Howe to Canada, a printer like Franklin with some of his earthy touch, who could fight a duel, argue a libel suit, rouse a mob, oppose union with Canada, and then, suddenly reversing himself, become the first Lieutenant-Governor of the new province of Nova Scotia—the tribune of the people, the great folk figure of the Maritimes. Charles Tupper, one of Canada's founding fathers, also came out of these Halifax politics, and lately came Angus Macdonald, a brooding Scot of sudden eloquence, Canadian Minister of Defence for the Navy. Whenever you meet a Nova Scotia politician you will find him, even in the teeming politics of Ottawa, of a distinct and settled type—more canny, more concerned about expenditures, more cautious, and generally tougher than the politicians from the more reckless west. Nova Scotia politics, centering in Halifax, is built of the hard Scottish race and it has lived long in a poor, hard country.

Yet I like to think of Halifax as more than a great port, a political capital, a sailors' town. I like to think of it still as a Georgian countess, strolling with parasol beside the sea, and beside her a manly, plump figure in three-cornered hat, scarlet vest, and riding breeches—the Prince Edward Augustus, Duke of Kent, his eye taking in every pretty ankle and every hill that could hold a cannon.

The Queer Lady

At the junction we waited for the branch-line train to Fredericton. I stood, for lack of other interest, examining some day-old chicks that were being shipped by express in cardboard boxes. Through the air holes I could see the fluffy, yellow creatures, and they set up a clamorous chirp.

"Pretty, aren't they?"

I turned to see a lady with a round, shiny, and freckled face, large and placid as the harvest moon. She smiled at me kindly, as if I were a small boy who was fascinated by his first sight of chickens. "Pretty," she repeated, and hauled some eyeglasses out by a gold chain and perched them on her flat nose, so that she could see the chicks better.

"So few things are pretty now-a-days," she said. To humor her, I agreed. And all the way into Fredericton she sat beside me on the dingy little train and talked about beauty. She spoke without emotion or expression in a steady, monotonous flow. I saw the other people in the car watching her.

"Something," she said, "has happened to the world. Not something temporary, like you read of in the newspapers, but something very deep. It is ugliness. People have the notion that America is ugly because its inhabitants can't be bothered to make it beautiful. That's entirely wrong, of course, entirely wrong. If it were only that! No, America is ugly, the towns and cities are ugly, because we want them to be that way. It is a positive thing. It is a passion for ugliness. It's an appetite! That's why we haven't one truly beautiful city in America and hardly a beautiful town. Fredericton is beautiful, but how many Frederictons are there in Canada? No, we have not only

219

lost the instinct for beauty but we have developed a genius for ugliness.

"Ah, yes! We work at it. We toil after it. We contrive ugliness in our buildings, our streets, and our rooms. Don't tell me! Haven't I seen them? The largest part of our income and our energy is devoted to the construction of ugliness. In the furniture business alone more talent is wasted to build ugly chairs and sofas than would be needed to rebuild the country. Architects sit up at night to design hideous buildings. Artists devote their entire lives to developing ugly designs for furnishings. Painters spend all their training to create ugly color schemes. Funny thing, though, everybody thinks they're beautiful. That's advertising. That's because we have been ugly in our souls and don't know any better."

"A passing phase," I ventured.

"Oh, no. You're quite wrong, young man. If it were that, it wouldn't matter. People can probably be as comfortable and sanitary in an ugly town as in a beautiful one. But the ugliness on the surface is only a symptom of something else underneath. Do you know what it is? It's unhappiness. We are ugly because we are miserable. A happy people produce beautiful things. But tortured people breed ugliness. You can look at a cathedral in England and be sure the men who built it were full of happiness, even if they never took a bath. Why, the stones of Canterbury and Durham are all laughing. Did you notice that? All laughing. But look at a modern skyscraper, or a modern village by the roadside, and you can see that the men who built them had no happiness inside them. And they were built before the war or the depression. I tell you, the people of North America have been unhappy for thirty or forty years. The people of Europe have always been happier. Look at their faces. Listen to them laugh. See the way they know how to live. The surest sign of unhappiness is the modern building of America, the modern living room, the style in women's shoes. The historians will look at these things and see what we were like. You re-

member what Keats said? 'Beauty is truth, truth beauty.' Well, we haven't either.

"It's queer though. They tell me the beauty industry is one of the largest industries in America. But we spend it all on the women's faces and legs. They look fine. But what a background! Well, I suppose nobody notices that, only the legs and faces."

We were coming into Fredericton now. The placid lady slid the gold-rimmed eyeglasses into her bosom and walked out of the car without another word to me. She was the ugliest person I had ever seen.

The conductor of the train, a sad little fellow with rheumatism, told me he had seen the lady before. Everybody knew her. She was a little crazy. "Paints pictures. But nobody buys 'em. You know—touched a little in the head, but does no harm."

CHAPTER ELEVEN

The Home Town

On the bank of the Saint John River at Fredericton I met an aged man. He was sitting on a bench, blinking and dozing in the sun. His clothes were worn and he was poor, but a gentleman and a United Empire Loyalist, with fine, deep-carved face.

As we sat talking there, between the river and the town, he swung into what was evidently his favorite speech—Maritime Rights, the ill treatment of New Brunswick by the rest of Canada. Like the Ancient Mariner, he held me with his glittering eye as he recited out of long practice a detailed and desperate account of the original Confederation bargain, by which the Canadian provinces were joined together. Finally, hammering his cane on the gravel path, he cried: "By God, we will have a square deal! We'll have our rights yet!" Then, tired out, he slumped back on the bench, and I left him there, snoozing by the river in the first frail sun of the spring.

Looking back now, I know, of course, that he was not a man at all. He was a spirit brooding by the river, the spirit, the genius and very essence of Fredericton. This little capital of New Brunswick is an old man, very poor, very respectable and intelligent, United Empire Loyalist to the core, blinking in the sun, shouting out suddenly that it will have its rights and then going to sleep again; for really it does not want its rights. It only asks to be left alone at the river edge. It doesn't want a new age and a new barbarism to disturb its reverie.

The new age and new barbarism have not disturbed it. The

twentieth century has not yet discovered it. Time somehow has missed it altogether, until you might say that this is the last surviving Home Town of America, uncorrupted and innocent as your grandmother, rocking on her porch chair.

You can only compare it to some of the little towns of England. If you stand at the end of the main street, in the well-treed cathedral yard, you will think you are in Gray's Stoke Poges, or in Burford, or in the churchyard at Stratford, by the Avon, where Shakespeare's bones lie, with the commoners', under the church floor. The Fredericton cathedral is a perfect reproduction of an old Norman church, with gaunt tower, clean-cut walls, and plain buttresses, almost lost among the foliage of great elms—an English church, built by men of English blood, out of long practice and a deep, well-hidden mysticism. The churchyard, as only the mystical English can make it, is the most pleasant and cheerful spot in town.

But Fredericton is not English. It is pure North American. It has brought the architecture, the furniture, the flavor of New England in its trek from the Thirteen Colonies after the Revolution, and it is still the kind of North American town that Emerson lived in. He or Hawthorne or Longfellow or Thoreau would have been perfectly at home here and, if smuggled in somehow today, blindfolded, would hardly know that their age had died. Yet English still because all these things came from England originally, from a little exile England in America.

Fredericton is the unmarred and unscratched relic, the perfect museum piece, and with that final rarity in our time, a complete unconsciousness of itself, for it has never been discovered, extolled, or exploited by the traveler. The old man blinks in the sun, shouts for a moment about his rights, and then dozes again, and the river flows by, and time flows by with it and nothing ever happens. It is the Home Town as it should be, where men can sit and dream, as they must have dreamed in the Athens of Pericles.

Fredericton lies on a gentle flat by the stream which bore the first settlers up here from the sea. All Canada was French then and the new settlement was called St. Anne's, until Lieutenant Moses Hazen and his British bully boys burned the village one cold February night in 1759, driving the inhabitants into the winter woods. No wonder the Loyalists built anew on such a site, when they found the charred remains of the old French town, overgrown with trees. Hard times they knew here, living on game and on the bark of trees, but the land was good and the river a clear highway to the ocean. No wonder either that it was chosen as the capital of the province of New Brunswick, for it was quiet, thoughtful, far from the centers of corruption, a good place for sound legislation.

Now, in summer, it is lost in meditation and in a soft tangle of verdure. Every street is lined with trees, every back alley and every yard. The trees are more precious to these people than gold, and when caterpillars started to devour them a few years ago the whole town rose up, levied new taxes, bought a gigantic pumping machine, and sprayed the invaders to extinction. Life to a man in Fredericton without the elms above him is unthinkable.

In neat, orderly squares this Loyalist town is laid out, a leafy graveyard in the center, and everywhere old rambling wooden houses, obese and expansive, with vests unbuttoned for comfort, basking in the shade—the kind of houses where America used to swing on the porch hammock and kiss its girl in the darkness, where dinner was at noon, with hot roast, and father stoked the furnace and split the wood, and a house was a home, not a camp on the route of march.

But the real repository of Fredericton's history and its genius—like a lavender-scented jewel box—is the Parliament Building down at the end of the main street, hard by the river, half hidden among the elms. Its square towers of brown sandstone, its absurd, elongated, and rusty dome inhabited by hordes of disorderly pigeons, its tiny size and enormous pretension, are like a poor gentleman who must keep up appearances and knows, as his neighbors know, that he has something better than wealth.

As you go inside this curious pile you will be greeted by the very caricature of a guide, in wrinkled uniform, an old man like the conductor of the Toonerville Trolley, friendly, toothless, eager to talk. He will show you the tiny octagonal anteroom with its gigantic portraits in oil, and he will stand back and regard it, head on one side, as if it were the largest and most magnificent chamber in the world. He will not know that this dark woodwork and paneling, this simplicity of line and stateliness of form, have a magnificence, not of the sort he imagines, not of size and wealth, but of a quality more valuable, a true architectural tradition, a solid dignity that flowed joyously and naturally out of men's minds into the materials of construction, before they had started to suspect and despair of themselves.

To enter the visitors' gallery of the legislative chamber, you pass another old guard, tilting on his chair, smoking his pipe placidly by the door, and you climb up a narrow, winding stairs in pitch blackness. This, too, is in accordance with the English tradition, and reminds you of the dark, winding stairs that used to lead to the British House of Commons gallery, before the Germans smashed it. But the Fredericton chamber is purely American, taken straight out of the Thirteen Colonies—a square room, with wooden columns, dingy purple hangings everywhere, a curtained dais for the speaker, huge crystal chandeliers, dark wooden galleries, plush-covered chairs, oil paintings of departed kings.

In just such a room, surely, the Declaration of Independence was signed, the Constitution framed! You expect the speaker to enter in three-cornered hat, knee breeches, and sword. It is a rude shock when he appears in a simple black robe and incongruous top hat, and the members of the legislature drift in wearing ordinary business clothes. They should talk here of

Life, Liberty, and the Pursuit of Happiness, of a Decent Respect for the Opinion of Mankind. You almost shudder when these modern legislators begin to talk about gasoline taxes, paved highways, and the sale of the potato crop. Yet all the formalities are observed: the sergeant-at-arms with the gold mace of royal authority, the speaker kneeling at his chair to pray for guidance, the antique language of British parliaments. All is done somehow with that surviving British instinct which, as it did in the young Republic of the United States, can take civilization into the wilderness, can rear parliament buildings in the woods, and perform ritual in the forest, among savages, without becoming ridiculous.

There is nothing ridiculous here and, among the members, no realization of their quaintness. They are simply making democracy work—the sort of little assembly of free men which has shaken the world so often. Still, there is a complete unreality about it, an utter isolation from the world around. Men here are governing, in suitable surroundings, the kind of simple society that existed in the last century, is dead now, but still walks around, like a disembodied spirit, in the heart of New Brunswick. This is the old Home Town of thrift, of balanced budgets, of men who still share the old illusion that you can't spend more money than you have, that two and two make four.

The library of the legislature is the final haunt of this old spirit. It is a noble room, yet to be discovered by architects and collectors—beamed, with high, sunny windows and glass book cases and ancient mahogany and such peace and quiet as this age has lost. It is like Faneuil Hall, like Mount Vernon, with the peculiar brightness, cleanliness, and cheer of colonial architecture. Here Jefferson could have written the Declaration, or Washington the Farewell Address. But it is not especially old. It has the touch of age because the design, the tradition of the eighteenth century were brought here by the Loyalists, who knew how to preserve it.

In a dark vault they keep their special treasures, all the old records of the legislature when this was a colony and not part of Canada, little rolled-up bundles of papers, all neatly labeled, records of the Matawaska Riots, the first appropriations and resolutions passed by the legislature long ago. Most sacred of all, to be brought out only on great occasions and handled carefully, an original set of Audubon's birds, which an old man will finger tenderly and then put back on its own shelf, within the locked vault.

When you talk to such men as this, or to an old maid who shows you the ancient books and documents, you sense a different set of values here in Fredericton. These people have a true culture, unconscious, sincere, and very deep, that comes out of their beautiful university on its hill behind the town, and lives in the daily life of the town. It is the kind of quiet, isolated, and unknown atmosphere which lived in New England towns and built the American Republic, and blossomed in American literature—a detachment, a leisure to think. It is a self-centered life to be sure, but concentrated on essentials, on realities, and not wasted, tattered, and diffused, as in the modern town, where everyone is tortured by the news of the outside world and whirled away in the wild currents from the city. Here an old man can fondle a portfolio of Audubon's birds, and a spinster can point out, one by one, the pieces of furniture, the old paintings, and the documents, with a simple delight in actual *things*. After half an hour in the library you know that your own life is a prodigal waste of lost motion, of grasping after ugly shadows.

It is no accident that Fredericton produced the prose of Sir Charles G. D. Roberts, our great Canadian interpreter of wild life, and the poetry of Bliss Carman, our finest poet. He lived not far from the Parliament Building, in a curious old wooden house, which got turned around by an oversight in construction, so that its back door faced the street. Carman, the product of this town, could rise sometimes to great music:

Was it a year, or lives ago,
We took the grasses in our hands,
And caught the summer flying low
Over the waving meadow lands?

In such a town, without straying from the streets, a man
could catch the summer in his hands, and the scarlet autumn
and the glistening winter and the surging spring, for they come
to the very doors of Fredericton, unafraid.

I left the Parliament Building with the feeling of a man who
has lived for a moment with his grandfather, and learns a sudden appreciation, reverence, and understanding of the old gentleman. On Queen Street the children were coming out of
school for lunch; soldiers were drilling in the old stone barracks where their great grandfathers drilled; the sun shone on
the white-painted iron Cupid, who clutches green dolphins on
the civic fountain; and up through the trees thrust the incredible spire of Wilmot Church, with a gigantic yellow hand at
the tip of it, pointing, like a traffic cop, straight to heaven. But
the strangest spectacle was in the lobby of the Barker House.

You will not believe it, of course. You will say it is a crude
invention, but that doesn't matter. The thing is there, before
you, in the lobby of the Barker House, in an undeniable glass
case—the stuffed corpse of a frog which weighed forty-two
pounds in life, is as large as an English bulldog, and sits forever grinning shrewdly at the world. He was found in 1885,
lived comfortably as a family pet for some years, coming home
for meals twice a day, until someone killed him by dynamiting
his lake for bass.

There are those who say he is a taxidermist's fake, no better
than Mark Twain's Jumping Frog, but you had better not sug-
gest it in the Barker House. I know myself, beyond question,
that he is real, for obviously he is just such a frog as would
live here, just such a unique and fantastic creature as would
refuse to conform to the sizes and standards of society, as

would spring out of the odd genius of Fredericton. There he sits grinning forever in splendid immortality, Frederictonian to the last grain of stuffing.

A little way down the block is the home of the venerable *Fredericton Gleaner*. The editorial office upstairs, in litter of paper and old desks and dingy toil and crusty old editor, is the very apotheosis of aboriginal North American journalism— such a place as Twain worked in, and Dana and Greeley or, perhaps, even Franklin. There they were turning out their editorial utterance for the first day of April, to denounce "the causing of false alarms of fire as a Fools' Day joke," and declaring solemnly in this year of civilization's ruin that "fire is a great enemy of man," and "there never should be unnecessary resort to an alarm. Otherwise the harmless joke is to be expected today and is generally appreciated."

Ah, Fredericton! That spot where Time lost his way and halted and could not rouse himself to move on—that fine old man, blinking by the river, demanding his rights and then dozing off again.

The Trees

Who can tell the wonder of Canada's trees? Who can know Canada who has not slept in the west coast forests and seen the clean shafts of wood, six, ten, and twelve feet through the butt, and felt the cedar's reddish, stringy coating, the fir's bark, wrinkled like a friendly face, the feather-foliage of hemlock, fit for making a king's bed, the flat juicy needles of balsam, the dark blot and sharp prickles of spruce, the lonely yew, unnoticed except by the woodsman's eye, the rare white pine?

Among the grim conifers, forever fighting to survive and forever doomed, the smooth limbs of maples search for the light, spreading jagged leaves to the sun, like supplicating hands, and in the bottom lands beside the streams the alders leap up overnight, with white-mottled bark, hand-painted. High in the coastal mountains the gray bowls of yellow cedar are as antiseptic in their emanation as the smell of a hospital. Down in Saanich, which the evergreen forest has not yet discovered, there are old oaks, with crooked arms, running across the hillsides like frightened gnomes.

Hot and still and pungent in the sun grows the pine of the interior, with deep red bark, darkly lined, and at the smallest cut it bleeds its clean-smelling sap. On the parched clay banks spreads the green mat of the juniper, crawling close to the ground, and in the mountain meadows the little blue spruce are like Christmas trees, shaped to order. For a thousand miles in weary blur sweeps the infinite family of the jackpines, scorned by men, and the open range is seamed with little poplars, their round leaves spinning frantically like tops, with a peculiar,

231

unmistakable whisper. Their cousins, the giant cottonwoods, seize every creek bed and make deep shade for the noon rest of horse and cowboy and the quiet ruminations of beef cattle. But harder, longer in the growing, longer in the burning, lovelier in mottled white bark or in darkest wine color, are the twin birches. In smallest cranny, without earth or nourishment, the dwarf firs eke out their lives alone, close to the sky, twisted and tortured by the wind. When spring comes the tamarack, strangest of conifers, puts out new needles like trembling green lace.

On the prairies live the starveling poplars, poor fuel and rotting fast as fence posts, but the only wood for a hundred miles or more, except the little windbreaks planted by the farmers, until the Manitoba maples crawl westward, and the prairie oaks and elms stand in noble groves beside the Red River. Then the leagues of stunted jackpine and spruce on the badlands, and at last the succulent hardwood forest of Ontario. Maple, with sweet sap for spring syrup, stout-hearted ash, oak, walnut, hickory, beech, and the universal tribe of willows spread generous leaves, making the woods open, bright, and friendly after the sullen conifers, and breathing a brisk, manly, hardwood smell. In the fields or on a village street the elms grow round and symmetrical, in graceful sweep, like big bouquets. But the pine and fir, after the west coast, are puny and haggard.

Loveliest of all trees in Canada, with a purely female beauty, is the eastern birch tree. It hides, shy and virginal, through the forest as if ashamed to show its naked body to man, and it moves in innocent nymph dance all the way down to the Atlantic shore. All night, against the forest gloom, the birches are pale ghosts in the moonlight, with far-flung white arms, but in the morning, if you look at them closely, you will find their bark turning to infinite warm shades of color from black to purple and coral pink, like a woman's rosy flesh. Up above, before the leaves sprout in the spring, the twigs seem to float, far off, in their own vapor.

And in the autumn what but fire itself can compare with the hot and ruddy glow of the hardwood forest, the fierce flame of color burning through the hills?

CHAPTER TWELVE

Fundy's Children

The bus from Fredericton that afternoon was filled with farmers' wives who had been to town for a day's shopping, and with soldiers going on leave. The farm women, stout, comfortable souls, severely plain, with none of the smartness of their neighbors in Quebec, shouted to each other the gossip of the road. A red-faced woman, with cheeks like twin raspberry jellies, told her companion that Al was supposed to be out of jail again. "But he'll be in soon," she screamed above the roar of the motor. "They'll all be in, the whole family." And I began to catch some intriguing snatches of information about Al and his relatives that set me in a lather of curiosity.

"Up to his old tricks, eh?" . . . "but his mother!" . . . "that woman he kept in St. John" . . . "his mother has the baby" . . . "the taxes they're puttin' on" . . . "I wouldn't mind the government spendin' the money if they'd only show a little more agony about it" . . . "in the depression they told us to spend money when we hadn't got any, now when you've got a few dollars they tell us you mustn't spend it, you got to lend it to the government" . . . "well, he'll be in again, you'll see. . . ."

Before I could get to the bottom of the mystery, the raspberry jellies heaved themselves out of the bus with a huge shopping bag full of parcels. It was a depressing thought as we bowled along beside the Saint John River, that I would never know who Al was, why he would return to jail or whether he was the father of the baby. But evidently everyone along this neighborly road knew.

The soldiers—boys, most of them, hardly requiring a razor yet—began to sing and everybody joined in the choruses. The driver took off his coat, and he waved to every traveler on the road. A deep gulf of caste used to yawn between the north bank of the river, where the original settlers lived, and the south bank, where the Loyalists considered themselves a somewhat superior breed, but now everybody seemed to know everybody else.

The Saint John River has always been the spinal cord of New Brunswick's life since the first days when everybody traveled on chuffing little steamboats and old Captain Sam Peabody used to bring up the freight, the passengers, and the news, stopping with a blast of his whistle at every farmer's wharf. The white-throated sparrow came about the same time as the ice broke and the Captain's boat waddled up the river for the first trip of the season, and the people said the sparrow sang: "Old Sam Peabody, Peabody, Peabody. . . ." That is how the Peabody Bird got its name. Few people remember that now, nor remember either a more notable character who once lived by the river—Benedict Arnold, whose neighbors did not like him. They burned him in effigy, hung a sign marked "traitor" on his door, and he disappeared down the river one night in a boat which, they say, he neglected to pay for. Much and varied human freight this stream has carried.

All along the road the little farms run down the river, and every mile or two, like a friendly traffic policeman in a broad white hat and red coat, stands a little river lighthouse. Now and then there are minute ferries that will carry you to the opposite bank if you blow a horn, hung conveniently for the purpose. Every few miles stands a village with church steeple piercing the forest of the river bank—lean steeples unlike the gay, glistening spires and domes of Quebec, quiet, drab villages, with English faces and no laughing eyes or red lips like the French villages on the St. Lawrence. Back of the villages roll the low New Brunswick hills, with the pink vapor-puff of new birch twigs hanging over them like a mist, waiting for the first leaves.

A land of little trees, as we measure them in Canada, but these forests, stretching in dark tangle from the Bay of Fundy to the St. Lawrence, have kept the people of New Brunswick. Swarms of logs, wallowing down the rivers in the spring drives, little mills puffing in the backwoods, spars for ships in the old days, planks for the great wooden fleets of the Maritimes, pulp for the modern paper mills—wood has always been the great crop of this country, while the cultivated farms stretch only in thin, frail fingers up the narrow valley. Woods, and wooden houses, and faded wooden churches and little wooden villages beside some little wooded stream—this is what you always remember of New Brunswick.

They are poor here, as poor as in Nova Scotia, and the towns often wear little paint on their faces, but they have bred a hard race of men, who, spreading throughout Canada, have succeeded richly. To the United States also they have exported many of their strongest sons, who could not find enough to do at home. With us in the West it is generally agreed that the transplanted New Brunswick politician, reared in these little towns, trained at town meetings, accustomed to pinch every taxpayer's penny and argue over every dollar, is the toughest and ablest in the country. Lord Beaverbrook came from New Brunswick, by the way, and so did Andrew Bonar Law, the only Canadian prime minister of Britain.

Through the New Brunswick woods run the innumerable rivers and up the rivers surges the New Brunswick salmon, one of the noblest of created things. On the Miramichi, on the Restigouche, the Tobique, Upsalquitch, Kedgwick, and Nipisigint they move in perpetual migration from the sea, to lay their eggs in the stream where they were hatched years before, and in no other.

To catch a single salmon—forty pounds, perhaps, on a light fly rod—is a worthy ambition for any man's life. The poor New Brunswicker gladly leaves this wondrous sensation to the stranger, and the stranger from the American city pays well for it, making the salmon one of this country's chief means of livelihood. The guides, the fishing clubs (with fishing rights for a mile or two of river auctioned periodically and often at fabulous prices) form such an industry that the native is content to abandon the best salmon waters to the mad anglers who care nothing for cost. To maintain this industry, millions of eggs are stripped from female salmon every year—as many as 5,000 from a single fish—carefully coaxed to life in hatcheries, the baby fish fed on liver and released into the rivers. All this in order that a tycoon from Wall Street may ship home a salmon in ice at a cost of something over ten dollars a pound, after the only happy and truly profitable days he is likely to know in the year. There are other rivers, however, where anyone may fish, the poor native or the poor visitor.

Salmon fishing in New Brunswick is not the kind of thing you write or talk about unless you have become a member of the order, have taken the vows, have entered the holy of holies and left the world behind. The layman can only stand on the shore and gape at the man in the canoe with the light rod, who has dedicated his life to a higher purpose. (But wait until we get to the trout streams of the free, barbaric West, even with worms for bait, if you know no better. Then we can all go a-fishing.)

This is old country with dozing villages, covered bridges, and old tales—like the legend of the Dungarvon Whooper, a huge and fearsome cat, as dangerous as a grizzly, which lived not far from Fredericton in the imagination of the settlers; the tale of pirates' buried treasure at Kingston Point; and the green light which rises out of the earth along the river and means sudden death to the man who sees it. It is a country of pinched and winding valleys like Matapedia, where the ripe autumn fields are walled in by fiery forests of maple, burning in harmless flame of color to the tops of the little mountains. It is the country of the world's most fantastic, mouth-twisting names.

Just try to pronounce Kou-chi-bou-guac, Washa-de-moak, Kennebecasis, Madawaska, Missaguash—Indian, beyond the white man's tongue, and probably beyond my spelling. Professor James DeMille long ago immortalized New Brunswick's choice of names in this jolly rhyme:

> *Sweet maiden of Passamaquoddy,*
> *Shall we seek for communion of souls*
> *Where the deep Mississippi meanders*
> *Or the distant Saskatchewan rolls?*
> *Ah, no! In New Brunswick we'll find it,*
> *A sweetly sequestered nook,*
> *Where the smooth gliding Skoo-da-wab-skook-sis*
> *Unites with the Skoo-da-wab-skook.*

Just quaint Indian names you may call them, but to me they have always seemed much more. They seem to mark a kind of secret understanding among all New Brunswickers, as if they were the pass words of a tribal unity which forever sets them apart, by secret vows, from the rest of Canada. Wherever he goes the New Brunswicker takes something of New Brunswick with him, treasures it, boasts of it, hangs on to it. His strange place names are the symbol of a fierce, tenacious grip upon this old land.

So we went down the river in the rolling bus, and at dusk, out of a flaming sunset, we came to St. John, New Brunswick's principal city. The desperate tide of Fundy was rising as we crossed over the river and in the narrow channel the falls were running uphill, inland from the sea, which is their odd habit.

Quabeet-a-wee-sogado, the Indians called this gorge—"the beaver's rolling dam"—and it is well known that the god Glooscap broke the dam and let the river run freely to the sea; but the Fundy tide, raging up thirty feet, pushes back the river current, which thus flows alternately in and out for six hours at a stretch. Only at the pause, when the tide is changing, can boats push through the gorge, and there is a sudden scurry of lumber barges, tiny steamers, and pleasure craft. You must hurry, for when the tide changes and the falls reverse themselves, the whirlpools are so fierce that anyone who falls into them is never seen again.

The city of St. John at the river mouth is a rare study in ugliness. It is ugly with the fascination of a person who is too ugly to be plain, too unusual to be dull. It has the fine, hard, deep-lined ugliness of an old Scotsman, with courage and shrewdness and strength in every line of it. I have seen a Scotsman selling candy in a store in the Pass of Killiecrankie, and a stone mason in an inn beside Loch Lomond, and a fisherman at St. Monance, and a woman peddling flowers in Edinburgh, who had faces exactly like the face of St. John. This Canadian city on the Bay of Fundy is a town from Scotland moved stone by stone, spire by spire, street by street, across the ocean. It is Greenock rising in its trim tiers of stone from the seashore. It is a minor Dundee upon the Firth.

St. John is as hard as any Scottish town, its flat, glum face made of brick and stone upon a round and barren hill. Like the Scottish towns that bore it, St. John clings to the sea, crowds against the beach and the slippery sea rocks, lives by the sea's bounty and asks nothing better—asks neither beauty nor vegetation, nor any soft delights of land. Up to the ends of the streets, beside stone quays like the quays of a Scottish herring village, the ravenous tide of Fundy creeps, brown and urgent, driving the sea gulls before it, lifting up the little ships that lie drunkenly on the mud, washing up to the very doorsteps of the houses.

Only a few green spires of churches, as dour as the frown of John Knox, break the line of stone upon St. John's naked hill. Only by a large public square and an ancient burial ground on the hill's hump does St. John admit the need of recreation, for its life is in the harbor, in the fleets of merchant ships, in the little freighters and fishing craft. There is no time for amusement, for decoration, for the earth. The sea is waiting at the door and the tide is rising.

Walking these stark streets at night, you have the feeling that the crowds of boys and girls, the soldiers in uniform, the sailors, are trying desperately, under a little speck of incandescence here and there, at a movie theater or a soda fountain, to overcome the settled melancholy of the place—a few moments stolen from the dark clutch of the city, saved from the scowl of this granite face. As I strolled through the town I came upon an old man, ragged and bearded, sitting on the curb and playing a fiddle. He wore a sign which said: "Blind, but happy." Perhaps you would be happier in St. John if you were blind.

But in the morning early, when I walked up the hill, across the square, and down the solemn streets of stone and brick houses, each cheek by cheek, but cold and sexless as a tombstone—just then, and for a brief moment, St. John seemed to relax and smile. As the sun rose it caught the windows and they gleamed suddenly, like sparkling eyes, a sly quick smile, the smile of a Scotsman with his joke. Then, as suddenly, the light died in the city's eyes, as if it were ashamed of being caught in a moment of weakness. Yet out at sea, when I got to the street end, the sun still shone on the glistening sides of liners and on the rusty bellies of old freighters that prepared to sail into the Battle of the Atlantic, and everywhere was bustle and cheerful sound, the noisy but well-ordered speed of a great world port of war. Only on the sea is St. John truly itself.

I walked back to my strange hotel. It was like a boarding

house on the south coast of England, years behind the times, but keeping up a faded gentility of crystal chandeliers, finger-bowls, and rococo ceiling. There I found the final triumph of the Old Land in this distant outpost. They served me kippers for breakfast.

Actually, of course, St. John is not Scottish. It is the product of a few Frenchmen who came here when this was part of Acadia and of many United Empire Loyalists who had lived long in the Thirteen Colonies. It belongs to the New World.

The first white man to see this coast, Esteban Gomez, was exploring for the King of Spain in 1525, before Cartier and just after Cabot, and he called it Deep Bay, Baya Fonda, so that it became in English the Bay of Fundy. Champlain, that ubiquitous traveler, who turned up everywhere sooner or later, sailed into the harbor here on the feast day of Saint John the Baptist, and gave that name to the river. But Charles de La Tour was the real father of New Brunswick.

What a parent! The French king gave him the fur trade of the river and he built his fort at the head of St. John harbor, where he prospered until a fellow named Charnisay established himself on the other side of Fundy, with his gorgeous wife. In a private navy Charnisay attacked La Tour's fort when the owner was away, but Charnisay had forgotten Madame La Tour. This lady, commanding her husband's fort, waited until the Charnisay flotilla was at the edge of the shore and then let go with her cannons, blowing most of the ships out of the water. Charnisay scuttled back across Fundy, but he returned two months later when Madame La Tour stood him off again for three days, until her men betrayed her. Charnisay killed all the soldiers of Fort La Tour and made Madame watch the shootings from a scaffold, with a rope around her neck, but he didn't kill her. He allowed her to die peacefully of her experiences three weeks later.

King Louis was so pleased to have the troublesome La Tours out of the way that he gave all the territory from the

St. Lawrence to Virginia into the keeping of Charnisay, who most inconsiderately got himself drowned from a rowboat. The king, changing his royal mind again, gave the country to La Tour, who had been in hiding while his wife was fighting and dying. Whereupon the widow of Charnisay sued La Tour for the remainder of her drowned husband's estate. La Tour, a man of infinite ingenuity, solved the whole difficulty and fooled the lawyers by marrying the beautiful Madame Charnisay. Thus ended in a perfect movie fade-out the incredible case of Charnisay versus La Tour.

After that nobody paid any attention to St. John until the British came and took it before taking the rest of Canada. Some tough New Englanders from Haverhill settled here to trade rum with the Indians, and liked it so well that they refused to join the Revolution, as the Americans had expected. Captain Stephen Smith, of Maine, was so enraged by St. John's loyalty to the English Crown that he sailed north and burned the fort to the ground. After the Revolution the Loyalists came, landing at Upper Cove on May 18, 1783, three thousand of them from twenty ships, and it was they who cut down the forest and laid out the city in hard right angles and Puritanical straight lines, with the scowl of a deacon of the Salem church.

These people took easily to the sea, wrestling with the tides. The sea waters rush in so fast that on the Petitcodiac River at Moncton the Bore rages inland over the mud flats in a solid wall of water four or five feet high. (And, strangely enough, not far off, is a public highway where your car starts to roll quietly up hill, or seems to, by an extraordinary optical illusion in a land full of contradictions.) Everywhere the New Brunswickers built their settlements by the hungry tides and launched their great ships of wood, among them the first fleets of the Cunard Brothers at Chatham. From the neck of Nova Scotia north to the Bay of Chaleur they put to sea in their frail fishing boats, and on the windy shore of rocks and tattered pines their nets are still strung today on cottage fences. The cod is drying on the racks, and the lobsters litter the prolific beaches of Shediac.

North and east, and cuddling into the shoulder of New Brunswick and Nova Scotia, lies Prince Edward Island, Canada's tiniest province, a single speck of garden in the sea. The inhabitants—like all island folk, with a character of their own —say it is the only truly civilized spot in America, where, in the pleasant farms and quiet villages, there is still time to live. We have it from L. M. Montgomery, who wrote *Anne of Green Gables* here, that fairies still live in the land which the Indians called Abegweit, "Floating on the Wave," a charming conceit.

"We are," says the mother of Anne, "not hide-bound or overly conservative, but we do not rush madly after new fads and fashions because they are new. We wait calmly until other parts have tried them out for us and then, if they have stood the test, we adopt them." And if you ask an Islander, in any part of the world, what island he is talking about, he will reply, in the words of the old Scot from Charlottetown: "Mon! What ither island is there?"

North again and across the Bay of Chaleur (Cartier's Bay of Heat) you are in French Canada on the Gaspé Peninsula, Quebec's round nose, forever scenting the Atlantic. Gaspé is a country of its own, French with an Irish mixture, where life has depended on the unfailing harvest of cod since Cartier planted among the wondering Indians the first white man's cross in Canada, and the French fishermen sailed here to take their salted cargoes home again across the ocean.

Still the fishing fleets come in, red sails against the evening sky, the sea gulls swooping beside them. Still the *"décolleur,"* with hand in giant mittens, rips the entrails out of the cod with one expert twist, throws the offal to the screeching gulls on the beach and the valuable livers into a vat. Still the cod lie on the drying racks or "flakes," and the beaches give off a smell which strangers find stronger than quaint, but which the fishermen grow to love.

Gaspé has been rediscovered—fortunately or unfortunately as you view these things—the white villages have been pronounced picturesque by artists, the fisher folk have been found charmingly primitive, and the attentions of the tourists eventually will make Gaspé primp itself and paint its cheeks and develop a self-conscious perfection.

Nothing, however, save the elements can touch the astounding and heroic spectacle of Percy Rock, the French Isle Percée, the pierced rock that Cartier saw beside the shore—a sheer hunk of naked stone, richly colored in soft reds, yellows, and greens, wallowing a few yards from the beach, like the hulk of a ruined ship, like a stranded whale, with a hole through it, blinking like a wild eye. Beside it, long broken from the main body, stands a single obelisk in the water.

The tourists cannot touch it, but in geological time Percy Rock is dying fast. John Mason Clarke, a great Canadian geologist, calculates that in precisely 13,000 years the wonder will disappear, pulverized by the sea. There used to be several tunnels through the rock, bored by the waves, but in time they were undermined and collapsed. On the seventh of June, 1845, as Phillip Le Boutillier was turning the key to his store in the village of Percy, he heard a shattering burst of sound, and saw a cloud of dust, with swarms of clamorous birds, rising from the sea above the rock. As the cloud settled he realized that the outer arch of the rock had fallen, leaving only one hole in it.

Even now the sea is hard at work boring still another, digesting the rock at leisure, all unknown to the swarms of gannets, absurd puffins with red-striped bills, cormorants, sea pigeons, and kittiwakes that circle in eternal round of quarrel and breeding, so that the white streaks of them look like a fall of early snow on the cliffs. Unknown also to the remains of billions of prehistoric lobsters and sea creatures embedded here, when the rock was heaved out of the ocean bed.

This is better pirate country, perhaps, than Nova Scotia, and ghost country, too, the best in America. Out on Bonaventure Island lived Captain Peter John Duval, who commanded the privateer *Vulture,* of five guns and twenty men, in the Napoleonic wars, and you can dig hopefully for buried treasure almost anywhere. From the Gaspé shore, looking southward, you can see the familiar phantom ship, crowded with pirates, which sails in from the sea, catches fire, and sinks with a roar of guns, a clank of chains, and the moans of the dying. Or if you happen to miss this spectacle, you can consult one of the great editors of Canada (whose name I will supply privately on application), and he will tell you, with obvious conviction, that he has seen the ship not once but twenty times in his boyhood here. The Irish of Gaspé still hear the banshee wailing on stormy nights and when the fishermen, afraid even to move their anchored boats, are gathered around, a Stranger will enter and say: "Is it here you are and the boats on the chains?" That means death for someone before morning.

Death is familiar here, for the Atlantic has driven ships upon these rocks and scattered their bones across these beaches since Cartier's time. It is one of the ocean's most populous graveyards. Times beyond number the villagers have watched some great vessel pound to pieces, close to shore, its crew and passengers in the rigging, and no one able to help them. Always the sea rages in, offering cod, but cutting away the land in payment.

The Geese

A band of geese went north today. They were high up, a little black V in the sky, but we could hear their honking. George Pudbury stopped his plowing and looked up, following the flight of the geese until they disappeared over the hill. The woman next door gazed over her clothesline, a wet shirt in her hand, and watched the flight. Old Jim Barlow, bent double with rheumatism, craned his neck to see. The children playing in the sand pile stopped for a moment and pointed.

All over Canada the geese were going north. In the natural channel of the prairies, between lake and mountain, you can hear their thousands at dusk, honking high, and then the intimate whisper of wings as they come down to land.

In the autumn they will come again and at evening drop down to rest in the stubble fields. From the distance you can see them feeding on the scattered grains of wheat, or you may find a solemn pair swimming in a puddle, but you will never get close to them. They are wild and will never come close to man, whom they do not trust. Nothing can tame them, nothing deflect them from their course.

Every spring they head northward, and south each autumn, the Canada Goose, noblest of birds. Everywhere, but especially on the lonely prairies, men look up and watch them, and never tire of the sight. In the flight of the geese they see the thing that everywhere is withheld from man. Without compass, without knowledge of geography or power of reason, the geese move certainly, over the thousands of miles to their habitation. No doubt here, no fear, no bewilderment. And men, doubtful always, afraid always, and in their civilization completely be-

wildered, see the geese and they know that here is something, a freedom, a surety that they had once long ago but have mislaid in the glut of living.

The geese know their way, over the trackless land, over men's cities and the empty tundra, while men, for all their roads, maps, paraphernalia of travel, their cunning science, are lost. The geese fly boldly into the darkness and the wilderness and it is friendly to them. Men flee from the dark and huddle in their cities, their tiny points of light behind flimsy walls.

Men look up to see the geese go over and they feel a terrible longing in their hearts. The plowman stops to watch them, the free creatures that are not doomed to the labor of the plow. The housewife watches them, who are free of drudgery. The old man sees them and the swift, bitter passage of his life. The child gazes at them in wonderment, not yet aware of their meaning. Pudbury, old Barlow, the woman next door, and the children all look up at the geese—at the unvarying passage, the certain destination, the sure journey that never ceases and never fails, while we are bound to the earth.

CHAPTER THIRTEEN

The Frontiersman

John W. Dafoe, editor of the *Winnipeg Free Press,* is the greatest Canadian of his time. The mark of it is on the outside of the man—the huge, roughcast figure, the shaggy head of reddish hair, the carved-stone face. It is in his slow quiet speech, his power of writing, his prodigious memory, his uncanny grasp of men and events, his refusal to accept office, honor, or rewards. It is in the record of his life. That record, because it is so largely the record of his time, must be examined by everyone who wants to understand Canada, where it came from and where it is going in the world.

For nearly fifty years Mr. Dafoe has been doing a large part of Canada's thinking. Day in, day out, he has sat down in his littered office and slowly, with the stub of a pencil, has scrawled his closely reasoned and documented editorials. These, for their accumulative effect on Canadian politics, might almost have been the commandments written on tablets of stone and brought daily out of the wilderness. What Mr. Dafoe said today will be said all over Canada tomorrow, echoed in other newspapers, stolen by scores of journalists, voiced in Parliament, often denied by the government and quietly incorporated in government policy. In his own field of Canada, Mr. Dafoe has been more influential than any corresponding journalist in the British Commonwealth—a last rugged relic of the days of personal journalism, when men like Greeley, Dana, and Watterson flourished in the United States.

Mr. Dafoe is a Liberal, but not a very constant one in the party sense. Always he has been more Liberal than the politicians of that name—old-fashioned in his economic Liberalism, perhaps beaten already by the march of an opposite idea, yet still believing, with a fierce religious conviction, in the rights of the ordinary man and the value of competition in human talent. The Liberal has been recognized by his Conservative opponents. When the Conservative prime minister, Sir Robert Borden, went to the Peace Conference, he took Mr. Dafoe with him. In every great Canadian crisis, the lonely man in Winnipeg is consulted by statesmen, gives his answer, and goes back to his pencil and his sheaf of copy paper.

More than any man in the country he represents the continuity of Canadian affairs since the days of Confederation. He came out of a bush farm in Ontario, when the Ottawa Valley was a wilderness, raised on the Bible, Shakespeare, and the old *Toronto Globe,* was teaching school when most boys are in the middle of it, and finally got a job as a reporter in Montreal. In Ottawa he reported Macdonald's speeches, was always in Laurier's confidence, and for twenty years has watched over the shoulder of Mackenzie King, with a look of general approval but some skepticism.

Most of the time he has sat at his desk in Winnipeg, a gigantic creature, sprawled over his copy paper, hair wildly rumpled. This was the ideal place for him. Winnipeg largely gave him his character. His character has largely made the mental climate of Winnipeg. To understand either, you must investigate both, and both are worth investigation.

Winnipeg lies alone on the empty prairie, thrusting itself suddenly out of the flat plains like a mirage. Being isolated, it has developed its own ways, its own thoughts, and its own looks, free from the monotony of multitudes. Winnipeg is still the West and far more western than the cities further westward. Despite its size and physical structure it is, in spirit, the frontier. Its inhabitants come out of the western soil, out of immigration, hardship, loneliness, and the hope of riches. They are frontier folk and many of them remember the buffalo herds.

They came first out of ships from Hudson's Bay, by the long river route of the fur traders, to the edge of the prairies. By 1806 the first white woman ever seen on these plains had stowed away on a Scottish ship, disguised as a young man, and, searching vainly for her lover, bore her child in a cabin at the mouth of the Pembina River. Next year Marie Anne Legimonière paddled up from the Bay with her husband and her baby, who was to be the mother of that fantastic rebel, Louis Riel. Then came the Scottish women of the Selkirk Settlement, plodding through the rotten spring snow, babies on their backs, a piper in kilts leading them. They had been expelled by the landlords of Scotland, who wanted their fields for sheep and they had seen their homes burning as they boarded the exile ships.

In Canada life was little better—wars of the fur traders, floods on the Red River, Massacre of Seven Oaks, cold, hunger, and months of living on buffalo meat, mixed with wild berries to make pemmican. But soon at the Hudson's Bay Company post of Fort Garry a vagrant seed of civilization took root in the empty soil and would some day grow into Winnipeg.

Gradually the fort produced a curious aristocracy of Hudson's Bay factors, who ordered suits from England, bonnets and gowns for their wives and even carriages, to be delivered by river boat a year later. Sir George Simpson, that fabulous fur trader, traveled like a Roman emperor in a fleet of canoes, a piper playing beside him, his Indian paddlers gay with feathers. Then, on the great man's arrival, there would be a ball at Fort Garry, with officers in military uniform, ladies in London frocks and long white gloves, dancing that reckless new step, the polka. In another hall the halfbreed Métis pranced in their moccasins, with plenty of rum, in freely distributed "regales," the customary hospitality of the Company. At Christmas there would be three weeks of parties, Indians dancing in war paint to earn a few cookies with currants in them, and dinners and flirtations, and Dr. John Bunn's famous letter to Donald Ross, at Norway House, recounting the great ball of 1848 when "all became hiccups and happiness."

There were months of loneliness between the celebrations, and in the mud-plastered log houses beside the Red River the Scottish crofter longed for home:

From the lone shieling of the misty island
Mountains divide us, and the waste of seas;
But still the blood is strong, the heart is Highland,
And we in dreams behold the Hebrides.

All the homesickness of the exile, the world over, is held in the wistful music of John Galt's lines, written in Canada.

The prairies filled up. The ox cart and York boats moved westward. Grain had been grown on the bottomless, rich muck of the Red River Valley. A few men had glimpsed the value of the lonely plains. But Canada's ownership of this land had to be established, and in strange fashion.

Riel and his Métis, the French-Canadians who had intermarried with the Indians, proclaimed their new republic of the West. They seized Fort Garry and raised a flag bearing the French fleur-de-lis and the shamrock. Riel himself—handsome, theatrical, like the villain of an old melodrama—made speeches, saluted the ladies, murdered young Thomas Scott, and for a year ruled a vast empire in the wilderness. Rebellion was easy until the redcoats came from the east and drove him into the United States.

He would appear again, that crazy young man, and a Conservative Government would hang him after a second rebellion. His hanging would enrage the French race, wreck the Conservative Party, elect the Liberals, launch the great career of Laurier, and cause other incalculable results to the present hour.

At last the railway came to the plains, then the surge of settlement, the grain sprouting from the Lakes to the Rockies, and Winnipeg the center of it all—Main Street churned into deep mud by horse and wagon, Portage Avenue still the trail westward to Portage, and the young journalist, Dafoe, picking ice out of the water barrel in his kitchen every morning.

Some old men and women still alive remember most of this history. Their square houses of warm yellow stone stand along the Red River, north of Winnipeg, hard by the massive walls, gates, and buildings of Lower Fort Garry. Their Scottish kirks stand there also with the stern look brought from Scotland, and many a gravestone tells of their wanderings, their loneliness and the days of starvation, when they begged a little meat from the halfbreed buffalo hunters.

Among the graves is the stone marking the burial of Colin Robertson Sinclair, whose father, without telling his mother, packed him off on a ship in Hudson's Bay and sent him home to Scotland at nine years of age for a year of education. The son never came back until he was 81 and then he raised a monument to his forgotten mother in St. John's churchyard, where he now lies beside her. "Erected," says the monument, "by her wandering boy."

A great story, the Scottish origins of Winnipeg, overlaid now by the deep strata of immigration from Europe, by the hordes of whiskered men who had never seen the Hebrides. Yet the flavor of old Winnipeg remains, and the attitude of the settler in a new land—the expectation of continuing growth, the willingness to gamble, the confidence of wealth. Why, this town has gambled through its grain exchange on every crop, on every season's rain and sunshine and hail, on every passing storm. Its richest men have watched the clouds in the morning and the look of the sunset, smelled rain in the sky, brooded over the reports of moisture, and staked their fortunes on the thousand miles of rippling yellow wheat stalks.

Winnipeg has never lost its grasp of the plow, its feeling for the soil, for weather, and for freedom. But it has reached out, selling its grain the world over, and it has had to think about the business of other countries, to ponder a drought in the Argentine, the Russian crop, the prospects in Hungary. Winnipeg, the frontier town, having world-wide interests, is the least provincial spot in Canada. It has a better grasp of national and world affairs than any Canadian city, except Ottawa, because it has to market its product everywhere.

You can sense this combination of the old west and broad modern ideas as soon as you reach the place. Whenever I land in Winnipeg, though it is usually forty below zero and a blizzard whipping down Main Street, I can feel a warm surge of friendliness and a sudden uplift of the spirit. These people, lost in their immense prairies, forced to make their own amusement and think their own thoughts, have a vigor about them, of the body and the mind, which makes a coastal Canadian feel frail and flabby. They have made their own culture also, of music, dramatics, and art, in the fashion of their fathers in old Fort Garry, because they had to. They have taken the bald-headed prairie and made parks and planted trees and reared up business buildings, fine homes, and a notable university.

Whatever they do, whether it be a patriotic campaign or merely a drinking party in Wellington Crescent, is done with a fierce energy. There is in dress, in language, in manners, in conversation, more than informality—a kind of jollity and recklessness which was born in the fort, at the old routs and balls. Winnipeg has seen boom and depression as sudden as the failure of a crop or the decline of a foreign market and is used to evil fortunes. Some authorities will argue today that the depression of the world's wheat industry limits the city to its present size or less. Perhaps it may, but the spirit of Winnipeg is the true hope of Canada—the forward look, the broad, world-wide feeling, the pioneer spirit, the willingness to gamble.

It is no accident, therefore, that Canada's best thinking in the last twenty years has come out of such a place. Out of it came Dafoe, and probably he could not have flourished anywhere else. It was he who gave direction and point to this thinking and persistently forced it by persuasion, by eloquence, and by argument, upon the Canadian people.

So wide is this man's range, traveling in person and by pen from London, Paris, and Geneva into the smallest prairie hamlet, walking with kings and never losing the common touch of Main Street, that his ideas are the common property of the nation, a large part of our current stock in trade. Any ideas on public affairs which, by chance, have found their way into this book, are very likely his, but he will not miss them, having plenty more. Never has he charged admission to the library of his mind. (But if you tried to steal a single clipping from his strange filing system, his rows of little drawers and boxes, I fancy he would stab you dead on the spot with his short pencil.)

Around him has gathered a little group of men who will carry on his work. Colonel Victor Sifton is that rare thing, an enlightened publisher with a public conscience. George Ferguson, Mr. Dafoe's assistant, has acquired the master's touch and outlook. Grant Dexter, at Ottawa, whom Dafoe discovered, is Canada's ablest reporter and master of facts, on whose shoulders cabinets weep regularly, almost every evening. Thomas B. Roberton was another of Dafoe's discoveries and, before his untimely death, wrote some of the few pieces of literature produced in Canada. His essays on the earthworm and the prairie shack can be safely recommended as the work of quiet genius. D. B. McRae was another who died young but at his best was sometimes as good and inspired a liar as Mark Twain.

Dafoe has always been happy in the ownership of the paper. Sir Clifford Sifton, the proprietor, let him say what he thought regardless of the business office, and in 1911 Canada beheld the rousing spectacle of the owner campaigning publicly against reciprocity and his paper fighting fiercely in favor of it. Today Sir Clifford's son follows the same principle. All these men live and move and have their being in the *Free Press,* which Dafoe made, and to see the old editor looming huge among his colleagues, or in the little group of Winnipeg oldtimers, who are commonly called the Sanhedrin, is an experience sharpening to the brain, warming to the heart.

These inward workings of a single newspaper would have no point here if they did not so vitally affect the whole outlook and history of Canada. Dafoe and his men have stood for something important in Canada, stood by it when others fled, kept it alive, and will yet see, God willing, its vindication and establishment.

Dafoe has fought, first, for Canadian nationhood and against what he has called the Butler Mind of Colonialism. He has grasped better than any man of his time the place of Canada in the world and, above all, the essential nature of men's freedom in this country.

His belief in trade and individual initiative taught him early the need of an open world. His belief in Canada's nationhood taught him Canada's responsibilities. On this foundation of thinking, Dafoe saw suddenly, and saw it whole, the meaning of the first world war, the follies of Versailles, which he watched at first hand, and the single hope of the League of Nations, which could undo them. That, more even than his impact on Canadian domestic politics, has been the chief work of his life, now emerging so plainly in the second world war.

Dafoe's editorials, cold with the drip of argument and written in the language of a man who was raised on the Bible and Shakespeare, are the record of Canada's relation to these problems and to the world. Anyone who read them between the two wars understands Canada and, very largely, understands the world. Let us take a quick look at them.

They reveal at once that Canada's foreign policy has been to dispense deliberately with a foreign policy, and from that have flowed many weird and terrible consequences. These Dafoe long foresaw.

He came back from Paris to dedicate his life to the League, to the idea of collective security, which, rectifying the mistakes of the Peace Treaty, could keep the frontiers open and make possible a trading world of free enterprise and free men. Everywhere he saw men tired of the war. He found an America which had not suffered enough to fear another war or to prevent its occurrence.

Year after year he maintained his lonely crusade. Year by year Canada grew more bored with this cosmic stuff and retreated more and more into the fool's paradise of isolation. We wanted to leave the world alone and we wanted Dafoe to leave us alone. We had not realized that we were no longer an infant nation, without the responsibility of power and without danger. We were not willing to grow up.

These twenty years of peace in Canada seem in retrospect a nightmare and a fitful fever, quickening to the crisis of 1939. Canada had struggled greatly for its right to manage its own affairs and had succeeded. There it paused. It wanted nothing to do with the management of the world's affairs, or even the Empire's affairs. In Mr. King it found perfect expression.

Mr. King began his foreign policy by refusing to fight the Turks in Chanak, in which no doubt he was right. He refused to have anything to do with the Locarno Pact. Finally Canadian foreign policy (or the lack of it) achieved the dismal formula which held that we would not be bound by any foreign commitment of the British Government, unless we were consulted first, and we would refuse to be consulted unless our interests were directly involved. Mr. King's head was now completely immersed in the sand and Canada's head along with it, by general agreement.

Then came the test of Ethiopia, when the world began to slide over the brink. For a moment Mr. King stood in the very center of the universal stage, with the spotlight of history focused on him. Italy was bogged down in its African campaign. The League, in its supreme crisis, had applied sanctions; its members had refused to supply the Italians with certain nonessential materials. In Geneva, Dr. W. A. Riddell, Canada's representative (probably with the Anthony Eden group of England behind him), suddenly rose to move that the League members refuse to sell oil or coal to the aggressor nation. This would mean Italy's collapse in Ethiopia, perhaps an Italian declaration of war on Britain.

Blinking in the spotlight, Mr. King repudiated Dr. Riddell and announced that Canada would co-operate with the League "in purely financial and economic measures of a pacific character which are accepted by substantially all of the participating countries." In Winnipeg, Dafoe, who knew that the world had now slipped over the brink, sat down with angry pencil and wrote that the League "was ushered into the darkness with assurances of the most distinguished consideration by Mr. Mackenzie King." He was right. The League never functioned again after the Riddell affair.

Mr. King will make his defense on the record in due time. It happened that I was in his office on the day when he heard, shortly after Dr. Riddell's repudiation, of the Hoare-Laval Deal, which proposed to carve up Ethiopia without further fuss. It is no breach of confidence to say that Mr. King was staggered and outraged by this monstrous arrangement, in which he was not consulted. In his defense it should be remembered that Dr. Riddell had not consulted him either about the oil sanctions.

There are those in Canada who insist, however—devoting most of their lives to these vain regrets and to their hatred of the prime minister—that if Mr. King had been firm in Ethiopia he could have forced Britain's hand and compelled the League to act. No British government could risk a breach with Canada in a crisis of that magnitude. A word from Mr. King, it is argued, would have forced Britain to stop, almost at its beginning, the cancer growth of anarchy which spread from Ethiopia across the face of the earth.

If that be so, the fault is not Mr. King's alone. He followed the views of the British government of appeasement, which was not prepared for war. He expressed beyond question the attitude of the Canadian people. They wanted no trouble. Never at any point in this long and bitter retreat from reality was Mr. King's ostrich policy seriously questioned by parliament or by the country—only by Dafoe and his friends, then few.

When Mr. King, by a wonderful feat of evangelism in Geneva, reduced the League to the sweetness and light of a Sunday school class, blandly construing it as an instrument of conciliation, not a weapon of force, Canada said this was all right, but not very interesting. The League had ceased to be practical politics.

When Mr. King's do-nothing foreign policy became so complicated and so unreal that he had to ask the House of Commons more than once not to discuss it at all, lest somebody take offense, there was no serious objection, and if Dafoe could hear the pitter-patter of scared mice in the marble corridors of Parliament, Canada did not care. We were staying out of Europe this time, like our neighbors, the Americans. We were acting more than ever before as an American nation. If the British were satisfied with things in Europe why should we worry on the other side of the ocean? "No commitments anywhere," said Mr. King in effect. "Parliament will decide everything if we get into trouble." That seemed good enough, and we nodded approval when, in an agony of inward revelation, Mr. King suddenly cried out:

The idea that every twenty years this country should automatically and as a matter of course take part in a war overseas for democracy and the self-determination of other small nations, that a country which has all it can do to run itself should feel called upon to save periodically a continent that cannot run itself, and in these ends risk the lives of its people, risk bankruptcy and political disunion, seems to many a nightmare and sheer madness.

Since our beginnings we had let the English make the foreign policy of the Commonwealth because they claimed to know how and, when we were needed to stiffen the backs of the few English statesmen who saw the truth, we were absent.

In Winnipeg, Dafoe saw that there was no escape. To the scandal of the Butler Minds, his pencil traced out his philippics against Baldwin, against Chamberlain, against appeasement. Day by day out of Winnipeg came the same unvarying chant, like Cato's wail against Carthage: "Hitler must be destroyed!" At Munich time, when Dexter in London scooped the world on the deal by several hours, Dafoe was not fooled. It meant war in a few months, he wrote, with no allies in the east. In a private speech he predicted categorically that Hitler would overrun all Europe, drag America into war, and threaten to destroy democracy everywhere.

By this time something had happened in Ottawa. Mr. King was a changed man. It is part of the façade of democratic politics to rationalize and reconcile all past acts, to admit no mistakes, to assume a perfect consistency, in the belief that the electors will not vote for a man who admits he was wrong. Mr. King has kept up a magnificent pretense of consistency, but actually the foreign policy of Canada has changed completely with the change in him.

He had been an appeaser of the appeasers, with a kind of mystical belief in the power of mere words and gestures, and he had judged Hitler, after a personal interview in Berlin, as a simple peasant who wanted nothing outside Germany. He was the perfect Municheer, as Dafoe calls them. But after Munich he knew what was happening as clearly as anyone, and began to see the part that he must play in it.

Sitting in his upstairs study, beside his fire and the lighted portrait of his mother, he told his friends of the black years ahead. Perhaps his deep gloom was not without a twinge of conscience, for his record in foreign affairs and in national defense was not the kind of thing a man enjoyed on his pillow at night. Still, he had represented the public view, if he had not led it.

At last, when it was too late to avoid war, we found a foreign policy. We found it on the day Hitler invaded Poland.

Canada did not go to war, as is widely supposed, merely out of a sentimental attachment to Britain. Half of our people had no such attachment by blood or tradition. Only about 5 per cent of us were born in the British Isles. The feeling for Britain was strong in us, certainly, even after two generations of separation, but not strong enough in itself, lacking other reasons, to make us fight another European war, unless we felt ourselves, the whole British Commonwealth, and the world's democracy endangered. Mr. King had said in Parliament that, two years before the Polish invasion, this country would not have entered a war in Europe. In London later he said: "Canada is proud of her position in the sisterhood of the British Commonwealth. But that position and association, had other reasons been lacking, would not have sufficed to bring Canada into a European war."

When Hitler went into Poland, Canadians, better than any inhabitants of North America, knew at last what it meant. We knew it instinctively, in our bones. We knew, almost in a single hour, that Dafoe had been right from the beginning. Like a man waking from a long sleep, Canada, almost in one breath, whispered: "This is It."

We knew it better than the Americans because we were a people of world-wide dependence. Far more than they, we depended on the markets of obscure nations everywhere, and especially on the British market. We knew it because we were a part of a Commonwealth which girdled the world and we believed in that Commonwealth as a practical thing, beyond sentiment. We believed in it, with all its faults, as a sound and useful force in the world, one of the few things you could tie to in a sea of anarchy. We saw the world falling to pieces and realized that the Commonwealth was the last stronghold of alliance left. If we did not enter the war, we must leave the Commonwealth, and that would probably mean the Commonwealth's end.

Above all, a vulnerable nation economically, a defenseless nation militarily, we saw that Hitler must be stopped before he could cross the Atlantic, or, at best, ruin our way of trade and our way of life. We knew what war meant, having lost 60,000 soldiers between 1914 and 1918, as many as our large neighbor. Now 400,000 veterans of those days were leaders in our business and professional life, and we understood with them that the job had to be finished this time.

With Mr. King the war had suddenly become a religious experience. He called it a test of Good and Evil, a challenge to the existence of Christianity itself. For once he seemed to feel a public issue deeply, passionately, and in personal suffering. As if to make up for the twenty years of delay, he threw himself wholly into the war program of the nation.

When the time came, only one man stood up in Parliament to vote against the Canadian declaration of war, made independently of the British government, made by Canada itself.

There is little use setting down in detail the figures of Canada's contribution to the war, for they change and increase monthly. As a rough measure of the war program, it can be stated at this writing that Canada is spending $2,500,000,000 a year out of a national income of $6,000,000,000 on its own war effort and on large loans to Britain, which is equivalent to an American expenditure of $30,000,000,000. Over fifty cents of the Canadian dollar goes, in taxes or loans, to the state.

Canada has a foreign policy now, but only for the war. It is not enough. What part will Canada play in the reconstruction of the world, given the defeat of the dictators? It can be an important part, out of all proportion to Canada's size, for Canada occupies a unique position, different from that of any other nation.

Canada is the only nation of the British Commonwealth in the Americas. It is the only British nation which has a permanent military alliance with the United States. It is the voice of the British peoples in the Western Hemisphere. It is the voice of the Americas in the British Commonwealth. It is a North American nation bound to the Old World by ties of blood, constitution, and interest. It is, in fact, the hinge between the United States and the British peoples everywhere.

This may sound rather too much like after-dinner oratory, but the facts show that the hinge actually works. It creaks sometimes, but it works.

At the Paris Peace Conference this fact first began to appear. The Canadian delegation always doubted the wisdom of Article Ten of the League Covenant by which members guaranteed each other's territorial integrity. It objected to some of the provisions for sanctions and flatly opposed a League control of such domestic questions as immigration and raw materials. This view, as it turned out, was more truly the view of the United States than the attitude taken at Paris by the American delegation itself. Canada was able to express at the conference the feelings of Americans because it knew them and shared them.

Again in 1921 Arthur Meighen, prime minister of Canada, went to the Imperial Conference and insisted on the abrogation of the Anglo-Japanese Treaty because it was disagreeable to the Americans. That was the voice of America speaking through Canadian lips.

At the Imperial Conference of 1937, Mr. King undoubtedly expressed the attitude of the American government on trade. Out of that expression grew the new trade treaties between the Commonwealth and the United States, which would have been impossible without Canada's willingness to forego certain advantages in the British market.

We shall not know for some time what part Mr. King has played between Mr. Roosevelt and Mr. Churchill during the war, especially in such projects as lend-lease, the destroyer deal, and the American use of British bases; but it will be found in the end to have been far more important than the public yet suspects.

This is all natural and inevitable. Canada is simply doing the obvious thing in its peculiar circumstances of geography and history. There is much more to do.

Canada has learned in this war that it cannot keep out of world wars, as it had hoped. It is turning to the Dafoe idea of collective security. We are a tougher people than we were. We have no illusions left. We do not expect a new heaven and a new earth to follow the war and we look for no miracles of international organization. While the League ideal is latent in all Canadian thinking, for the present Canadians' minds are concentrated chiefly, when they are not considering the war, on the prospect of a working agreement between the English-speaking peoples.

Perhaps because we are close to the United States, know its power, and trust it, we more than any other people desire— as a start anyway—a firm understanding embracing the United States and our Commonwealth, strong enough to resist another attack on the democratic idea and upon us. Out of that a world system could grow, but, failing it, all Canadians feel, nothing of permanent value can be hoped for.

Without the co-operation of the United States, Dafoe said in a lecture at Columbia University as far back as 1934, "Canada's sacrifices and the sacrifices of all the English-speaking peoples and of all the nations which profess the democratic faith, would be fruitless." And another great Canadian wrote this: "Unless the Americans go into the war and suffer in it they will come out of the conflict, however they come, hating Britain and perhaps hating us, and all our previews of the shape of things to come will be lost visions out of the ivory gates to mock the hopes of better times. And the same argument goes for Canada, too, in its own degree, according to its own circumstances, and for all of us in our place in our little souls."

These two extracts, I fancy, sum up the belief, deep in the heart of every Canadian, that the only hope of maintaining democracy and a tolerable life in the world is by the deepest and fullest co-operation, in action and in spirit, between the English-speaking peoples. Most Canadians will not ask the name of it or the form of it. They want the substance, as they have experienced it themselves on this continent.

For Canada this co-operation is essential, whatever happens. A breach between Britain and the United States would make the position of Canada almost impossible, with its interests, material and emotional, in both these countries. Dafoe long ago realized that and saw in the League idea the only permanent solution of Canada's problem. An Empire centralized in London having been rejected by Canada time and again, he saw that the conflicts of opinion between the various British nations could be ironed out best, and perhaps only by a world-wide organization embracing the United States.

In such a world as we now inhabit and in such a loose Commonwealth, the British peoples, he thought, might find it possible to work together permanently only with some such machinery of joint action—fighting in League wars, on the principle of collective security, rather than in Empire wars. In 1937 he set out this conception thus:

The differences on foreign policy from one Dominion to another, and between Britain and the Dominions, must be accepted as facts; and whatever disruption results from this can be harmonized inside the framework of a strong and effective League of Nations, although without that framework the difficulties might perhaps become insuperable.

The future of the British peoples, he said, did not lie "in a unified imperial foreign policy unless that policy is also a League policy."

These are bold words, disagreeable to the Butler Minds and, up to now, little appreciated and seldom observed by the Canadian people. The idea behind them will survive this war, if Germany is defeated. The problem will remain. The solution will become imperative. In that solution the part of Canada can be great if Canada proves great enough for it, because the British Commonwealth cannot endure without Canada's adhesion and Canada's close ties with the United States.

Winston Churchill foresaw these things years ago when he wrote:

The long, unguarded frontier, the habits and intercourse of daily life, the fruitful and profitable connections of business, the sympathies and even the antipathies of honest neighborliness, make Canada a binder-together of the English-speaking peoples. She is a magnet exercising a double attraction, drawing both Great Britain and the United States towards herself and thus drawing them closer to each other. She is the only surviving bond which stretches from Europe across the Atlantic Ocean. In fact, no state, no country, no band of men can more truly be described as the linchpin of peace and world progress.

Mr. King, for his part, called the Ogdensburg agreement

"part of the enduring foundation of a new world order, based on friendship and good will. In the furtherance of this new world order, Canada, in liaison between the British Commonwealth and the United States, is fulfilling a manifest destiny."

Manifest destiny has undergone a marvelous metamorphosis. So has the mind of Mr. King. So has the mind of Canada.

Canada will never lapse again into the position of nationhood at home and a colony in world affairs. Never again will this country take its foreign policy, complete and beyond question, from London. The folly of refusing to accept responsibility, to make commitments, only to find that we have responsibility and commitments everywhere, has been burned into the Canadian soul by the second world war. Never again, having feared actual attack for the first time in its life, will Canada leave itself without defenses on both oceans.

The war has remade Canada economically and industrially. It has built a stronger nation than we ever thought possible in our time. Greatly led, Canada can play its great part in the next peace, as the hinge between the democracies which will have to shoulder, whether they want to or not, the load of a ruined world. No man will have done more than Dafoe to prepare Canada for its manifest destiny.

The Canadian

We picked him up on the Cariboo Road, in central British Columbia, south of the Hundred Mile House. His face was ringed black with sweat and dust, he carried a seventy-pound pack, and he looked about twenty—a tall, handsome blond boy.

He didn't talk much at first, just sat back in the car, resting. He had walked 25 miles since morning, had come 400 miles from home so far and had 300 miles in front of him. He never asked for lifts and 72 cars had passed him that morning. By Lac La Hache he had helped some people get their car out of a ditch, but even they didn't invite him to ride. Young Franz Schmolding walked on alone, too proud to ask a favor from a Canadian.

When he spoke we knew he was a foreigner. He spoke good English in excellent grammar, but there was an edge of foreign accent in it. After thirty miles of travel we got his story out of him. He was Swiss. His family had been ruined by the Depression, had lost their prosperous lumber business near Zurich, and had come to northern British Columbia because they liked the mountains, the green valleys, and the foaming rivers that reminded them of home.

The Schmoldings bought an abandoned farm and made it yield. Four years have gone by and they are still on the land, clearing a few acres every year, buying more cows. A few months ago they got a radio. Ah, that was an event! Not a new radio, of course, but it worked, and they could get the news. In another year they would be able to apply for naturalization and become Canadians.

It would take a long time to get the land into shape, Franz

said. *A hundred years at least. Sometimes his father grows impatient at the wild land of Canada, remembering the shaven hillsides and well-trimmed fields of Switzerland, and the dwarf, gray cows grazing up to the edge of the snow. Franz had to take his father to a doctor because he seemed to have heart trouble, but the doctor said it was nothing but nerves. Schmolding was working too hard, trying to tame the land before he died.*

Franz knew better and could wait. He was not leaving the land now. He was going to earn wages in the logging camps of the coast and pay for new machinery, more cows, more land. Next year he would come back and settle down with his parents, his brothers and sisters on the farm. That was the great discovery of the Swiss family—a man could own all the land he needed in Canada. At home, Franz said, the land was always mortgaged to the banks and a man seldom owned it outright, no matter how hard he worked.

This country, which is deplored by half its native-born inhabitants, which is ridiculed, abused, and often butchered and devastated, looks good to Franz. He doesn't want to go back to Switzerland, where the ground is all tamed and fenced and groomed like a garden. He wants to tame a new land for himself.

But most of all, he wants to become a Canadian. In another year he will apply for his papers. Already one of his sisters has married a Canadian farmer and her baby will be a Canadian. That is a start. Soon Franz will vote. That is the great thing, the vote. Often at their dinner table the Schmoldings talk about the day when they will vote as Canadians.

Yet Franz had noted one disturbing fact about Canadians. They seemed rather sad. They rushed about the country. They never sat still. They made a lot of money and spent it and were always broke. They didn't relax like the folks at home and have a good time with a little music, a little wine. Was all America like that? Well, maybe people would get over it, after

the war. Maybe they would settle down on the land and be happy again. The land was so rich and there was so much of it empty.

We dropped Franz at Clinton because we were going no farther. He walked on down the dusty road, whistling, asking for no lifts—a tall blond boy from Switzerland, a Canadian.

CHAPTER FOURTEEN

The Men in Sheepskin Coats

The postmaster of Gimli, Manitoba, is named Tudni Thorsteinsen. He is an old man now, with curly gray hair, a face which may properly be called beautiful, and fine, clear eyes.

He has held his official position for fifty years, since he came to Canada from Iceland. His daughter does most of the work at the post office now, and this gives him time to complete his memoirs. He writes them on a typewriter in the Icelandic language and then translates them into English. When you sit in his little house, across the village street from the new brick post office, and listen to him read the records of Gimli, you can still see in his old eyes some of the immigrant's lust for land, for settlement, for crops, for building. In this neat and shiny sitting room you can see, as well as anywhere, how the blood of foreign races has been poured into the earth of Canada, and guess that in time it will grow a new race here, indigenous to this country, against all calculations and against all race prejudice.

At Gimli everybody is Icelandic. The old folks speak only the language brought with them from home. At the refuge for the aged down the street only one inmate can speak good English. But the younger folks understand both tongues, and many of them have succeeded in the business, professions, and politics of Winnipeg. Two of them have gone to Oxford as Rhodes Scholars, one into the Canadian government.

Mr. Thorsteinsen is proud of his people and sets down their record faithfully on his little typewriter. Meticulously, as if

every date and fact were terribly important, he told me—and
waited for me to note everything down at length—how the
Icelanders came to Gimli and settled here by Lake Winnipeg
because they could fish, as they had fished at home. Through
the window now I could see the fish nets hanging on the picket
fences and the poplar trees of the garden. By boat in summer
and by dogsled on the winter ice the Icelanders go out on the
inland sea for their fish harvest, as they used to go into the
Atlantic.

Slowly, waiting politely for me to write it down, the postmaster of Gimli read from the record—the first trek from
Winnipeg by flat-bottom boats on the river, the original settlement in cabins of poplar logs and sod roofs, long before his
time, the poor crops of wheat and potatoes between the stumps,
the starvation, the epidemic, the desertion, the trek to better
lands in the States, the dispersal of the whole colony until only
ten people were left. Then the return, the arrival of new immigrants from home, the first school (ah, he was proud of that!),
the founding of a weekly paper, the appointment of a postmaster, the building of wooden houses, the new road to Winnipeg.

Every date the old man had noted down, and the number of
houses in the village every year, the names of the people. Here,
for Tudni Thorsteinsen, was the foundation of a new nation,
the record of a whole race. In the village of wooden cottages,
with the fish nets drying on the fences, he saw the beginning
of something great. Now he hurried to set the record down
before he died, so that the greatness of it would never be lost.

"Why is it," he said, "that they can take the census this year
and they call us still Icelanders? Why don't they call us
Canadians?"

No use to explain that the government wanted to know the
racial origin of the Canadian people for its own purposes. Before he died, Tudni Thorsteinsen wanted to be a Canadian on
the record, as he was by right of settlement, of toil, and of

loyalty. This was his last chance, this census. He would hardly live to see another.

I left the patriarch of Gimli and walked down the main street. It was early spring, the ice too rotten to hold dogsleds, thick enough to keep the fishing boats at home. The young men were mending nets and tinkering with their boats by the shore, and I thought I could distinguish them, if I saw them again, from any other Canadians. They had a clean, lean look about them, and were as neat as their trim little town and of quiet, earnest expression. The girls, often blonde, were generally large and handsome. The whole place had an air of extraordinary cleanliness about it—people who had endured for a thousand years or more on a barren island in the Atlantic and counted themselves wealthy on this poor land by the lake side. At the drugstore Jean was drinking a milk shake and talking in English to some of the Gimli youngsters. The boys and girls talk English only. Canadians all.

Down the road towards Winnipeg—the road where old Thorsteinsen used to travel for two days by ox cart to get to town—we came upon a young man riding a bicycle. On the handle bars sat an aged woman with a scarlet kerchief over her head and a shawl about her shoulders. "Ukes," said the lady from Winnipeg, who was driving us. The square faces, flat noses, and high cheekbones showed their nationality. They had come in the great immigration from the Ukraine.

We stopped the car and offered the woman a lift, her son evidently being exhausted by the extra burden on his bicycle. She stood smiling at us shyly, a lined, bony face for an old master's brush. She could speak no word of English, but her son explained that she had been to church six miles up the road and he was bringing her back as far as his farm. She would have to walk six more miles home.

She got into the car, grinning with pleasure, and settled herself into the back seat, rough hands folded, and at all our questions only smiled again and shook her head. Never would she learn the language or understand this country. Her hands told her story plainly enough. She was a beast of burden, and content.

When we came to her home, twelve miles from her church, she pointed at it excitedly, for fear we would pass by. We stopped and let her out at a huddle of squalid barns and a dirty-looking shack—queer contrast to the neat houses of the Ice-landers. She bowed to us and smiled again and trudged through the barnyard, up to the ankles in mud. She had not missed the weekly church services.

Closer to Winnipeg, on the east bank of the Red River, and opposite the original Scottish settlements, we could imagine we were in a foreign country. Bulbous church domes and twisted spires rose above the little poplar woods, the architecture of Byzantium, brought by long and tortuous passage into the prairies of Canada. The squat log houses were covered with white plaster and the doors and window frames were painted blue or red. Exactly the same houses glisten white beside the Danube as you drive down through the flocks of geese to Budapest.

There were glimpses here by the Red River—the white plastered houses, the church domes and cupolas, the women in scarlet kerchiefs and shapeless skirts—that could be moved bodily into central Europe and no one would know they had ever been away from it. A few of the more successful Ukrain-ian farmers had torn down their plastered houses or used them for barns, building new houses of Canadian style—universally hideous. They were beginning to learn the ways of the country.

In the railway station of Winnipeg you can still see the immigrants occasionally, their belongings done up in blankets and bed quilts, their children clustered around the women like scared chickens, but not many of them now.

In the spring of 1892 the station master of Winnipeg beheld two bearded men in woolly sheepskin coats who tried to speak to him, but could utter no word of English. They were Ivan

Pilipiniski and Vasil Leynak. They got jobs on a farm and in the autumn they disappeared. They had spied out the ground for their friends in Galicia and presently they returned with hundreds more like them. The great trek had started.

Forty years ago the stations from Montreal to the Rockies were crammed with these people—Sir Clifford Sifton's tide of settlement that built the prairies. The Men in Sheepskin Coats, as Sifton called them. For a time they would become the chief political and economic fact of Canada.

All over Europe Sifton searched them out and brought them here, regardless of blood or tradition. On the lonely sweep of the prairies they would cultivate the ground, said Sifton, raise crops, enrich Canada, and breed a new Canadian race. Time and soil and weather would wear down by erosion their separate characteristics and shape them to this country.

Out of the Ukraine they came and Galicia, out of Germany, Norway, Sweden, Holland, Poland, Italy, Austria, and the Balkans. By the census of 1931 only 51.86 per cent of Canada's population was British in origin, 28.22 per cent French, and 19.93 per cent from a dozen other races. In 1871 the British had made up 60.55 per cent, French 31.07, and the other races only 8.39. Ever since the others have grown steadily, and the census of 1941, when finally analyzed, will probably show that slightly less than 50 per cent of us are Anglo-Saxon, many of whom have come from the United States.

In the last census Canada had 2,927,990 people of French origin; 2,741,419 English; 1,346,350 Scottish; 1,230,808 Irish; 473,544 German; 228,049 Scandinavian; 225,113 Ukrainian; 156,726 Hebrew; 148,926 Dutch; 145,503 Polish; 128,890 Indian and Eskimo; 98,173 Italian; 46,519 Chinese; 23,342 Japanese.

The new census will show all groups increased, but the general proportions not largely changed (though most groups are more prolific than the Anglo-Saxon) because there has been no significant immigration in the last ten years.

The melting of these elements in the crucible of Canada is not as rapid as might be supposed. The French are confined mostly to Quebec, though they have spread lately into northern Ontario, New Brunswick, and the prairies. Of the other continental European stocks, 60 per cent are on the prairies, living often in their own communities—little isolated clots of foreign blood, not readily absorbed. Yet so widespread is the penetration of these strains that you will come upon a Ukrainian church, with mosquelike dome, on the hill above the Niagara shelf. You will find Russian peasants chanting their hymns by a wild river in the Canadian Rockies, a German family putting down its winter barrel of pigs' knuckles and sauerkraut in Kitchener, Ontario, an old Chinese vegetable grower smoking his opium in the Dry Belt of British Columbia.

A Canadian Mosaic, John Murray Gibbon called this mixture of bloods, in his fine study of our people. Most Canadians do not attempt to understand these other races. They are peasants laboring by the roadside, or a Uke kitchen maid to do the heavy work of the household, or that perennial nuisance, the naked Doukhobor, or the Oriental Problem. Only a few men like Gibbon have troubled to investigate these strange inarticulate, shy people, have encouraged them to develop their own native arts and handicrafts, their music and dances, to enrich the Mosaic of Canada.

A land as empty and rich as Canada was bound to fill up, and to fill it up has been one of the basic policies of all Canadian Governments since Durham's time. In his report, which turns out to be one of the most prophetic and wisest documents ever written by a British statesman, he clearly foresaw that Canada could not become a nation while its people beheld greater activity and larger opportunity in the United States: "On the American side all is activity and bustle. . . . The ancient city of Montreal will not bear the least comparison, in any respect, with Buffalo, which is the creation of yesterday." Everywhere he saw "evidence of our own inferiority," and this was the first official record of the inferiority complex which has dogged us as a people to this day.

Durham saw Canadians living "almost without roads, in mean houses, draining little more than a rude subsistence from ill-cultivated land and seemingly incapable of improving their condition" and they "present the most instructive contrast to their enterprising and thriving neighbors on the American side."

But, within a few years, Charles Dickens uttered an equally shrewd observation of Canada which is still valid today: "Few Englishmen are prepared to find it what it is. Advancing quietly; old differences settling down and being just forgotten; public feeling and private enterprise alike on a sound and wholesome state; nothing of flush or fever in its system, but health and vigor throbbing in its steady pulse. It is full of hope and promise."

How few Englishmen until this very day are ready to see us as we are! "Ah," cried the Scot, Sir John A. Macdonald, "an overwashed Englishman, utterly ignorant of the country and full of crotchets as all Englishmen are!"

By the two opposite views of Durham and Dickens, by alternate despair and high hope, Canada built its population. Not long after both these distinguished visitors had left, Americans were coming into Canada, finding it a good country, even while Canadians continued to pour into the United States. By 1900 there were over a million Canadians in the United States, a fifth as many as in Canada. Between 1881 and 1891 more than half a million Americans came to Canada. In those days, when the world's frontiers were open, the forty-ninth parallel became so imaginary a line that Goldwin Smith, a noted English journalist who had settled in Canada, wrote in 1904 to Lord Rosebery:

"The customs line is a pure nuisance and some day must go. . . . As to the political line, nature has probably made up her mind; and if she has, she will have her way."

Today, more than two million Canadians are in the United States and 350,000 Americans, whose parents were born in the United States, live in Canada, in addition to the fully absorbed American immigration of the old days. Yet the political line remains. The core of Canadian nationalism, which could endure despite this free exchange of people, which could remain unbroken under the successive layers of race out of Europe, must have been stronger than Smith realized, stronger than most Canadians had dared to hope.

From the United States we received our first immigrants in the United Empire Loyalist tide of Anglo-Saxon people, and in successive waves out of the American prairies. The English, next to the French, have been our largest strain, coming direct and by the American route. They and their descendants have no special home, being everywhere in our country. The accent of Oxford and of East End London is heard from coast to coast, never dying this side of the grave.

The first generation of English, especially the gentry, usually keep their ways and often their clothes. You can see them growing fruit in the Okanagan, fishing for salmon at Cowichan, directing companies in our cities, or living on pitiful wartime remittances from home, without complaint, in lonely homesteads among the mountains. The gentry still wear tweed coats from a West End tailor and the unmistakable look of Bond Street. They are handsome of face, charming of manner, sportsmen all, maintaining civilization in the wilderness and, as the Englishman does everywhere, organizing society, entering public service, and laboring in charitable enterprises with a stern sense of obligation. And you will find every one of them, who can pass a medical examination, in Canada's armies.

Their sons show no trace of England and have little knowledge of it, and without a new supply of English immigrants the old English flavor of Canada will be doomed.

From Scotland came the next wave of settlement and washed

clear to the Pacific when Mackenzie reached the salt water on foot and Fraser's flimsy canoe floundered through the unknown torrent of Hell's Gate. Everywhere the Scottish people have succeeded, in city, in village, on lonely farm, and in Indian trading post, until you cannot mark their special place in Canada. You cannot go anywhere without finding them. So many of us still feel their blood that Canadian soldiers often prefer kilts to trousers, and the pipes skirling on a Canadian street as the troops march by will set all our hearts thumping.

In the village of Quesnel, British Columbia, four hundred miles up the Fraser, I have seen a Scottish piper leading a parade of cowboys and Indians to a rodeo and no one considered him or his music out of place. A friend of mine camped last year on a forgotten lake in the outer wilds of Ontario and was awakened by a strange sound to observe a Scotsman, in kilts, playing his pipes sadly beside the water, merely because he enjoyed the old music and the old memories. If you walk up Parliament Hill at seven o'clock almost any spring evening you will hear the same wistful strains coming from an open window of the Center Block, as Tom Reid, M.P., gets in a few licks after dinner.

Since Hugh McQuarters fired the cannon which killed Montgomery in the mean street of Lower Town, since the disbanding of the Scottish regiments and their marriage with the pretty French girls (who bore them children with Scottish names and no language but French), since the days of the starving settlers on the Red River, the Scots have claimed a large share of Canada. No one grudges it to them. Three generations removed from the old land, we still in dreams behold the Hebrides.

We are Irish, too. Out of Ireland's famines came many of our ancestors and there were more of them than Scots at the time of Confederation. Always the Irish were great breeders and great people to stick together. Only an Irishman like Thomas Talbot could have conceived such a fantastic settlement as Port Talbot, Ontario, where, in his castle of Malahide, like an eagle's nest on a cliff, this dashing soldier cooked, milked, farmed, baptized the babies, married the young folks, read the Sunday services, and made sure everyone came to church by sending a bottle of whisky around after the services. We have had other great Irishmen in Canada—Baldwin, the real father of popular government, Edward Blake, our finest legal mind, D'Arcy McGee, the poet and darling of Confederation, who was murdered by the Fenians for his love of Canada, Thomas Shaughnessy, the railway builder.

We had, in fact, a kind of Irish period, followed by a Scottish period under Macdonald and Brown. One of the most pleasant relics of the Irish period, which Mr. Gibbon rescued for his book, is the series of advertisements published by R. J. Devlin, in the Ottawa papers seventy years ago:

I have a lot of Grey Goat Sleigh Robes at $6 each. They are lined and trimmed but if there is any worse lining or trimming in the country I should be pleased to see it. Of course, with a raging Protectionist Government in power, people can't expect much for six dollars and in this case I think their expectations will be realized.

Also:

One coonskin coat, price Fifteen Dollars. It is not a good-looking coat. It is not even a good coat unless it possesses some hidden virtues of which the undersigned is unaware. It is good enough, however, to keep out fifteen dollars worth of cold. I have two cloth coats lined and trimmed with fur. At a fair valuation they would be worth forty dollars each. Measured by the Golden Rule they might be squeezed down to thirty. Measured by the state of my bank account, I offer them for fifteen dollars each, no questions asked.

But the Irish, for all their whimsy, knew their business. Devlin's store, the property of his descendants, is still one of the best in Ottawa. Not far off, another great Irish character, Grattan O'Leary, speaks in one of the most powerful editorial voices in the country and the most eloquent. Up and down the Ottawa Valley you will find farmers still talking in a rich brogue like the old man we bought strawberries from not long ago, who paused in his task of erecting a platform for a country wedding and dance that night, just as if life were still like that. I suppose it is always like that for the Irish, and happily few English-speaking families in Canada are without their warming drop of Irish blood.

The Germans have come here steadily from the earliest times. In 1750 the English King acquired 300 settlers in Germany and sent them to Halifax, where their first settlement is still known as Dutch Village. They were soon moved to Lunenberg and there they have remained German by race but Canadian by conviction. More Germans came up from the States with the Loyalists, and in Dundas County, Ontario, were settled as a buffer between the French Catholics and English Protestants. In all directions their fat farms spread, with toil and thrift and understanding of the soil. Even their names have taken on Canadian sounds. Kountz became Coons; van Keugh is now Cook; and Merckle is Merkley.

Berlin, Ontario, which became Kitchener in the first World War, is a manufacturing city of importance, and I have heard a member of Parliament from there—pure German by breeding and looks—crying out in sincere agony of soul to the House of Commons for a larger army to fight Hitler. On the prairies are later German settlements, many of them grown up between the wars, when we thought Germans the most desirable immigrants from the Continent of Europe. Many of them are loyal to Canada. Many of them want to see Germany win the war, but Canada has had no serious trouble with them and no sabotage worth mentioning.

Out in the Cariboo gold fields of British Columbia I have lately watched a little German settler pleading with the judge

to grant him Canadian citizenship and make him "a British."
But when asked for his views on the war he replied that he
had not made up his mind. His application was rejected. Next
day we gave a lift to a young German who said a man wouldn't
be worth much if he didn't hope his own country would win.
It is notable, however, that in this war there has been no race
hatred against the Germans already in this country and no
anti-German riots, as in the last war.

On the farms, in the mines and the lumber camps, you will
find the Swedes, Norwegians, and Finns—prodigious workers
—and on the prairie land the Russians, with their strange
churches, their peasant women and chunky daughters, their
love of pageantry and song. The Italian laborers built a large
part of our railways. The Jews have their own districts in
large cities like Montreal.

So they came, swarming through our railway stations, the
whiskered men in sheepskin coats, the tired women with
bundles, the scared children, each of the Ukrainians with a
handful of the Ukraine earth wrapped in a handkerchief, to
be thrown into his grave. We saw them for a moment, trudging through the stations, crammed into the stinking colonist
cars, then disappearing into the immensity of the prairies.
Sometimes we saw them standing in their fields by the railways, gazing at us stolidly as the train passed, or their women
working barefoot among the vegetables, outlined against the
flat horizon. When they appeared timidly at concerts and village fairs to sing their folk songs and perform their lively
dances, we were amazed. Why, these people actually knew
something, knew things that we had forgotten or had never
learned! And presently we saw their daughters marrying our
Canadian boys, who were glad to get them, and a pure-bred
Icelander became Minister of War Services in the middle of
our greatest war.

We heard their strange names—Ruthenians, Galicians,
Ukrainians, Jugo-Slavs, Rumanians, Bulgarians—and we

called them Bohunks or, if they were swarthy, we called them Wops.

Many strange people, beyond our comprehension, have come to us in this tide. Out of Pennsylvania early in the nineteenth century came the Russian Mennonites, followers of Menno Simons, strict pacifists and great farmers. Their scattered settlements stretch to the Pacific Coast, and you will find them living among the giant fir stumps of Vancouver Island, where Canadians failed to make a living. They brought the flax into the Red River country, they paid back their settlement loans to the government, and some went to Mexico because they would not send their children to Canadian schools. More came to Canada after the first world war, terrified of the Bolsheviks. A hundred thousand of them are farming here now.

The Moravian followers of John Hus came from the States a hundred and fifty years ago and there are still settlements of them near Edmonton. But strangest of all are the Doukhobors.

These were the Spirit Wrestlers, who left Russia to be free to worship God in their own way, to wait for the coming of Christ. So soon was He expected to arrive that they marched chanting through the prairie snow, stark naked, to meet Him. The tale of their wrestling with the spirits and with the police when they became unruly, their settlements, their quarrels, desertions, betrayals has been recognized at last as a minor epic and set down in a fine book by James Wright, a young Canadian. *Slava Bohu* he called his history—the Doukhobors' familiar greeting, which means "God be with you."

There is a strange irony in that phrase. Trying to find God, the Doukhobors have roamed the prairies, penetrated the Rockies, and are still wrestling with the Spirit on the banks of the Kettle River in British Columbia. What incredible leaders they have thrown up! Peter Veregin, the First, a patriarch who lived among women and was stronger than any man, who built towns, sawmills, jam factories, irrigation systems, was blown to pieces by his enemies with a time bomb in a railway coach, and buried by the Kootenay gorges under a little mountain of stone; Peter Veregin, the Second, who drank, whored, raged, fought, and thieved through the country and appeared like a gentle saint, with prayer and sermon, before the unsuspecting colonists.

What agony the Wrestlers have suffered for the Spirit, marching naked through the snow of winter and the summer heat, locked up in foul jails by bewildered constabulary, who couldn't persuade them to put on their clothes, burning school houses, imprisoned on a lonely island in the sea because they would not send their children to school, defying the laws of Canada as stubbornly and dumbly as cattle!

Not long ago I visited their settlements in southern British Columbia and talked with them in the big brick community houses that old Peter had built. The young people talked excellent English and, in a crowd, would hardly be distinguishable from Canadians. The wife of the house wore her hair in the latest fashion, with a snood to support the curls, and her fingernails were painted scarlet. But on a bench, close to the gigantic Russian stove of brick, sat an old woman who might have come from Russia yesterday. Shriveled under her kerchief and shawl, she watched me with dull eyes, understanding no word of our conversation.

"There is no difference between us and Canadians," said the young wife. She told me proudly that she had made a trip to the prairies not long before and traveled first-class and nobody suspected her nationality. Religion? Ah, well, there was no real difference there either. Only that the Doukhobors had no priests. Her husband, who spoke poor English, but drove a truck for a Canadian sawmill, listened to her and nodded, but he didn't seem so sure about it.

The Canadian people in the Grand Forks Valley regard the Doukhobors as a problem and a pest. Most of them have settled down now, the original pure communism dying out—and with it Veregin's old drive, which turned the bare bench lands into gardens. Now the Doukhobors, absorbed too well into our ways, are getting jobs at wages, are letting their orchards die for lack of water, their lands run down for lack of cultivation, their houses for lack of paint.

Some still wrestle with the Spirit. In Grand Forks, at least up to recently, one of the Wrestlers used to walk about, unnoticed, with a headdress of oranges and other withered fruit, sewed into a flour sack, to mark the fact that he had been to heaven and returned with the Word. Down on the river bank, trying to grow food on the gravel soil, the exiled Sons of Freedom have settled, squatting on this useless land because the Canadianized Doukhobors do not want them. Still they refuse to accept Canadian laws, still invite the government to arrest them, still are ready to suffer for their belief in a godly anarchy. No one knows when they may come swinging down the road, men, women, and children all naked as God made them, to scandalize the modest Canadians. The Sons of Freedom are a minor sect now, and in a few generations all the Doukhobors will fade into the Canadian Mosaic.

In British Columbia also is another problem much harder to solve, perhaps insoluble—the descendants of the first Chinese who were brought in to build our railways, the fecund Japanese whose immigration has been limited to a "gentlemen's agreement" but who have overcome that restriction by an unmatched capacity for reproduction.

The last census, as noted before, showed 46,519 Chinese and 23,342 Japanese in Canada (nearly all concentrated in British Columbia) but the Japanese are notoriously underestimated by their refusal to register. Probably there are more of them now than the Chinese, who, lacking wives, have actually declined as the old men went home to China to die. The second generation of Chinese, divided equally between the sexes, will grow fast.

Already these Orientals control most of the truck gardening

industry of the coast cities, have made great inroads into fishing and into retail business and offer a competition in low living standards that no white man can meet. Regularly, every year or two, British Columbia conducts a crusade against them, with newspaper editorials, resolutions in the legislature, frenzied speeches, and always with the same result—none whatever. Every year their farms spread further into the Fraser Valley, their shops appear in the better retail sections, their homes in the residential districts, their young men and women in new automobiles. There is no hope either of their absorption or their decline. Forever a white race and a yellow race are fated to live beside each other on the Pacific Coast, and the white race can only hope that in time, as they acquire our habits, the Orientals will lose some of their fertility and will adopt our standards of life.

The first world war and then the Depression dammed the tide of all immigration, but a trickle has continued. Lately Hitler, driving skills and brains out of Europe, has given us exiles as valuable as the old craftsmen who brought the arts of the continent to barbarous England and the original Pilgrims to America. The great Bata shoe industry, forced out of Czecho-Slovakia, has established itself under ideal conditions of labor and living, in Ontario. Not far away a refugee glove industry has succeeded. On the Pacific Coast a Czech refugee has demonstrated the commercial use of our neglected hemlock forests. These are but the first of many who want to follow.

When the war is over Canada expects to see another large immigration movement like that of Sifton's times. Largely, we think, it will come from Britain. Britain tired by war, its class system shattered, many of its people impoverished, will see in Canada a chance to start over again. How to absorb them, how to find jobs for them when thousands of Canadians are released from fighting services and from war factories, will be one of Canada's largest postwar problems.

Yet Canadians from the earliest days have wanted more population, have built their towns, railways, and public services to serve more population, and require more population to carry the load of taxes. Always immigration has been accepted as a basic need in Canada, a constant policy, and its interruption was regarded solely as an emergency until the Depression ended. We know instinctively that more people must come here, that we cannot forever hold so much of the world's surface and so much of its wealth, unused.

In 1864, Sir Wilfrid Laurier—then young and unscarred by the world—said this: "Race hatreds are finished on our Canadian soil. There is no longer any family here but the human family."

Sir Wilfrid lived to see his own French race bitterly divided from the rest of Canada. But in the long run, on his side of the argument, are important exhibits. There are among others the old postmaster of Gimli, and that young Swiss boy, striding down the dusty road, whistling, not asking for a lift.

Father's Plow

The wheat is fat and heavy on the prairies. The stalks bend under the weight of the grains. Little waves seem to flutter across it as the wind blows, like ripples on a smooth green sea. Now there are faint tinges of yellow, waxing and waning. Each grain is swelling and hardening and sucking up the last fertility, the minute chemicals and richness of this prairie earth.

Piled together, these grains will make four hundred million bushels. Too much wheat, they say. Too much wheat, say the sleek, well-fed men in the Château Laurier. Too much wheat, say the clever men in the East Block. Too much wheat, say the frantic men in Parliament. Too much good food here on our rich prairie earth.

The wheat knows nothing of that. It grows and swells and ripples in the wind. And in the fallow land the white horses, three abreast, pull the harrows, making ready the ground for next year's crop. The horses know nothing of the wheat surplus. They only know that the midday sun is hot and there is dust in their eyes and that by the brook, among the little poplars, there is shade and rest at noontime. The lean farmer follows the horses, trudging through the dust, his face black with dirt and sweat, and he only knows that he has plowed this ground and will soon feel the good yellow grains in his hand. He only knows that he has labored here and produced good food that men need in their bellies.

Too much wheat, the other men say. We must not grow so much wheat, they say.

If we only had a different financial system we could sell our wheat at a good price, the crazy men say. There is no solution, the clever men say. Wait a while, the frantic men say. The farmer doesn't know about that. He only knows that he broke this land with his plow long ago, that he can make wheat grow, that other men who grow nothing and produce nothing become rich while he is poor.

Too much wheat, the other men say, the men who have never felt plow handles, nor the whip of the blizzard, nor the dust and sweat in their eyes. We must cut down wheat acreage, they say, as if it were just bookkeeping, as if it were just a charge on a piece of paper. The farmer knows it is more than that. It is rich land, pregnant with fertility, soil full of goodness, and its crop is solid substance, not statistics. It is the ultimate wealth of the world. To destroy it, to limit it, to waste it, violates laws far deeper than economics, and faith that cannot be set down in a ledger.

Out there somewhere on the prairie is a piece of land that my father broke. There were Indians here then—Pound Maker, Red Cloud, Big Bear, and the exiled Sitting Bull— and men in feathers and blankets used to come to the sod-roofed cabin for a pinch of tobacco. There were buffalo then, endless herds of them. But my father and other men fenced off the land, broke it with their plows, and planted it, and watched the first crop ripen, and felt the grain in their hands, and knew it was good.

Acre by acre they broke the land and every year they had a little more grain to trade for the things they needed, and hungry men across the sea ate the grain, paying for it gladly. Life was hard then and lonely—a sod cabin, a few horses, a sheep dog, and maybe a sweetheart in England who would come out some day. But my father and the others were well content, because they could see the grain growing. Life made sense to these men. They were free men as men can be only when they feel their own earth under their feet and see the growth of the seed they have planted. They were happy men because they were producing something the world needed. Only crazy men would have said then that they could ever produce too much food when the world was hungry.

But today, the clever men say, there is too much wheat. The land that our fathers broke and harrowed and sowed must stop producing food in a world where most people will go to bed tonight with pains of hunger. My father shot buffalo here. Let the land go back to buffalo. Your father was wrong, they say, to make the land produce food that the world needs.

The farmer pauses there in his field, in the dust of his fallow land, and looks across the rippling sea of grain with the tint of yellow in it and he is sick at heart. He has grown the wheat, he has performed the real miracle, done the real job, and clever men, who have done nothing but talk, tell him that it is foolish and wrong to make the land yield. The farmer is baffled by the smooth talk of the clever men, the shrieks of the crazy men, but with an instinct deeper than their wisdom and their lunacy, he knows that this land was made, between the mountains and the lakes, made by the patient chemistry of nature through millions of years, to bear, to produce, to feed hungry bellies.

CHAPTER FIFTEEN

Drought and Glut

We sat on the running board of Hearn's truck. The old man had insisted on laying his torn sweater coat across the running board so that the mud wouldn't get on my trousers. Now he leaned forward and picked up a handful of the drying spring earth and rubbed it between his fingers to show me that there was no speck of grit in it. The best land in the world, he said, this ancient lake bottom of the Regina Plains.

Hearn had grown old tending it, plowing it, reaping it, mining it. He didn't look like the farmer of the movies or the cheerful harvest scene on an advertising calendar. He wore a peaked cap, like a locomotive engineer, black with machine grease, and mechanic's overalls, patched in a dozen places, the suspenders on them held up by nails for buttons, his feet in rubber boots. His hair was long and white, his face stretched taut, like rawhide, his eyes narrow and wrinkled from the sun. This lean, stooped man, sitting beside me on the running board, rubbing the soil between his fingers and calling it good, was the chief problem, the most bitter tragedy of Canada.

Around us, barren and bare, stretched the thawing plains of Canada, out to the infinite horizon. Specks of houses dotted the land, and, stark against the flat sky, stood the grain elevators with their jutting shoulders, like giant men. Miles away, so far that it seemed like a child's Christmas toy, a little train waddled across the land with a solid puff of smoke. These were the prairies that had once been our chief producer of wealth, the greatest single fact of Canadian life, and were now on relief.

I looked around Hearn's farm, the work of forty years. His square house was almost bare of paint now. The barn had listed, as if the wind had been too much for it. An old tractor and odds and ends of farm machinery stood before it in the mud, and a young man was working at them with a wrench. Some white chickens wandered about the front yard, among the leafless shrubs that had once formed a plot of garden.

The old man followed my glance.

"Pretty bad, eh? Well," he said, "it's not as bad as most. See those houses up the road? Every one of them's on relief. The women haven't enough clothes to go to town in. Hell, many's the time kids around here couldn't go to school—no shoes. See that white house over there? One pair of shoes between three girls last winter. They took turns goin' to school in 'em."

He picked up another handful of earth from the road. "This year she didn't freeze into the ground. Ought to be froze deep down for moisture. I've walked over it, up and down, every foot, testin' it, but there's no moisture. Like puttin' a wet rag between two hot stones—no moisture below and hot sun above. She dries right out."

Nine years he saw the land dry out, the best land in the world. Nine years there was no crop in a territory larger than many European countries. Nine years, always hoping, they sowed the seed and watched it sprout green in the spring, like a faint green wave of water color across the prairies, and then watched it head out when it was only a foot high—not worth threshing. They cut it and fed it to the cattle. They cut the Russian thistles, too, and the cows ate them and starved and had to be slaughtered. The horses grew too weak to work. Wells dried up, sloughs became dusty depressions in the baked soil. The land blew away in dust storms, drifting like snow to the tops of the fence posts, so that men worked with handkerchiefs stretched over their faces, and automobile headlights were burned all day on the roads to penetrate the darkness.

Nearly all the farmers in this district were on relief, drawing a few dollars a month while their clothes wore out. Families were without sufficient blankets in the fearful prairie winter. In the spring children walked to school barefooted through the dust. In southern Saskatchewan, which had been one of the most prosperous farming regions in the world, people lived worse than the poorest peasantry of Europe.

Anne Marriott, a prairie poetess, described it after long and dismal observation:

> *Wind mutters thinly on the sagging wire*
> *binding the graveyard from the gouged dirt road,*
> *bends thick-bristled Russian thistle,*
> *sifts listless dust*
> *into cracks in hard grey ground.*
> *Empty prairie slides away*
> *on all sides, rushes toward a wide,*
> *expressionless horizon, joined*
> *to a vast blank sky.*

"Hell," old Hearn said, "I've seen a cow starving to death and dropping in her tracks a hundred yards from an elevator full of grain. But we never went on relief in this family." He was mighty proud of that. "Don't know how we did it, but we kep' goin' somehow. The chickens gave us enough to pay for groceries. But everything ran down. In 1929 I bought eleven thousand dollars' worth of machinery. Thought nothing of it. Paid cash for it. You couldn't work these two sections with horses—just me and one boy. That's the boy over there by the barn, the others went east. I put them all through school in those days. Well, sir, the machinery's all worn out now. We make it run. We patch it up, but we never know when it'll break down. Ought to throw the whole lot of junk out by rights. We're gettin' it fixed up now, best we can. We'll be seedin' in a couple of weeks."

"Aren't things getting any better now?" I asked.

"Well, we had a crop last year. A good one, headin' out fine. Hail got it. Fifteen minutes and it was flat on the ground. Yeah, hail."

He said it not with despair, but with a kind of dogged fatalism which was worse. I was glad I hadn't been here to watch this family in the fifteen minutes when a year's work, and every hope of a few dollars, some new clothes, and new machinery, were beaten into the ground by the hailstones.

Now they would seed again, working all day and half the night, with headlights on their broken tractor, though there was no deep moisture in the soil. Maybe rain would come in the summer and see them through. They would seed again now and watch the green spring surge and hope for a crop, even though they could sell it at only a few cents per bushel above the cost of producing it, even though every elevator, barn, and woodshed from the Lakes to the Rockies was bursting and running over and dripping yellow with unsalable grain.

Hearn started to roll a cigarette clumsily in his grimy fingers. When I offered him a store cigarette, he accepted it eagerly. He had not seen many of them in the last ten years. I thrust the whole package into his hands, feeling swinish and mean to own anything when these people, better people than I, the people who had made Canada, were destitute. He took the cigarettes, reddening with embarrassment, but glad to have them, and added quickly: "I'm not meaning to kick, understand. We came here of our own accord. I came from Nebraska, myself, and thought I was lucky. We were, before the drought, and then the war. Should have moved up north or out to B. C., or back to the States. But I'm too old to move now."

He drew the smoke deep into his lungs and laughed hoarsely.

"They call us the Wheat Problem now. I read it in the papers and I hear it on the radio. They talk a lot about us back east. And that's all—talk."

Yes, I had heard them. Week after week, month on month, I had listened to the men in Parliament protesting about the Wheat Problem, and harassed cabinet ministers trying to answer them in figures, ciphers, statistics, until wheat had become a weird abstract puzzle, an impersonal sum in mathematics, and all these people between the Lakes and the Mountains were mere entries in a relief record, figures in a book. Here by the dirt road was the Wheat Problem in the reality of human beings and broken lives. Here was a man who worked harder than any laborer in the factories of Ontario and he was just able to keep off relief, being a little luckier than his neighbors. Here was a man who had to plow, disc, seed, reap, and thresh two or three acres merely to pay for a small mechanical part to repair his tractor, when it could be bought for a fraction of the price on the other side of the American boundary, the tariff wall.

He spoke of some obscure part needed for his tractor now. It would cost $25. If he could get it from the States, without paying the tariff, it would cost maybe $10 or $5. This is the tribute that the prairies pay to the eastern manufacturer, who, in return, must keep the prairies on relief.

"Leave us alone and we won't ask for relief," Hearn said. "We could get by this way, even with drought now and then, if we didn't have to pay two prices for everything and sell at any price offerin'. Thousands of dollars I've paid those boys back east. Now look at that tractor. Just junk."

"What's the answer?" I said.

"God, I don't know. Mind you, I'm no Red. I'm no communist. I got no use for this Social Credit bunk and all like that. We just want to make a living. Not to get rich, just to make a living, if they'll let us. We can get crops again. The rain'll come again. But something else has happened now.

Where can we sell the stuff? I've watched this thing pretty close. Before the war we were losin' out. Germany was growin' wheat. Italy was growin' wheat. Everybody was growin' wheat. No matter how much it cost to grow, they grew it, and we were losin' our markets. Can we ever get them back?"

He peered at me with his shrewd, tired eyes, thinking that I must know something, coming from Ottawa. "Will we ever be able to sell our wheat again?"

What could you say to that? The harassed men in Ottawa didn't know. Nobody knew. It would depend on whether the world had sense enough to trade again after the war.

What a cycle was here in forty years! Forty years ago the plow had not cut most of this prairie land. It had lain untouched except by Indian and buffalo since it emerged out of the preglacial seas. In forty years it had run the whole gamut from settlement to boom to destitution. In forty years the prairies had risen and fallen.

And what ingenuity, toil, and sheer luck had gone into this land!

In the spring of 1843 David Fife, a Scottish farmer living near Peterborough, Ontario, asked his friend, George Essen, who was going to Britain, to send him some samples of wheat. Fife was a man who liked to experiment with new seeds.

Essen forgot all about Fife until he was on the point of sailing back to Canada. Then, seeing a grain ship unloading in Glasgow, Essen begged a couple of quarts of wheat, and these he took back to Peterborough. Fife sowed the seed in the spring, but as it was evidently fall wheat, only three sprouts came up. Around them Fife built a fence. He didn't know that enclosed within the fence was the whole economic future of Canada.

One day the family cow stretched her neck over the fence and started to eat the three stalks, and she had nibbled one of them when Mrs. Fife drove her off. Had she eaten the other two, we might have a different Canada today.

The remaining two heads of grain matured, ten days earlier than any other wheat that Fife had ever seen. Ten days meant the difference between safe maturity and freezing in such a climate. He harvested forty grains of this precious stuff, stored them in a teacup over the winter, and planted them in the spring. This time he harvested a pint of seed and, on the third year, half a bushel. He called it Red Fife, for its color.

Red Fife, shipped out of Ontario in 1876, was the foundation of the Canadian West. In many parts of the dry prairies only a desert plant can produce a crop, and it must mature in a little more than a hundred days of rapid growth before the fall frosts. The old wheat strains would be useless there. Without Fife's seed, grain might never have spread past the Red River Valley.

Where did those three original grains come from—three grains of spring wheat in the quart of fall wheat which Essen had begged from the grain ship in Glasgow harbor? No one knows how they happened to be in the ship's cargo, or by what magical accident Essen managed to pick them out of a shipload. It made the Canadian government think.

Dr. W. S. Saunders, of the government's experimental farms, got seed samples from every wheat-growing district of the world, grew them, tested them, crossed them. He concluded that the three grains of Red Fife had come out of a little-known district of Galicia. Even it could be improved. The prairies needed wheat which could resist rust, which could mature still more rapidly and grow still farther north.

Dr. Charles Saunders, son of the original experimenter, tested the innumerable samples left by his father. One grain in a little bottle he was going to throw away as useless, then decided to plant it as a matter of routine. This seed grew and he crossed the grain with a variety from India. The cross produced Marquis Wheat, which matured in about 100 days and resisted rust. That was one of the most useful things ever done in North America.

Marquis spread across the entire prairies, and fields of it marched into the north, where the season was too short for any other variety. Go north fifteen miles and you lose a day of growing season, but with Marquis the danger line moved back so far that Canada's production of hard wheat, of the highest quality known, became a sudden new factor in the economy of the world. Year by year the government scientists still improve on the old strains. Mrs. Fife did a good day's work when she drove the cow away from the little fence in the back yard.

The prairies were all but empty at the turn of this century, when Sifton started his immigration campaign. They filled up in one of the fastest movements of people in history. The men in sheepskin coats swarmed through Winnipeg, headed west, were lost against the horizon, but presently were driving their wagons to town, loaded with wheat.

The Canadian Pacific Railway had stretched long ago to the Pacific Coast. It wouldn't earn enough money to pay for the grease of its axles, they said. Soon it was not big enough to carry the grain. Branch lines spread over the prairies like fast-spun spider webs. These were not enough. Another transcontinental railway was thrust across the plains and a third, in an age when a railway was considered the solution of all economic and political problems. (Two of them were destined to go broke and fall into the government's hands, but no one foresaw that then.)

Cities were built, new provinces. Legislatures and governments were created with all the trappings and gold braid of an ancient system on this empty land. Innumerable wooden towns sprang up beside the railways and the red wooden grain elevators stood everywhere, with square shoulders against the sky.

Presently Regina, a Royal Northwest Mounted Police post, where Riel had been hanged in the jail yard, found itself the capital of Saskatchewan with a domed parliament building beside a slough, dammed to form an ornamental lake. Trees, shrubs, and flowers grew around it where the buffalo had grazed a few years before. Saskatoon to the north expanded out of the river bank like a mushroom.

To the edge of the Rockies the plow turned up the land, turned up the old grasses and "prairie wool" that had fed the buffalo and then the cattle—for which nature would take a terrible revenge later on in dust storm and erosion. In the foothills, in sight of the mountains, they built the rollicking, ten-gallon, hair-pant, and joyous town of Calgary, where business men wore cowboy hats and high-heeled boots, and R. B. Bennett, living at the Palliser, wore cutaway coats and striped gray trousers, on his sure way to the premiership of Canada and the British House of Lords. North again, almost at the edge of the tundra, they laid out Edmonton, with Jasper Avenue running, paved, for miles into the prairies; and then built another parliament building for another province, until at night its lights twinkled on the river like a Rhine castle.

There was no limit to the prairies, their production and their population. All the world wanted this hardest of wheat. The only problem was to grow it and that seemed to be no serious problem either. No trees and stumps to clear, no preparation. You thrust your plow into the virgin ground and scattered the seed and in a hundred days or so you reaped it and sold it and denned up comfortably for the winter.

Wheat! It was like the old cry of gold. It was better than gold, easier to get, surer. Wheat—and the plows tore at the ground, the grain poured into the elevators, into freight cars, into the bellies of ships, into the stomachs of European cities, into the mouths of brown men and yellow men across the sea. Wheat to make a man's fortune in a few years, so they built poor houses and flimsy towns. Soon they would move on again.

The wheat boom was the largest economic event so far in Canadian history and transformed the whole character and future of the country. Here was a commodity which could be traded in the world market, for anything Canada desired. It could be grown cheaply and well, of assured quality. It brought cash. At once the rest of Canada felt the stream of prairie wheat coursing through its veins. The new farmers wanted machinery, furniture, clothes, food that they could not grow, everything but wheat. Central Ontario and Quebec, which had been deep in hard times almost since Confederation, suddenly began to boom, too. The new prairie market must be kept for Canada, must be hedged with tariffs. The farmer must buy in Canada even if he had to pay a higher price, and the farmer did not protest much. He was making money.

Far from the prairie land, but fattening on it, grew a rank growth of middle men and a complicated machinery of marketing—a grain exchange in Winnipeg, where fortunes were made and lost with every change of weather; terminal elevators in Fort William and Vancouver; farmers' co-operative pools, handling millions of dollars monthly; wharves on the Great Lakes and the St. Lawrence; the Welland Canal; fleets of grain ships in all the world's oceans. Men grew rich and lived in the West End of Montreal or in Wellington Crescent or on Shaughnessy Heights because wheat would grow for the sowing on the old buffalo lands. Canada became one of the world's chief traders, an important nation, without suspecting it.

The first world war only quickened the pace. Wheat prices broke all records and still the warring nations of Europe could pay the farmer cash. He could spend the winters in Vancouver or California, build a new house, buy a car. Always he planted more land until the sea of grain, washing from lake to mountain, covered forty million acres. Nearly two and a half million people lived among it and a large part of Canada on it. There was to be no end. A hundred million dollars the wheat brought in, then two hundred, three, four, and finally almost half a billion of cash money, in a little country of less than ten million people.

Nature waited her time and struck suddenly, with searing drought, with rust, with grasshoppers. The land which should never have been plowed, which should have been left in its natural grass to feed cattle, blew away on the hot wind, year after year.

Another strange thing had occurred, which nobody had foreseen. For the first time the world did not want the wheat. European countries were growing their own, growing inferior wheat, at enormous and uneconomic cost, with government subsidies, so that they would have food when war came again. The world was in the early stages of the wasting disease called autarchy, and the Canadian prairies were the first to fall by it.

The wheat grew again after the long drought, but now it piled up in the elevators, unsold. The government had to buy it from the farmer so that he could live, paying him a starvation price, and soon the taxpayers of Canada found themselves with millions of bushels on their hands, found themselves gambling with millions of dollars in the world market. The prairie towns grew dilapidated, years without paint, and looked gaunt and sick beside the railways. The whole wheat industry was on a government dole. The farm machinery ran down. Thousands of Canadians in Ontario, Quebec, and British Columbia were idle because the prairies no longer could buy their products.

The new war did the rest. All the old European markets were closed by blockade. Only Britain could take Canadian wheat and Britain no longer paid cash. Canada had to loan Britain in 1941 about a billion dollars worth of goods, without receiving cash or goods in return. The Canadian taxpayers were carrying the wheat industry, paying the farmer little more than the bare cost of production, and even though new elevators were built and temporary sheds along the railways, they could hardly hold this glut of useless food in a starving world. The harassed men in Ottawa chanted over and over again that the farmer was the first casualty of the war, as if that honor should satisfy him.

Since the time of David Fife, Canada had tried always to grow more grain—always another acre, another bushel. It was more than sound economics. It was almost a religious conviction. It was feeding the hungry of the world, as the Lord desired. Now, for the first time, all this process, all these convictions, had to be reversed. For the first time, with a sense of despair and a sense of sin, Canada bonused its farmers to grow less wheat, to leave their land fallow, to refuse the Lord's bounty.

Desperation on the prairie brought queer results. First, in the early twenties, there had been a farmers' political party which held the balance of power in Ottawa and disintegrated. Then, as the depression deepened, came the weird phenomenon called Social Credit, with its mountainous and glistening prophet, William Aberhart, of Alberta. This strange man quoted alternately from the Old Testament and the jokes of those old-fashioned almanacs that advertise liver pills, thus assuring himself of the liver-pill vote and the support of the Godlike. He declared on the authority of the great prophet himself, Major Douglas, of England, that everyone could have a dividend monthly without paying for it. He set the whole world watching for him to pull the largest economic rabbit in history out of the hat. He denied that his system was inflation or, alternatively, totalitarian control of everything when, of course, it had to be one or the other, and in the end proved nothing but a way to get elected. He was searching, as the late and beloved Professor Pete McQueen said, in a dark room for a black cat that wasn't there.

Yet somehow, despite everything, with loans from the national government, with relief, with writing down of debt, with poverty everywhere, the prairies kept alive, sowed their crops in the spring and waited for a sane world to return.

"What I don't see," Hearn said, as we sat there on the running board, "is how we can ever get a square deal out of those fellas. It was bad enough before the war. Now look at it."

Two of Hearn's sons had gone to Ontario to work in war factories and they were the portent of a silent but mighty change in the whole balance of Canada. From the beginning it had been a delicate balance, the constant struggle between the protectionist cities of the east and the trading farmers of the west. Gradually the farmers had been losing out, until the protected cities had to bonus them so that they could still live and pay high, protected prices.

The war has undermined the balance still further. By industrializing Canada it has concentrated economic power, political power, and population more than ever in the manufacturing areas. It has shifted the whole fulcrum of Canadian life eastward. It has built a new vested interest in the principle of protection on top of the old interest. It has created new factories and new towns which will want to sell manufactured goods, not wheat, after the war, which will want to control the Canadian prairie market more than ever when the war machinery must turn to peacetime goods. The position of the farmer, like the position of those fishermen in Nova Scotia, is weakened daily as Canada becomes less of an agricultural, more of an industrial nation, with all the problems, sores, and social strains of industrialism.

Hearn is not alone in his alarm. In the head offices of the farmers' wheat pool in Regina the best minds of the wheat industry are desperately worried also. They see the prairies losing ground in the economic struggle and the political struggle. They know, as the puzzled men in Parliament know, that there is no cure for the prairies, no solution, no hope, no way of avoiding a slump in population, the collapse of towns, the decline of cities, the abandonment of farms, unless there is a return of world trade and foreign markets.

So today the prairie waits, with bulging barns and elevators,

for the day when it can seed again as the Lord intended. Deep
in the souls of these people is a strange love of their grim
land that makes them loath to leave it—the love of distance,
sweep, and elbow room, the love of the rich soil between their
fingers and under their plows, the pull of loneliness and the far
horizon.

Here is a bitter sight for Canadians crossing the prairies.
The land turns like a vast platter as the train speeds across it—
in winter white and cold, with men in sheepskin coats driving
in box sleighs and shivering on the station platform; in spring,
black and glistening with the dark water of melting snow; in
summer, green with the first wheat sprouts; in the autumn,
burning yellow, when the stooks lie in endless pattern and the
threshing machines belch chaff into the wind.

Good land. The best in the world, Hearn said, and reminded
me again that there was no speck of grit in it. This lake bottom of the Regina Plains, he guessed, went down thirty feet
in pure black muck, almost no end to it. He had never fer-
tilized it, yet the crops were as large as ever when there was
moisture for their roots. But no farmer in this district owned
the land any more, Hearn said. The mortgage companies
owned everything. They didn't foreclose now because they
could make nothing out of the land. If it ever became valuable
again, the companies would take it over quickly enough, and
the men who had plowed it, reaped it, toiled on it, would have
nothing, unless the government intervened. They lived now,
around here, on relief and on sufferance.

"The other day," the old man said, puffing his store cigarette down to the last quarter of an inch, "they came around
and asked me to buy war bonds. They said the idea of war
bonds was to reduce our consumption of goods, so we could
pay for the war." He laughed hoarsely again, "Reduce our
consumption of goods!"

His wife was watching us from the window of the house
now, a gaunt woman in a faded pink dress. The chickens picked

at the drying mud of the abandoned garden patch. Hearn's son hammered a bolt in the worn-out tractor. These people were asked to reduce their consumption of goods, while the rest of Canada was in the first fever of a war boom, wages at an all-time high, retail sales smashing all records, the country dropsical with a false war prosperity.

"Yeah," Hearn repeated. "The fellow said we had to reduce our consumption of goods. That's what they call economics."

All the prairies have not suffered so much. Some districts, avoiding drought, have never been without crops. Some farms, able to grow other crops besides grain, have managed fairly well. Where it is possible, cattle are being raised. But the per capita income of the prairies before the war was about $188 a year, 60 per cent of it from agriculture, and of this 60 per cent 47 per cent was wheat.

The prairies have other sources of income besides wheat. They have coarse grains, cattle, hogs, dairying. In southern Alberta they have an oil industry sufficient to supply most of their needs. In the north they are opening up mines. A fifth of their income is derived from manufacturing, a remarkable growth in the last twenty years. The war has given the prairie cities even an air of prosperity with soldiers everywhere, and the flying fields of the British Commonwealth Air Training Plan.

There is room yet for more diversification of crops, more self-containment, better management, and better use of the land in place of "wheat mining." But if the prairies produce more of other crops, they will only offer new competition for the farmers of the east and of British Columbia, who already are drowned in surplus and have not received even the bonuses of the prairie farmer. No matter how the prairie economy is changed, no matter how crops are changed, the only real hope of maintaining the present population and the present position of the prairies in Canada is the return of the wheat market.

This is wheat land. This is the crop that nature intended

most of it to grow. It is the only crop that much of it will grow. An economic world, seeking cheap costs and greater wealth, would grow much of its wheat here.

Perhaps the decline is permanent and much of the land must go back into pasture or be left, abandoned and empty. Perhaps Canada must reverse the process of forty years and move many of the people out of the prairies. No one dares to face it. Governments pause and argue, and deal in figures and theories and statistics, and utter patriotic slogans, and wait for the war to end and the return of an economic world.

"Maybe," said Hearn, "I've sounded too blue. Feeling a little down today. I've just been over the land again and there's no moisture and the tractor needs a new bull pinion. I suppose we're lucky we're not being bombed. It's all right for a young man. If I was young, I'd move up north. They get moisture there. I'm too old for that now, and my last boy wants to join the army. Too late to move. But remember this."

His shrewd, wrinkled eyes looked hard into mine. "Remember this, my friend. Wheat will come back. Always has, from the time of Moses in Egypt. They'll want this wheat. They'll need it. They'll buy it. And we can grow it. This is the best land in the world. Not a speck of grit in it, even thirty feet down. Look at it. Feel it."

He held up another handful for me to rub between my fingers. Then he flung his arm towards the horizon which lay around us, in a taut, dark line, a circle joining the flat sky. It was the best land in the world.

As I got into my car, Hearn saw some newspapers on the back seat. "Finished with them?" he asked. I handed them to him. They were three days old. "That doesn't matter," he said. "We're in no hurry here and we don't see many papers. We like to keep up with the times."

I left him on the lonely road, and a mile away I could still see him standing there, watching me, a dark dot against the sky, the white papers clutched under his arm.

Never Go Back

As soon as we reached the hill at the edge of the town, we knew there was something wrong. Why, in my boyhood here it had been a long, steep hill, good to coast on in the winter, a formidable climb in the dust of summer. Now it appeared less than twenty feet high. Everything had shrunk.

When we came out to this town in British Columbia from Ontario it had seemed a substantial place. You had to own a saddle horse to get around at all. (My father bought Dock, with his potbelly and wall eye, from an Indian on the main street, against the bidding of a drunk, who only wanted to raise the price for fun, and got it up to $27 cash.)

Now I saw, in one bitter glance, that the town had never been large and always been ugly. So splendid it had seemed to a small boy from Ontario and so wild! We used to stand in the snow, on the sidewalk outside the Nugget Hotel, and watch the cowboys lining up in front of the bar, with all its mirrors and glitter, and old man Hodges serving the liquor in his white apron and red vest. It had seemed to us, shivering in the cold, like the luxury of an Oriental court, like the opulence and sin we had read about in books. Hodges and his customers, we knew, were going straight to hell, and the thought of them roasting there, forever, fascinated us. We pressed our noses against the cold glass to watch them, half expecting some of them to fall down dead at any moment.

When the ladies from the little houses at the edge of the town paraded through the street in the afternoon, in ostrich feathers, furs, and silk dresses, their faces all painted up, we

*knew who they were, and we knew we were living in a desper-
ate place, a wild west town. The only drawback was that nobody
carried a gun or shot anybody.*

*Still, old Tex undoubtedly was a Bad Man. He was broken
down now, with a bad cough, and he always smelled of whisky.
Tex cleaned out Coulter's livery stable, sleeping in a little room
like a box stall that smelled of horses. It was well known that
he had fled from the States when the law tried to get him. He
had shot dozens of men, we were quite sure. Of course, he
was gentle with us, drunk or sober, and used to let us do his
work of currying down the horses (all except Bud, the thoroughbred), but we knew that some day Tex would go bad
again and shoot up the town. (They found him dead one morning in his little room and not even a gun beside him.)*

*The town was full of cowboys then, in big hats and fur
chaps. One day I got a big hat and an old pair of chaps (they
were badly moth-eaten and held together with shoe laces) and,
riding down the street, reining in Dock's head to make him
prance, I experienced an ecstasy never recaptured again. We
were all hard western characters then, even at twelve years old.
I played hookey from school for two months to hide in the
stable and brush Dock down and currycomb him until he
shone, but I could never get him to move faster than a slow
trot.*

*Now there were no cowboys on the streets, just men in or-
dinary clothes. Coulter's livery stable had been turned into a
garage, and men worked there at a dismantled truck. Not a
horse in sight.*

*Scharsmidt's bakery was gone, too. We used to sneak in
there after school, when it was twenty below zero, and warm
ourselves by the big oven, and old Scharsmidt, the German
baker, would grumble and give us each a hunk of his new
bread, all hot and steaming. On a cold day now I can still smell
the warm smell of the bakery, the new bread. Sometimes we
drove with Scharsmidt in his sleigh out into the country while*

he delivered bread and then, if there were any tarts or pies left over, he might give us one each for carrying the bread into the little cabins of the settlers. Once they used his sleigh, because it was the best in town, to carry George Middleton out to the cemetery, where we had watched them blast out the frozen ground with dynamite. We watched them let the coffin down with new ropes from Mr. Elwell's store. Then we rode back with Scharsmidt, and he gave us a tart each to help us recover from the funeral.

Elwell's store was properly regarded as the finest outside Vancouver. Three clerks were needed to serve all the customers. And what a smell of candy in tubs, molasses, coal oil, and buckskin! We would take a long time choosing the candy out of the big glass jars so that we could eavesdrop on the cowboys who used to sit around on the barrels, beside the stove, while Elwell, in his high stiff collar and black coat, would make speeches against reciprocity. The Indians sat apart, at the end of the store, never moving or changing expression for hours.

Elwell's store was still there, but the front had been covered with shiny tile and there was a Neon sign in front. It belonged to a chain-store company from the Coast. There were no Indians now, but clerks in uniform green coats. Next door the Nugget Hotel, that haunt of gilded vice, turned out to be a little wooden building that needed painting. The bar was labeled "Coffee Shoppe."

We didn't stay long. I tried to tell Jean what it had been like when I was a boy, but she didn't believe me. Our car went up the great hill at the end of the town as if it were only a little rise in the ground.

CHAPTER SIXTEEN

The Promised Land

Let me come to British Columbia in the spring, in the lush first days of April. Let me go to bed in the frozen prairies and wake among the green maple leaves, the swelling catkins, the uncurling ferns, and the blossom of old orchards beside the railway. Or blindfold me and stand me on the rear platform of the train and I will tell you, by the smell and the very feel of the air, when we pass through Golden and Revelstoke, when we reach the sagebrush country of Kamloops, when we are breathing the brave stone smell of the Fraser canyon and the meadow airs of the Chilliwack Valley. Every station and siding, every brook and field and little farm I would surely recognize by instinct, though I were blind. This is our own incomparable land.

Better still, let me steal in by night, lying, sleepless, on a lower berth, watching the moonlight skim the Thompson, the velvet hills of the Dry Belt, the lights of lonely farm houses, the bands of cattle staring at the passing spectacle of the train, and the mare with her new foal gazing from the meadow. Let me lie there and see the billows of smoke playing among the stone cliffs, and the dark, calm mass of forests and the awful bulk of the canyon at Hell's Gate.

Then, as dawn breaks, the canyon widens suddenly and there are the fields of the Pacific coast, deep green, rank, overgrown, and succulent, each with its own mountain in the corner. There are the wild currant blossoms dripping red and smelling of all the Aprils of the ages, the fierce growth of bracken, the white plumes of elderberry, and everywhere the hungry forest, marching back, with scouts of fern and alder, with shock troops of fir and hemlock, upon the settler's clearing. There in the broadening river are the great rafts of reddish cedar, the sea gulls roosting on them with wise and ancient look. There at last is the ocean and the unreal, flat shape of ships, the smell of the salt water, and the mountains dropping into it at a single leap.

Wild and upheaved, and forever changing, forever new, is this land. What hopes our fathers had for it! This was a land fit for men to live in, not just to struggle and exist in—men who had bleached in the prairie suns and frozen in the prairie winters, men who had stifled in the crowded, used-up air of eastern cities and the old world, men who wanted to be alone and free.

Captain Cook had seen it from his ship, and brought back strange stories, and before him, the Spaniards. They had seen the incredible green of the coast, its soaring forests to the water's edge, so thick that even the Indians feared to enter them. They had seen the mild and pleasant climate and growth everywhere.

Captain George Vancouver tried to put it down in words on May 7, 1792, but only succeeded in saying:

To describe the beauties of this region will, on some future occasion, be a very grateful task to the pen of a skillful pane-gyrist. The serenity of the climate, the innumerable pleasing landscapes, and the abundant fertility that unassisted nature puts forth, require only to be enriched by the industry of man with villages, mansions, cottages, and other buildings, to render it the most lovely country that can be imagined; whilst the labor of the inhabitants would be amply rewarded in the bounties which nature seems ready to bestow on cultivation.

But neither the Spaniards, Cook, nor Vancouver had reached the open lands beyond the coast jungle, the uplands of clear air. Mackenzie saw this hinterland, walking westward to the sea, and Fraser as he rode down on his river, churned like a cork through the rapids ("gazing at each other in silent congratulation at our narrow escape from total destruction"). The men who searched for gold on these rivers saw it, the immensity of the interior. Gold had brought them here, our first flow of population, brought the first railway wallowing down out of the mountains to Gas Town, but much more than gold was found—a land different from any in Canada, larger, wilder, as if it belonged to a different continent.

Here, it seemed, was the good life of freedom that all men sought, without the toil of other places. Here were timber and minerals and all crops throve. In the sea and streams the fish teemed for the taking, in the woods game for the hunter.

In such a land all men could be rich. They swarmed into it, cut the trees, plowed the ground, blasted the rock, plundered the sea, and reared up their cities so fast that, in the back yards of Vancouver today, you will find ten-foot stumps of the virgin forest that was alive a few years ago. With such resources they built the highest standard of living Canada has ever known, the most extravagant governments, the heaviest taxes, the largest public services, the happiest life. Built it, thinking nothing of the future, of wasting resources, as if there could be no end to their wealth, as if forests would last forever, as if mines could never reach bottom, as if the fish could breed without spawning.

Always there were more resources. Unlimited resources, the politicians assured us at election times, and that was good enough to win an election—unlimited resources, boundless future, no need to conserve or think about tomorrow. Only now do we begin to suspect that there may be an end. We have lived in almost a continuous boom that started with the discovery of gold on the bars of the Fraser and finally swelled up into the skyscrapers of Vancouver. Now we suspect that it may not go on forever. But we look again at our abundant land and we laugh at such fears.

Meanwhile life is good in British Columbia and unlike the life of the prairies or the east—so unlike it that, crossing the Rockies, you are in a new country, as if you had crossed a national frontier. Everyone feels it, even the stranger, feels the change of outlook, tempo, and attitude. What makes it so, I do not know. The size of everything, I suspect, the bulk of mountains, the space of valleys, the far glimpses of land and sea, the lakes and rivers, all cast in gigantic mold. They make a man feel bigger, more free, as if he had come out of a crowded room.

We cannot go back to our old homes east of the mountains. In our hearts we never recross that barrier.

From the beginning, when they debated the advisability of joining the United States, British Columbians have been part of Canada in constitution, in law, in the written word, but not much in the spirit. From the beginning it was the land of men who wanted to get away from everything, to start afresh, to be on their own. Only now does British Columbia begin to feel the pressure of the outside world, the regimentation of modern life, the dead weight of convention, the facts of hard economics, and the responsibilities of Canada. This thrust of men who were determined to be alone and free has paused for the first time. The British Columbia which was a magic dream for us all is fading into the light of common day.

Yet there is much of it still left, despite the dead growth of cities. There is untouched wilderness larger than half a dozen American states. There is sanctuary always close at hand if you seek it. The land is so upturned by mountains, so cut by river and lake, so heaved up, as if a hand had stirred it suddenly before it cooled, that a man can be lost to his fellows in a hundred yards and the world's armies could be hidden in a few leagues of valley or forest. There is the witchery of it—

the endless variety, changing with every turn in the road, with almost every valley and hill. Always there is something lost behind the ranges and men must seek it out.

British Columbia starts with the Rockies, and even they, hardly changing through the ages, are always different. So often I have threaded them by train and automobile, and they never seem the same. Never, though I should live to be as old as they, shall I lose the small boy's excitement as I watch the two puffing engines rounding a curve far ahead in the narrow canyon, the red glow of their fires at night, the uncoiling lights of the train. Always the old miracle is undimmed—that men can travel, that railways can be built, that engines can bore through this solid stone and emerge safe at the other side.

Best of all, ride in the engine cab. Stand by the engineer as, with cunning fingers, he moves the throttle up a notch and eases on the brake while we round a curve—gently, so that no soup may be spilled in the diner. Watch the fireman as he peers at the solid flame in the engine's belly and tosses a bucket of sand into it, to clear the soot. Now see how the shafts of the headlight, solid as steel, drill a clean circle through the darkness and throw monstrous shadows on the rocks. The bell clangs as we slow down for a little town in the night and the whistle shouts hoarsely across the land. The engineer leans out the window and waves to the section man, blinking in front of his little red house. Now the monster gathers power under your feet, like an animal straining and puffing at the leash. We are over the divide, rushing downhill towards the coast.

Always, since the first engine rolled down to the sea, since our fathers waited and longed for the coming of the railway, always from the days when we heard the engine whistle in the night and cowered deeper in our childhood beds, the railway has been close beside us in British Columbia. Always the echo of the whistle from the mountain, dying faintly in the far darkness, has been the urgent sound of British Columbia, full of memories, full of hope, full of all the unutterable longing, loneliness, and freedom of this land. We listen to the whistle and, in our memory, we can see the mountains and the rivers and the toil of our fathers. We can see our own lost youth.

Now we drive through these mountains by car. We have built hotels of exotic luxury, pictured in every magazine and travel folder, where soft people can look at the mountains and think they are seeing them (never knowing that the mountains can be seen only on foot, after labor and sweat, or on horseback, with the creak of leather and tinkle of steel bit, or lying down among the little spruce trees in the darkness). We have built paved highways through the canyons, with planned vistas of height and depth and distance, from Banff to Windermere, from Lake Louise to Golden and through the deep forests of the Big Bend, up to the cobblestone town of Jasper.

But in a car you can never feel the Rockies. You are insulated from them by glass, steel, rubber, and speed. They become moving pictures only. It is best to see them on foot or horseback, better to know one little valley or a single peak than to remember a blur of a thousand miles. Still, to many of us the Rockies will always be a toy train, burrowing like a mole through the living rock, whistling boldly among the crags to keep up its courage.

Row on row, like a series of sea waves, the mountains roll westward so that the Rockies never really end until they drop straight into the ocean. West of the first wave lies the East Kootenay Valley, the placid Windermere country, the beginning of the Columbia's wide wanderings. This valley, to the United States border, is friendly with the hot, aching smell of pine in the summer and the red glow of tiger lilies by the road and always the backdrop of blue peaks.

Then, behind the next western wave, is the deep trench of the Columbia on its southward swing, and its tributary Arrow, Kootenay, and Slocan Lakes. They lie close to the abrupt edge of the mountains, fed by the snow, very like the alpine lakes of Italy, and little white stern-wheel steamers chuff about them with a fine air of self-importance. (And, oh, the shuddering siren whistle of them in the night, when a little boy thought a fearful giant was bellowing with anger in the hills!) By the lake shore are pleasant, easy-going towns. Deep in the fume-scorched hills is the furnace of the Trail smelter, forever flaming in a hellish chemistry of zinc, silver, gold, and lead. It is ghastly by day, but by night it shimmers like a fairy city, its lights all swimming in the Columbia.

Another wave of mountains, and in the next trough lies the Okanagan Valley, that excellent contrivance of nature and man, where the worthless sagebrush soil, with a trickle of water brought in flumes out of the hills, has sent an orchard flowing, unbroken, for a hundred miles. Blessed and fruitful valley of homes among the apple trees! Of cheerful, well-groomed towns, of lakes like Kalamalka unbelievably blue, of rich fields and fat cattle! In the spring it is a rolling, frothing sea of blossom between the hills, and in the autumn the apples bend every branch, and there is a heavy apple smell everywhere.

Here is refuge. Here is the true sanctuary of British Columbia. Here is a distinct race of men, basically English, who have found what they were looking for, who would never leave, even though times are hard, apple prices low, and the largest fruit industry in the British Empire struggling for survival. Here are people who dare to *live,* a lost art in most places, and the sight of them in their orchards, in their shady houses, however poor, or in their jolly towns, will make you want to flee here and escape.

Strange people live in the Okanagan, the odd ones who want to live in their own way. Deep in some random valley you may run across a great house, furnished with antiques from England. Outside Vernon is an ancient Swedish potter, making beautiful bowls and jugs of glistening pottery but refusing to sell, slamming the door in your face (though he is desperately poor) unless he likes your looks. At Wallachin, at the far north end of the valley system, every man went to the last war, leaving miles of orchard and irrigation works to decay, and now a few trees thrust out despairing leaves and die one by one on the bank of the Thompson, because the soldiers never returned. At Naramata (the very name is like the trickling sound of water in the orchard) lives Carol Aiken, who proved himself a good poet and able stage director, built a summer theater at enormous expense merely to produce plays for his own amusement, has now turned to the creation of a large garden and lately dug trees for it in the forest, loaded them on a truck, and calmly broke down all the telephone wires of the district on his way home. Nobody cared. In the Okanagan they live.

Westward again roll the waves into such a turmoil of mountains and narrow valleys that there is only one clear pass through them to the southern coast, and only one road, along the canyon of the Fraser. The last wave stops suddenly at the sea. Along its edge, on narrow bench and river delta, the mountains always within reach of their hands, live most of the people of British Columbia.

Among the cities of the world that I have seen, Vancouver has easily the best setting. Men who have seen more than I generally agree. That Vancouver itself has never been worthy of its setting is the fault of our haste, our fury, and our appetite. In a thousand years, perhaps, there will be a city good enough for this site, but hardly before.

You come into Vancouver along a broad arm of the sea, which probably was once the mouth of the Fraser. Between Burrard Inlet on the north and the present three-tongued channel of the river to the south, Vancouver sits upon an ancient delta, heaped up high by the prehistoric river and once deep in rank forest. Across the inlet the North Shore Mountains seem as close as stage scenery, leaping suddenly out of the water, in mottled blue and green, until they turn white, like old men, at the top. Always the mountains rise up flat and unreal at the end of every main street and lie in deep reflection upon the water of the harbor. There the ships come from China and Japan, from all the oceans of the world, the white liners, the rusty freighters lurching along like revelers out of a bar, the ferryboats, as pretty and fresh as girls on a beach.

Into the harbor thrusts the green nose of Stanley Park. It was one of the few sensible things done in our youth, the preservation of this sweep of timber in the center of a large city, with its beaches, rocks, and cliffs, undefiled. Five minutes from Granville Street and you are in the virgin forest, if you want solitude, or in gardens of flowers, pleasant lawns, and little lakes. When you see the size of the original trees, the solid wall of underbrush, the dismal jungle, you wonder how Vancouver could ever have been cleared, how men could have found room here to live or even pitch a tent. Many men in Vancouver today, and not so very old either, can remember when most of the city was the same kind of wilderness, with no path through it.

From the sharp seaward jut of Stanley Park at the First Narrows, the North Shore Mountains threaten to fall on you and upon the frail thread of the suspension bridge which joins the two shores. To the westward floats the dark whale shape of Vancouver Island in the Gulf of Georgia. North of it, the sharp white peaks of Howe Sound, and everywhere the speckled dots of little islands, with a faint haze, a water color wash of blue over everything, and then the fire of the sunset across the sea.

Better still, come here at night. Then the lights race like fireflies up the mountains, the single light of the chalet winking at the top, the lights of ships and boats moving out of the harbor straight below you. Over to the east the skyline of Vancouver is ablaze, all ugliness blotted out. It is a combination of shadow, bulk, and light to be found in few places. Budapest is counted grand, but is a toy beside this. Paris and its river are pygmies. London a drab sweep of chimney pots in the darkness, the Danube at Vienna a poor flat stream, and Quebec a mere height of land beside the river. Only in the new countries can you find such spectacles, in San Francisco, in Rio, so they tell me, and in Sydney.

Stand at the top of Grouse Mountain as the day ends and look down on the harbor. It has become a small green plate. The ships are no larger than matches. The park is a dark smear on a map, leaning into the sea. The mass of the city, sprawling southward to the mouth of the Fraser, looks like a child's city of building blocks. Now the lights start to come on, row by row, street by street, in square pattern, sowed like grain across the swelling land.

Carlyle could have written a book from here, a larger *Sartor Resartus,* tearing the roofs from this city, exposing the life beneath them. He would have much to say about the contrast between this wild hillside and the streets below, on which you could almost toss a stone. Down there men struggle on the streets, never pausing to think that here, in plain view, the wilderness has not changed for ten thousand years. Great city with its noise and fury! Tiny city, little circle of lights, frail glow, slight rumble of sound, lost forever in the vast silence of these hills!

The fathers of the men on those lighted streets lived in the wilderness and counted it home. Now men flee from it, seeking the lights, huddling in these little lighted spots in the midst of the darkness of the vacant land.

In the chalet of Grouse Mountain, built of peeled cedar logs, I met an old man of ruddy, English countenance, smoking by the stone fireplace. Said he: "This building is built on the principles of construction that it took our ancestors hundreds of years to perfect, little by little, the kind of building the Norsemen built in Scandinavia and brought out here with them. It is well and truly built to last a thousand years. Look there"—he pointed to the lights of Vancouver—"look down there and tell me how many people living there can build anything with their hands, or know anything about the arts that our ancestors have learned through thousands of years, the kind of art that goes into a building like this. Why," said he, waving his hands at the lights of the city, "we can't build anything in a scientific sense, in a political sense, in an economic sense, in a spiritual sense, that will last ten minutes!"

We stood by the window watching the wink of the lights. "Yes, look at the lights, sir!" the old man said. "Look down at the glimmer! It may well be the twilight of civilization. Did you ever think of that? From all we can learn of the world today—war, revolution, decay, decline of population and birth rate—we may be in the first stages of the end, beyond help and rescue. But this building will stand here, and the principles of construction in it, for ten centuries, if they let it alone— long after the lights down there have all gone out. It is well and truly built. Civilization down there is jerry-built, flimsy and unbalanced. The lights will go out."

He stood gazing gloomily at Vancouver as if the lights might go out at any moment.

When the sunset had drained out of the Gulf, the sweep of lights and reflections in the water, the shape of mountain and the last glow of the sea (despite the old man's forebodings) are too perfect to be contrived by accident. They must have been planned by some artist who knew how to improve on nature.

Yet all this is sheer accident. Since it was Gas Town, a sawmill beside the salt chuck, since the earlier day when Captain Vancouver sailed up here and met the Spaniards off Point Grey and left his name on all this territory, the town has grown furiously, tumultuously, recklessly, the greatest boom town in Canada.

Back from the harbor it pushed, street by street, not pausing even to blast out the stumps, building its skyscrapers a few yards from the original wooden shacks. You may turn off Granville or Hastings Street today and, in two blocks, find yourself among run-down wooden slums that belong to a frontier town. You may step out of the unspoiled verdure of the park and find across the street the dilapidated hot-dog stands that belong to some cow town on the prairies.

Slowly the brawling boom town grows up, builds great homes and gardens, lays out parks everywhere, plants new trees to replace the old forests, clears its beaches, yearns after architecture, and wonders whether the square matchbox of the new City Hall is truly beautiful.

From the day when Captain Vancouver found that the Straits of Juan de Fuca were not a river mouth, as Cook supposed, and, following them, discovered the Fraser and Burrard Inlet, Vancouver was bound to be great. Geography and economics had conspired to lay their fingers upon this spot beside the sea. It was the western end of the natural pass through the coast mountains. It was the mouth of the river. It had to be the end of the railway. It had to drain out the products of the whole hinterland back to the Rockies and beyond. Into its safe harbor must come the Pacific ships, and the Panama Canal would bring it close, by competitive shipping cost, to Europe. It could not help becoming, if it had wanted to, Canada's third city, as it may ultimately become one of the great cities of the world.

Vancouver has lived by the legend of continual growth and feels ill if it is not in a constant state of expansion. The North American disease of proliferation and giantism has become chronic here and seems like normal health. Size, population, business appear as the end and supreme object of civic life. Already Vancouver holds half of British Columbia's people— a top-heavy and dropsical arrangement, but Vancouver never suspects that. It is always getting ready to move into a larger house, a better street. It is always thrusting new streets and miles of new houses into the second-growth that the loggers left a few years ago.

Lumbering, mining, fishing, agriculture, all come to focus

here and build upon the back of the producer the parasitical growth which is the substance of all cities. It is a quick and startling growth and out of it has come a quick and startling aristocracy of pure wealth. Vancouver is ruled today by able men who took the raw resources of the hinterland and converted them into money, into the economic strength of Canada. They are still close to the original tools of their hands, still thirsting with the old thirst for expansion. Tycoons flourish here who once worked as laborers, miners, lumberjacks, fishermen. The aristocracy of Vancouver is never far from the mountains, the woods, and the sea; and there is in it a strangely boyish and innocent delight in its wealth, its power, and its big houses. The Vancouver Club at noon, filled with men newly rich by their own efforts and earthy; the lavish parties in Shaughnessy; the saga of MacMillan's ships, canneries, and mills; the sudden millionaires of lucky gold mines; the political machine which runs British Columbia—all contain a certain frontier gusto not to be hidden by pavements and expensive tailoring.

The core of the old town beside the water, of Gas Town and the great fire, still remains and dies hard. Nothing happens in Vancouver without some old-timer hurrying to the phone to tip off Roy Brown at the *Sun,* and no old-timer dies without an obituary which tells of life among the stump clearings. Though a new generation has come, a proletariat and a big city's contrasts of riches on Marine Drive and reeking poverty in the East End, though there are new economic and social pressures seldom mentioned in print, the rulers of Vancouver still retain a wonderful and naïve faith in the old days, a belief that boom is normal and mere stability intolerable; still hope for the return of good times when the city is already obese and dripping with prosperity; still believe in their own legend.

Vancouver, living on its hinterland and dominating British Columbia, has set the tone of British Columbia's thinking. This part of Canada has never paused to conserve, to question, to doubt the future. When a royal commission of experts warns it that its prosperity is thin and brittle, being built on foreign markets and on resources now used up at an appalling rate, no one pays the least attention. Hew down the forest, dig up the precious spots of agricultural lands between the mountains, gamble on the latest mining strike, scour the fisheries, build big houses, expand and make money—there is the spirit of youth everywhere, and Vancouver is young.

None of the elegance of Montreal is here, none of the stability of the Maritime aristocracy, and little of Winnipeg's broad view. Still, life in Vancouver has been better for the ordinary man than in any large Canadian city, than in most cities anywhere.

Climate alone, the mild green winters (you get used to rain and fog) draw Canadians to it from all over the country and, in bad times, fill it every autumn with the jobless off the freight cars. In the cool summers every man can have a garden, can bask on a beach or sail a boat. There is outdoor sport for everyone. Young folks leave the Vancouver gardens in bloom and swarm up the North Shore Mountains to ski. Old men bowl in the park or play endless outdoor checkers on a twenty-foot checkerboard, meditating each move by the hour. In the summer evenings Vancouver strolls in the park to listen to band concerts. All public services are of the best. Houses are cheap to build, living costs low, wages high. Vancouver still manages somehow to keep many of the advantages of the small town. It is, in fact, a boisterous small town growing out of its clothes.

Vancouver has always thought of little but Vancouver. Always British Columbia thinks of British Columbia. Even when it was richer than any province, enjoying a better living, spending twice as much money through its government, British Columbia maintained the grievance, and governments got elected on the proposition that British Columbia had been unfairly treated in Confederation; was, indeed, a kind of Cinderella, sitting beside the ashes in the marble fireplace of the new Hotel Vancouver.

A few months ago some of us were coming west, and in the diner at breakfast, the talk turned to the Hotel Vancouver, which, being a state-owned institution, is open to free discussion. After I had expatiated at length on my simple rustic prejudice against the decorative scheme of this great hostelry (which most people find beautiful) and had risen to a considerable height of eloquence, the stranger at the other side of the table remarked politely: "I'm glad to hear your opinion of the hotel. You see, I happen to have been the architect."

After that I resolved never to speak out loud again about any tiny flaw in Vancouver. Such is the civic loyalty of the place that you can never convince anybody that your only interest is in a better Vancouver, a city as splendid as its setting. To men who have seen it mushroom up from among the stumps, who remember when Hastings Street was on the edge of town and Shaughnessy a good place for blackberrying or brook trout, Vancouver is a flawless growth, just right as it stands.

It will change, despite them, and very fast. In fifty years it will be as different from the present city as the present city is from Gas Town. In a thousand years one would like to come back and see what men have done with this unique site, this noble opportunity. They could build here the finest city ever inhabited by our species.

But it is not British Columbia. British Columbia lies far beyond the pavements and the last lights of the Pattullo Bridge. It lies behind the mountains. It lies along the narrow coastal inlets, in little pulp mill towns and fish canneries up to Prince Rupert and the Alaska panhandle.

No one has seen it who has not lived with it, worked with it, tramped it on foot, ridden it on horseback, camped far off its roads and trails, felt its good earth in his hands.

When I am far away from British Columbia I like to think

of those things. I like to think of camp beside the cold Skagit, the big trout, the white specks of goats on the mountains, the smell of a grizzly; our camp by a shallow lake just behind the coast range, after a long trek across the badlands of stunted trees; that other night by Big Creek, when we had come across the empty Chilcotin plateau and danced for sheer joy in the autumn moonlight; or fishing under the falls of Mahood, soaked to the skin and dizzy with the whirl of water; toiling with pack horse over Allison Pass in search of a grazing spot in the twilight; sleeping in a coast forest with the wind roaring above and the ghostly creak of branches; lying on the sea beach in the dawn with the smell of low tide; making camp beside a fairy lake on the Forbidden Plateau, three deer watching not twenty yards off; riding through a Cariboo blizzard; driving down the north road through two feet of snow at Christmas; picking lilies in the spring woods of Vancouver Island, picking roses in December; sawing stove wood for the cabin and smelling the spring sap of fir and cedar.

A lifetime is not long enough to explore this country. A man is too small to feel its size. The poet has not been born to sing its song, nor the painter to picture it. As we try to explain it we can only use the stilted phrases of Captain Vancouver or lapse into the gibberish of the tourist advertisement.

"What is B. C. thinking?" Pat Terry always asks me, looking up from the city desk of the *Sun* as I come to town. "Not Vancouver," says Pat. "Hell, you can build a city like this in a night. It's the country that counts. You can't build it in generations. What of the country?"

What of the country? We shall try to see. But remember always its youth, its boy's mistakes and boy's dreams, vanities and disappointments, its boy's bravery and imagination. There was no Vancouver sixty years ago. There was nothing worth mentioning forty years ago. At the turn of the century British Columbia was still a country of happy fairy tale, where all men could be rich and fortunate. Twenty years ago Vancouver was just beginning to hit its stride; the young scientists of its university were unlocking the chemistry of the interior ores; the lumbermen were beginning to ship our lumber across the sea.

Yes, young. But I am glad to have lived here before it grew old, while we could still feel our fathers' freedom in it, while we could come again and again through the Rockies and always look out on this land with a wild surmise.

She's Quiet Tonight

It is all quiet tonight on the fire line. Out beyond the fringe of green trees the fire is still burning, but she burns low. She has gone into the ground, down into the pitchy roots of old fir stumps, deep down into the soil, smoldering, sullen, ready to spring up with the first breath of wind.

Little patches of flame leap up now and then, run through the dried bracken, sink down again into the fields of gray ash. Sudden flames stream out from dead snags with a shower of sparks as from a rocket, and die as suddenly. A tortured tree trunk glows steadily against the night sky, far off, like a red-hot poker.

The fire has become a personal enemy, up and down the coast, a living thing with a will and a character of her own. We think of the fire that way—a cunning, calculating creature, full of tricks, only lying low now, ready to strike when we turn our backs. We call the fire "she."

She started in the logging slash and flamed up like burning gasoline, with a sudden hiss and then a steady roar. She ate the young fir growth at a gulp. She crawled slowly into the green timber and waited there a while. In the distance she looked like a thin, hot wire in the night sky. Then the wire suddenly grew thick. The red glow oozed out over the sky as if blotting paper were sucking up red paint.

"She's crowned!" Pete Haramboure said. She had leaped into the tops of the big trees and every fir needle swelled up and burst into a tiny puff of gas. She shot across the crown of the forest in a single flame. You could hear the roar ten miles away, like a train going over a steel bridge. She traveled

329

more than a mile a minute, and chunks of flaming wood blew on her wind far out into the sea.

But she's quiet tonight. At the edge of the fire the settler, a stooped man with sunken eyes, sits on the steps of his cabin, and watches the smoldering red line just beyond his rail fence, the darts of flames that come and go. He is too tired to do anything more. His wife and children have been moved out to the coast long ago, but he stays on, hoping that somehow his homestead may escape. Just a puff of wind is needed to send a wall of flame against the fence, the barn of cedar shakes, the cabin with its two rooms and shabby furniture—the work of years. The settler grew old clearing this land, foot by foot, blasting the stumps, burning up the old logs. The fire was his friend then. Tonight or tomorrow it may drive him to the sea. His cow grazes between the stumps a few yards from the rim of fire and ash. They are safe, the settler and his cow, until the wind comes.

Up the logging road the little firs that used to stand together, thick as hair on a dog's back, are black skeletons now, millions of them, mile on mile. In the big timber it is like driving into the pit of hell. Our headlights only penetrate six feet through the blue smoke. We have the feeling that there is no road ahead only a cavern. Through the murk a burning snag flares like a torch and is gone. Here and there in the purple darkness patches of flame glow faintly and fade out. Little tongues of fire lap the side of the road close to our wheels. Here an old fir is burning slowly from its roots to its highest branches a hundred feet up. The flames have cut a huge gash in its trunk and the wound is bleeding fire. Before the night is over this growth of five centuries, this tree that has toiled up above its fellows, crushed its weaker neighbors out, will crash to the ground with a brief flare of sparks. Beside it the other great trees are standing, black and dead with their feet in a sea of ash. A few days ago this was a pungent grove, deep in sword ferns. She crowned here.

Pete Haramboure worked four days and four nights without closing his eyes until he couldn't speak, couldn't understand what men said to him. His face and body were as black as the trees. With bulldozers, with mattock and shovel and axe, Pete and his loggers cut the fire lines, pushed the logs aside, turned up brown earth, but the fire line is narrow. Give her a wind and she could leap that easily enough. With miles of hose Pete and his men fought her and stopped her within ten yards of slash that would have exploded like a box of matches —fought her until their line of retreat was nearly cut off, they felt the hot breath of her on their chests, and their hair was singed. Then the wind dropped.

Pete has taken a shower and put on a clean shirt and he sits on the steps of the cookhouse, but he cannot eat. He cannot go to bed. "You guys better get some sleep," he says to the others. Their faces are black except for red rims around the eyes and they look as if they were made up for a minstrel show. But they cannot go to bed. Over the earth hangs the smoke and the fire's breath and the sense of her presence. She is cunning. She is waiting. She is quiet tonight, but if the wind comes she will awake. Pete wets his finger and holds it up and stirs uneasily on the steps. He can feel a gust of air on his wet finger.

CHAPTER SEVENTEEN

The Lotus Eaters

To be frank, I am unable to write about Victoria, British Columbia, with that same judicious poise and lack of enthusiasm which has marked these pages so far. I fell in love with her long ago, as a boy. This puppy love has only grown with the years into the settled attachment of old age and long daily companionship. I am but one of many. Even with a toughened traveler like Kipling it was love at first sight, and, sighing like furnace, he added a reckless prose poem to the long chant of her praises.

No one who has entered the Inner Harbor of Victoria, so far as the official records show, has ever wanted to leave again. It is the normal, accepted ambition of most Canadians to spend their last days here. This is the island where Ulysses met the sirens. This is the land of the Lotus Eaters, and many of those original inhabitants are still here.

You come to Victoria, with a cloud of sea gulls, down the Gulf of Georgia, flecked with its little green islands, and along the Straits of Juan de Fuca, glistening before the blue line of the Olympic Mountains on the Washington shore. On the southern point of Vancouver Island, to your right, Victoria suddenly appears, like an arrangement of toy houses, an architect's dream of the perfect human habitation, rising tier on tier from the sea upon a green hillside. It looks like the south coast towns of England. It looks like an artist's picture from which every disagreeable feature has been carefully removed. It looks like the ancient island habitation of the Blest.

Vancouver Island was named after the British navigator who circumnavigated it, but for years a fierce controversy proceeded in the Victoria newspapers to prove that he was really a Dutchman in disguise. In any case, his name, attached to both the island and the mainland city, is the cause of endless confusion among strangers, for the two Vancouvers have nothing to do with one another.

Vancouver Island (or Vancouver's Island as a few of the ancients still call it) snuggles like a wet spaniel into the side of the continent. Its southern tail lies well below the forty-ninth parallel, close to the American coast. The wise old factors of the Hudson's Bay Company saw its importance long ago, and when they knew they would lose the Oregon boundary dispute and have to move out of the American fort of Vancouver, they sent young James Douglas up north to establish a new seat of power. He founded Victoria and hung on to it, and the international boundary swung around it, by an intricate channel, among the islands of the Gulf. From the houses of Victoria you can see the brown stretch of San Juan Island, over which we almost went to war.

Victoria was Britain's assertion of control over the northern half of the Pacific Coast—an assertion still maintained widely with an English accent. The fort was established just in time. Before long the miners of California's '49 were swarming up here on steamboats, in rowboats and canoes. Gold had been discovered on the Fraser River. Governor Douglas found his little palisaded fort on the beach surrounded by a city of tents and a mob of adventurers from all over the world. So close was the new town's connection with the Americans—there was no connection with Canada—that when the time of decision came, the local legislature of the colony debated long and earnestly a union with the United States or with the new Dominion of Canada. You can still see the absurd little wooden buildings, shaped like a Chinese pagoda and known in their day as the

Bird Cages, in which a few bearded men in tail coats decided to extend Canada to the Pacific Coast.

It took some time to make Victoria part of Canada. The process is far from complete yet. From the earliest times it was an English outpost, with an English naval base near by at Esquimalt, with English people finding here, in the warm climate of the Japan Current, a perfect replica of Devonshire or Cornwall, finding the surroundings, vegetation, and even the giant oak trees that they had known at home. It was far from the cities, the people, and the problems of Canada, nearer to London in spirit than to Montreal.

Victoria became an English town in happy exile. It had none of Quebec's history, Montreal's wealth, the push of Winnipeg, nor the appetite of its young neighbor, Vancouver, which has always appeared here as a parvenu. Victoria was an English lady of good country breeding. She rode a bicycle to town for shopping, grew roses, served tea every afternoon in the garden on an antique oak table, while her husband—a tall, lean man in tweed coat and baggy flannel trousers—wrote letters to the *British Colonist,* on Broad Street, denouncing the German Kaiser, or announcing the first wild lily of April, in the woods of Cadboro Bay.

Once a year they dressed in a London frock and a tail coat and watched the lieutenant-governor drive down Rockland Avenue in a cocked hat and gold braid to open the legislature while guns boomed a salute across the harbor. Occasionally they danced at Government House or fished in the Cowichan. There was nothing to worry about more serious than the civic debt or the dry weather of August, very hard on the roses. Early life in Victoria must have been the final perfection of country life everywhere. Hearing of it, the English headed towards it by pure instinct and, for a little time, made it their own. Not for long.

The legend of the English town still persists but, like so many things, Victoria has outlived its legend. It has become modern. It has even recognized its own quaintness, which is fatal, and sold it to the tourists, who have never seen the original. Some of the original is left, not in any physical form that the visitor is likely to notice (for he will not look into the odd nooks and crannies as we do), but in a surviving, hard remnant of the old spirit.

Sometimes still you will come across one of the real old Victorians, that separate and distinct race of creatures, not quite English, never entirely Canadian, but rooted like the oaks of Saanich in this soil. You will recognize the old Victorian by his carefully careless dress, of tweed coat and flannels, by his speech which is not English but certainly not North American; but more, by a beautiful, natural, and wholly unconscious insularity. Nothing exists north of Nanaimo or south of the Straits, save vague rumors of strange jungle tribes. Nothing matters much except the weather for growing flowers, for golf, for salmon fishing, or for trout. The British Empire, of course, can be taken for granted and will see that the world gets along all right, and if it needs help, the old Victorians gladly would die for it. The immediate question, the Empire being secure, is whether those silly duffers, the city council, are going to cut down the beautiful wild-broom bushes in Beacon Hill Park.

Alas, so few of the old genus are still alive. For years Victoria resented the belief, common all over Canada, that it spent its time drinking tea and playing golf and writing letters of protest to the *Colonist*. Now, in a world like this, you wish that the story were only true. It has never been true, of course, but there was enough truth in it, there was enough truth in the accepted caricature of the early Victorian, to make the place seem like a happy never-never land to all Canadian visitors, and so English to American tourists that I have been asked more than once if the King didn't keep a summer palace here for his holidays.

Even now Mr. Walter Davenport, of *Collier's*, can come to Victoria and write solemnly that he could not get his shoes shined failing an appointment with a shoeblack, who had to

attend balls at Government House. But the distinct civilization of Victoria certainly is perishing, the thing born in the wilderness when English life had to take root here, grow strong, or die. A rich and valuable strain is going out of the Canadian breed.

Something new is taking its place. Instead of an English culture, as the outside world supposes, we are developing here a strange combination of the naïve and the sophisticated. To Victoria have come refugees from all the countries of the earth —from England again, from eastern Canada, from the United States, from Europe, from the Orient. You can find here, in some obscure house by the sea, unknown to his neighbors, a retired rubber planter, a richer trader from Shanghai, a forgotten Hollywood actor, an American millionaire, a Czech physician, British admirals and knights to burn. This has made Victoria one of the most tolerant and easy-going places on earth. Nobody cares what you say, what you think or, least of all, what you wear. (We are probably the worst-dressed place on the continent, another cause for rejoicing.) But Victoria is a rich city, despite its lack of industry. It has the provincial government payroll and it has the money of its retired men, so that it is able to support stores, hotels, and generally a way of life more luxurious than those of any comparable Canadian city. Man for man, it is probably the wealthiest place in Canada, its people the best kept, its poverty the least.

Towns take their character usually from a few men. After the ebb of Early Victorianism, this was Benny Nicholas' town. That great-hearted man, sitting in his untidy editor's office at the *Times,* pecking out his editorials on an antique typewriter, wasting his time on crowds of useless visitors and his money on anyone who asked for it, gave Victoria its intellectual flavor for some thirty years. When he dropped dead in the middle of an editorial, the light of a civic era went out.

Benny Nicholas, of Victoria, was this sort of man: A poor lunatic called on him one day and said he was Christ risen from the grave, and Benny, treating him kindly, sent him on to the leading Christian minister of the town for a quiet talk. When the minister telephoned an hour later and protested bitterly that he had had to receive a crazy fellow, who called himself the Saviour, Benny retorted: "How do you know he wasn't? Last time He came you fellows in the church crucified Him."

Benny taught Victoria tolerance. He educated Victoria, stirred it, attacked it, ridiculed it, and sought to make it Canadian. It was an uphill job and he was never able to complete it, never able to break down the local caste system of the old families, the Union Club, the Government House clique, from which even a prime minister might be excluded. But he laid the foundation and the work goes on.

What a job it is you will realize if you can spare the time to stroll over the flower-hung Causeway, and listen to the legislature of British Columbia at work in its grisly marble chamber, which is usually regarded as the last word in Greek architecture. The legislature governs this separate economy of British Columbia, the separate territory, separate interests, and separate mind lying between the barrier of the Rockies and the ocean, and you would think at times that the barrier was impassable.

Our politics, hidden away here, have seen rare moments—the "Revolution" when the crowds stormed into the Bird Cages to demand justice from Canada in our early years; the day when the legislature walked out on the lieutenant-governor (that "obese and shiny monster," the paper called him) because it didn't like his new premier, Joe Martin; and that memorable occasion when Joe and Dick McBride pushed each other out of the opposition leader's chair, and Dick ended sitting on the desk.

Always the core of British Columbia politics has been the feeling, bred in the little colony alone on the forgotten Pacific Coast—and whipped up by politicians to win elections—that

Canada has never been quite fair to us. Since McBride's time we have been demanding "Better Terms" from Canada, as if it were another nation, and compiling endless legal briefs to argue, in highly technical language, that the pact of Confederation has never been equitably administered. The government of British Columbia won its elections for a great many years on the promise that some day Canada would give us justice—we who have been better off than any part of Canada.

Never since the days of Fort Victoria have we felt really a part of the spiritual fabric of Canada and even as late as the last depression a politician could talk about secession without being thought altogether insane. Always there have been men to argue that, without the drag of Canada, we could be more prosperous and happy. However, the new war is teaching us many things. It is teaching us that Canada is bigger than British Columbia, and that only strong, unified nations can survive.

British Columbia politics, however unbalanced on the subject of Canada, have been forward-looking and more progressive in social legislation than the politics of any other province, have developed a strong socialist party, and also have spent the taxpayers' money and contracted debt with an unequaled lavishness. Only the extraordinary basic wealth of the province and its income from natural resources could have supported such a structure, or tolerated the expensive political machines, with their faithful campaign-fund contributors, the brewing and liquor interests, for so long.

It has been a pleasant, tight little world, the politics of James Bay, with wondrous sham battles over things that didn't matter. That it should be all disrupted by the war and lose its point and glamour and public interest, is rather sad. The provincial government here, like all the provincial governments of Canada, has surrendered its importance and its power to the Dominion for the duration of the war and probably will never get them back again.

The real English touch of Victoria is to be found not in the city itself, but in the country around it, on the Saanich Peninsula. There, among the green spring fields and gnarled oaks, or lying on a summer haycock (no one has lived, said Ellen Terry, until he has slept in a hayfield) you might be in Kent. Even the Channel is there, with moving ships—our Gulf of Georgia.

In the October stubble you should easily find Keats's female Autumn, her hair soft-lifted by the winnowing wind, for it is with us a season of mists and mellow fruitfulness so like England that I fancy the poet would hardly know, if set down here now, that he had left home. If Keats were in my workroom now, as these lines are written, if he could look over the ripe fields, the rolling land, the blue haze in the pockets of the little hills, the gulls beating in, white from the sea, to follow the plowman and scream for worms, the pheasants croaking hoarsely, the quail advancing in single file, the first brown leaves fluttering down from the oaks, the yellow pumpkins on my vines, the fat onions, the red apples, the grinning tomatoes, the whispering of dried corn stalks, the English hedges, the last roses—if Keats were here this evening, he would admit, if pressed, that this was the Autumn he wrote about, this close bosom friend of the maturing Saanich sun.

Our October is a brown man, rough and countrybred, and he never ventures into the city yonder. He lives among stubble fields, swinging over them with giant strides, and in the deep woods you can hear his steps rustling among the dry oak leaves. You can hear his muttering sometimes through the branches that are getting bare now, and the sound of his panting through the firs.

He is a crisp, blunt man, October, but there is no guile in him, none of November's treachery, nor the deep gloom of December, the fickleness of the spring months, the soft decadence of summer. October is blunt, but you can see his smile on the ripening squashes and marrows, the happy flush of his cheeks is plain on the late apples, and sometimes if you listen carefully you can hear his jolly whistling in the song of the last meadow lark. And though he may go about glumly some days in a coat of tattered mist, and perhaps complain roughly in the croak of tree frog, in the evening the face of October will light up in the west with a vivid glow between the oak trees and you know, if you live in the country, that he is your friend.

Victoria and its countryside are only a small point on the southern tip of Vancouver Island. For nearly three hundred miles the island hugs the mainland shore in dark sweep of timber, rising to a backbone of mountains and glaciers. Most of it is uninhabited, much of it unexplored, a jungle in which you might often hope to travel a mile or two a day at best, without a trail.

Along its eastern shore clings another peculiar civilization of British origin—the exiles who found Victoria too metropolitan for them and now may be discovered in little overgrown farms, in lost and tumble-down houses amid the oak furniture and fine old silver of England. You need not be surprised if the man who emerges from the listing cowbarn has been a colonel in the British army of India, who came here originally to fish in the Cowichan River, or if the woman in the shapeless dress speaks in the unmistakable accents of Mayfair. Your neighbor down the road is probably the nephew of a lord.

Duncan used to be regarded as the most English town outside England and probably was, but even here a generation of new Canadians, sons of the old English settlers, cannot be prevented from growing up. Yet you will still find on the streets of Duncan some of the old breed.

I took a skeptical friend of mine from Winnipeg up there not long ago, bragging of our island civilization. On the first street we found a man in khaki shorts and the invariable tweed coat. My friend from Winnipeg began to look interested. Down the next street strode a lovely Colonel Blimp, with fly hooks all over his tweed hat. My friend gazed at him with innocent prairie admiration. And on my honor, with sworn evidence to support it, we found in the liquor store an old English gentleman in shorts, six inches of cotton drawers, and those long, shiny boots that the Life Guards wear on sentry duty at Whitehall. My Winnipeg friend capitulated and bought the whisky.

These folk, make no mistake, are the salt of the earth. They have known how to live—tea on the lawn, tennis at Koksilah, pleasant dances in the Agricultural Hall, the fall fair, everyone working on hospital committees, everyone feeling a public responsibility that is bred in England. A caste system, certainly, a frank recognition of gentility, but in a larger sense, democracy proving itself by results in a happy daily life.

Best of all, see them in the autumn when the Spring and Cohoe salmon are swarming into Cowichan Bay, and a hundred rowboats and a few Indians' dugouts are fishing, every fisherman wearing the special black and white sweaters of the Cowichan Indians, everyone punctilious in sportsmanship, careful of the rules, and modest in the great catch.

To the island streams, as up the mainland rivers, the salmon return in the cycle of nature which man can never understand. Four years they have been at sea, lost no one knows where in the outer reaches of the ocean, and then, when their appointed time has come, they surge back to their own rivers, each fish to the stream where it was hatched, and to no other, as has been proved over and over again by tags attached to their bodies. For a month they wait in Cowichan Bay, rolling, wallowing, leaping from the water in the last ecstasy of their lives, as if they knew that life soon would end.

With the first rains and the rise of the river, they rush into the fresh water, recognizing their own stream with sure instinct though they have left it years before as babies—knowing the sand bars where they were hatched and seeking them out now like their ancestors that have come here through the ages.

Up into the shallow trickles the female salmon writhes, though she is half dead now, battered and already rotting. Finally, just able to thrust herself upon the sand, she squeezes the eggs from her body, the male struggles in and fertilizes the little red globules with his milt, and, their cycle complete, the salmon die. On their carcasses hordes of immaculate white sea gulls feast through the lavish autumn.

About this process there is a perfect rightness that men have long sensed—the urgent quest, the sure finding, the production of young, the certain end. Happily the baby salmon goes to sea and happily returns in four years to his death. Gladly he has lived and gladly dies, and lays him down with a will— on the Cowichan, on Campbell River, and five hundred miles from the sea on the remote bars and tributaries of the Fraser.

At Cowichan, watching the perfect life cycle of the salmon, men seem to have learned a rhythm in their own lives, seem to have found a sense and meaning in life not common elsewhere. The salmon, perhaps, teach them how to die.

There are some fishermen, of course, who merely go a-fishing. I have seen rich men at Campbell River who boasted that they had spent two or three thousand dollars to catch their first fifty-pound Spring. I have seen them rising in the cold, an hour before dawn, day after day, and sitting, chilled and damp, in the stern of a rowboat while a guide rowed them around, waiting for a single jerk on the line. While I have always held that a two-pound trout on a fly rod was far more rousing sport, I have never regarded the confirmed salmon fisherman with hostility, but only with a deep compassion. For this madness there is no cure. Men will come from Texas and Iowa and California to feel a Spring on their lines, to be photographed at the official weighing station, to win a button from the Tyee Club.

The highway of the island goes north from Cowichan along the shore, close to the beach, where you can see the mainland mountains across the Gulf, large as the Rockies. It curves through the little farm clearings; past miles of blossoming broom that spurts out in May like an arrested fountain of gold spray; among the second-growth trees that have already blotted out the scars of old logging; into the ageless virgin timber of Cameron Lake, all that is left of the old forest beside the highway.

This land is rough yet, with fence lines untrimmed, stumps yet to be blown, houses yet to be painted. Give us time. It takes more than one generation to make a farm here. Give us a thousand years, as they have had in England, and we will make this landscape more beautiful than England's, for we have not only the makings of the foreground, the soil, the growth, the sea, the English climate, but we have as well a background of mountains and glaciers. In time it will be another England and another Switzerland combined, but long after we have gone. In our lifetime it will always be wild, and men's clearings mere footsteps in the forest.

Fifty-nine years ago William Todd came to the island. He had a gun, a shovel, a saw, an axe, and a goat. He cleared a few yards of land by a lake. He tethered his goat to a tree and watched to see that the cougars didn't get her. He built a cabin of cedar logs. He cleared more land with his hands, piling up the logs to burn in great piles in the winter. He struggled with shovel and axe in the thick mat of roots. He planted his first crop, fifty hills of potatoes. He got a cow and rowed her milk seven miles down the lake in an Indian dugout to trade it at the general store.

Fifty-nine years he labored, and today his farm has thirty acres cleared; about half an acre per year, a life's work in this jungle. The log cabin has grown by stages into a large and gracious house. There are big barns outside, and machinery. The two-foot maple trees that he dug out of the forest and planted in front of his door cover a circumference of two hundred feet, making shade in the summer.

Todd's son inherits a fine farm, but Todd is too old to reap the reward of it. That will go to the son and the son's son. In three generations, Todd says, the place will be about right. Often I have sat with him by the fire, and the old man, still tall and straight, with coal-black beard, looks out on the clearing with content. He can remember when he had nothing but a hundred square feet of clearing in the forest, with a goat tethered to a tree, and his gun propped against the trunk.

At Christmas they came to Todd's house and remembered the old days—Crazy Wilgress, who lives with his bees down the lake and eats nothing, apparently, but honey and lettuce; the Indian Colonel and his deaf wife with her ear trumpet; the ruined English family who came here expecting to find the land like England; the German count who went about his place stark naked for reasons of health and lifted the goat up to his wife's sickbed so that she could milk it.

After a few glasses of Mrs. Todd's plum wine old Wilgress would give his imitation of the one-armed Frenchman reciting the "Charge of the Light Brigade," they would drink solemnly to the King and the Empire, they would remember that lost land of England over the sea, which they would never see again, and Todd would never suspect that his life had been a complete success, accomplishing more for his country than the politicians and the men who counted themselves successful.

Yes, give us time.

With desperate longing men clear this land, cut down the forest, sell it, and live on it, but the forest still surges up again. This coastal vegetation of British Columbia has a terrible power of growth, which defies the strongest man, and yet a strange serenity, and a peculiar flavor of its own.

In the spring the sword ferns suddenly uncurl in brown, shaggy knots. The thick bracken and the frail maidenhair appear. White trilliums shoot up overnight. A smell of sap and growth wells up out of the wet, matted earth. Then the succulent, growing forest is friendly and welcomes you.

In summer its springy floor is dry. Underfoot the rank

leaves of salal, the thick bed of fir needles crackle as you walk. The forest is parched, utterly still, as if it were panting and sweltering in the heat. There is no sound but the hum of insects and the faint distant drumming of a grouse, which is part of the silence. Soon there will be a blue haze over the forest and the faint smell of smoke. Fires up north. The forest is turning grim now and you begin to fear it. No power in the world like a forest fire on the wind.

In the autumn the maples turn to big puffs of pure gold against the forest's dark mass, and the first leaves start to flutter down shyly, until they form a thin yellow mat on the ground. Soon the forest, drinking in the rain, comes to life. The great trees fling wild arms against the sky, two hundred feet from the ground, shouting in a frenzy. Down below, the creak of branches in the dusk is like a ghost sound in an abandoned house. When the rain comes and nothing within miles is dry, and you are lying under a wet tent in wet blankets, with a roar of sound above, the forest is like a cunning enemy, crushing you, blinding you, entangling you, and sucking you into its maw.

Cut it down and it rises again. Clear your land with labor of hand and dynamite, spend four or five hundred dollars an acre on it, drag out the old stumps and the network of roots and underbrush—still the forest is watching from the edge of your clearing. Go away for five years and it will march in again. Some day, when men grow tired, it will reclaim every inch of this coast. Hundreds of years ago fire burned across half of Vancouver Island, but now only a few charred stumps are left among the growth of new jungles. Nothing can hold them down.

Another type of men, as different from the English exiles as a separate race, struggles with the forest.

Rolf Erickson hangs his bottle of precious saw oil on a branch. With thin, double-bitted falling axe he chops a gash into the six-foot trunk of a Douglas fir, grunting at every stroke. His partner, the little Finn, does the same on the other side. They work silently in flannel undershirt, short overalls, and calked boots. Into the holes they fit the steel hooks of their springboards, and on these flimsy perches, eight feet from the ground, they chop their undercut, neat and smooth as if it had been done with a single stroke. It will make the tree fall where they want it, within a yard.

From the other side they saw their main cut until there are but four inches of the trunk left. Then, with a yell of "Timber!" they drive their steel wedges into the cut and run back quickly into the forest. The two-hundred-foot column of wood, the growth of five hundred years, shudders for an instant and then goes over with a retching sound, the sound of torn wood cells and little trees crashing, and a hollow boom as the great trunk hits the ground.

Now Rolf saws it up, saws it from below where it straddles the other timber, to prevent its splitting, his saw resting on the handle of his embedded axe. Far off he can hear the whisper of other saws and the constant whistle of the donkey engines on the railway. Soon the high rigger will be along, climbing the selected spar tree, with axe and saw dangling from his belt, topping it a hundred feet up, clinging to it as the trunk sways like an uncoiled spring, rigging cables to it, block and tackle. Presently the hook-tender with his choker-men will wrap cables around the throats of the cut logs, the whistle punk will pull his signal wire, the donkey engine drums will turn. Then three logs, choked close together, tails lashing in agony, bare ends blank and huge like the faces of sea monsters, will be hauled into the air, dragged in crazy dance through the tortured forest, and landed as neatly as kindling sticks on the flat cars.

Watch your signals . . . stand clear of the line's bite . . . beware the stem-winder and the widow-makers . . . race along the logs on calked shoes . . . swing your hooks into her

. . . and away before she can drop and crush you like an insect . . . highball her through, for the train is waiting.

Like a brown snake a mile long, the logs curl through the bush to the sea, leap into the booming yard with a white dash of water and settle down, conquered at last, the centuries of growth finished, fit now only for men's uses, forever lost to the wind, the winter rain, the spring flow of sap, the company of the forest.

Soon the tugs will drag the booms down the Gulf and the headsaws will eat the wood with fearful appetite. Behind is left the churned-up ruin of the land, the pitch smell of branches, bark, and little trees in a deep welter where the forest once stood. In the fall these will be burned over, with a blast like a blowtorch, to remove the fire hazard of the slash. Nothing will remain but the blackened earth, where the ferns grew and the trilliums and yellow violets beside a dark brook.

For miles and miles out to the horizon the forest land is flattened and blackened as men harvest this crop. But see, among the old black logs, some green is sprouting—bold sprouts of willow, alder, maple, and nameless brush; at last the squat thrust of fir and hemlock seedlings. In a few years this will be impenetrable second growth. Nine out of ten trees must die to make way for the strongest, but in the end the forest always wins, if men will leave it alone, without fire, to its work of reproduction.

Tough men, our coastal lumberjacks, and, like so many others, unlike the world's picture of them. Small men, mostly, wiry, agile as monkeys; living in Gargantuan style on such food as you will hardly find in the best hotels; insisting on shower baths and clean sheets for their beds; going to town, going to the Vancouver Skidway for a binge, and, with a fierce lust for the woods, returning always to them; cutting them, loading them, despoiling them, and yet, in a curious way, loving them.

Far to the north and west the untouched forest stretches to the edge of the Pacific. There men have cut only a few tiny nicks into its side—the little canneries and mining camps, clinging to the cliff edge, the Indian village on the clam beach. All else is the silent, hungry growth of wood, the surge of sap.

A few miles from the logging camps, the donkey engines, the railways, the devastation, you will come upon such pleasant and quiet spots as Comox, like an English town beside the sea, and the blue sweep of Comox Bay, with glaciers behind it, lovelier than the lakes of Italy. To see it in the dawn is to look at an ocean as still as an oil painting, and as vivid.

Down by Qualicum, as we drive southward, the sun is cutting the Gulf like light through a polished gun barrel, and the porpoise form of Texada Island swims black in the water. Now morning smoke begins to curl from the tin chimneys of the cabins, where the neglected roses grow on the porch. Parksville is awake, and an old man stands blinking in the little vegetable garden that he has hewed out of the forest. On the Malahat a doe and her mottled fawn stand gaping, with upraised ears, and from here you can look across the Arm to the dog's tail of the Saanich Peninsula, curled up into the Gulf.

Victoria will be just getting to work as you drive down Government Street, the civil servants pouring across the Causeway, the English exile lady tending her roses, her husband taking pen in hand to address to the editor of the *Colonist* his opinion of the German dictator and of the pressure of the city waterworks.

The Buckskin

Joey Joseph, of the Three Horse Reservation, sat on the cowboys' bench in Michael O'Shea's kitchen. "How many dead people you said in the war?" Joey Joseph said. He had not come to talk about the war. He had come to sell his buckskin pony, but this had to be done with a decent delay.

"Hundreds of thousands killed in the war," Michael said, and tried to keep his eyes off the buckskin, tied to the porch rail.

Joey pondered that for a long time and asked again: "How many you said killed in the war?"

"Hundreds of thousands," Michael said patiently.

Joey thought about it again and then he said: "By God, that's too many dead people!"

"Look, you want to sell that horse?" Michael said.

"Maybe," Joey said. "I dunno. Worth hunnert dollars. Easy."

"I'll give you twenty-five," Michael said.

They settled at fifty. Joey went out and took off the saddle and bridle and stored them in Michael's barn. He stood for a moment running his hand along the buckskin's back. He had raised it from a colt, kept it in his house through the first winter, broken it. Up at Quesnel and at Ashcroft it had won all the cowboy races. Everybody knew Billy, Joey Joseph's horse. But Joey wanted to buy an automobile. He could get one for fifty dollars at Lillooet, a 1929 Ford. It would run. Joey pictured himself driving into town with his wife and his mother in the back seat. Certainly a man must have an automobile.

He walked down the road towards the reservation, but

stopped to look back at Billy. The buckskin's ears were up. He whinnied to Joey, but Joey turned around and walked on as fast as he could in his high-heeled boots.

That night Billy jumped the corral fence and was at the door of Joey's cabin in the morning. Joey rode him up to Michael's ranch, bareback, and tied him to the porch. Michael put the buckskin in a box stall, but in the night he kicked it down and Joey found him at his door again next day. Again Joey rode him up bareback and handed him over to Michael. Tonight, he said, he was going to take the bus down to Lillooet and get his car. He told Michael to tie Billy up better. Michael tied him up better, but in the night he broke the halter and started down the hill.

Next morning early Joey rode him up to Michael's place, bareback. No one was up at the ranch yet. Joey went to the stable and got his saddle and bridle and put them on Billy. He went into the kitchen and left something on the table. He mounted Billy and galloped down the hill. When Michael got up, he found his fifty dollars in crumpled bills on the kitchen table.

That is why Joey Joseph never did get his automobile.

CHAPTER EIGHTEEN

Cariboo Road

It was midnight when we crossed the Fraser at Hope. Behind us lay Vancouver, asleep in its bed. In front of us the Cariboo Road, frosty in the autumn. A few miles more and we could smell it—the first stinging, sharp smell of the Dry Belt, of sage brush and pine tree, mixed with the smell of parched clay earth. In little more than a mile, the coast jungle ended abruptly and the open interior began.

We breathed the new dry air hungrily. "It's still here!" Jean said. After our long absence we almost feared it would not be here, unchanged, the Cariboo, the other world we used to know. I stepped on the gas.

There was fog in the canyon of the Fraser. A thousand feet below us, in the black trough, a false white river of mist rolled along. Deep down under that the true river rumbled. We should have stopped. To drive through a night mist on this road, cut thinly into the living wall of the canyon, is madness, but we were always mad on the way to Cariboo. At the end of the road the great plateau was waiting and the house of Michael O'Shea.

Through Yale we drove, and not a light to be seen by the river—old Yale that had been the beginning of the road in the gold rush, crammed with miners and fancy ladies. Nothing left of it now but a few ruined cherry trees and the wooden church. No light at Boston Bar either, no light on China Bar or Jackass Mountain (what stories in these names!) and little Lytton sound asleep. They had never slept in the old days, from one year's end to the other, not when the gold rush was tramping up the Cariboo Road.

With logs and flimsy props they strung the road along the walls of the Fraser, lashing it to the rock with wire, and on the flats they twisted it around every rock and stump in their haste. From Fort Yale, where the steamboats stopped, to Barkerville their ox teams and six-horse stagecoaches hardly allowed the dust to settle all summer. They came on horseback and on foot. They pushed their possessions in double-ended wheelbarrows. They fought the Indians who rolled stones down on them from the cliffs. They were massacred at Black Rock and drowned in the river. But the rush went on to Cariboo.

On Williams Creek they had found gold and panned out great nuggets in Stout's Gulch, in Antler Creek, Lightning Creek, and Lowhee, and hit the glittering bedrock in Barker's shaft. There were 500 miles of forest, desert, and canyon to the coast, but distance was nothing with gold at the end of it. Toil was nothing, or danger. They scrambled up the river bars, they cut their incredible trail by the Harrison, they built their toy railway between the lakes, they laid out their new road in the canyon. By '62, millions of dollars were coming out of Barkerville, under armed guards, in nuggets and dust. British Columbia had been discovered by the world, was coveted by the Americans, and had become necessary to the projected nation of Canada.

No such wild adventure in Canada's history as this rush to Cariboo—the steamboats on the river rapids, the laboring freight convoys and lumbering oxen, the German girls in silks and satins on their way to the dance halls, the first steam tractor, which wouldn't work, the pack camels imported from China, which scared every horse and mule team into the river, the fortunes made and lost, the emptied creeks, the ebb of the tide down the broken road.

On the very bones of the gold road the new Cariboo Road is built. In places you can see abandoned stretches of the old road itself, narrow with steep grades, clinging to the canyon side, and a few ruined houses that once glittered with light as the stagecoaches stopped to change horses. Now, in the evening, when the shadows move suddenly down the mountains, and the mountains turn into a flat wall of darker darkness at arm's length—then even a stranger, standing by the old road on the lip of the canyon, with the steady gurgle of the Fraser down below, can surely hear the sound of the stagecoaches rattling along in the dust, the beat of hooves, the marching feet.

Perhaps the canyon of the Fraser is not beautiful, like the gracious river that drains the eastern half of Canada. The Fraser is too furious, stark, and lonely for mere beauty. It is angry with the scowl of black hills and the welter of riven stone. It is melancholy with perpetual shadows and gouged with fearful wrinkles. Through this dark canyon forever bores the river, deepening its trench, boiling, swirling in brown and frenzied tide, raging at every jut of rock, cutting down cliffs and tearing at the thin islands of stone that lie in it like the funneled shapes of battleships. Forever it moves and churns with steady power and sure purpose, a roar deep in its throat. It is jealous even of the single wind-blown pine tree at its edge, and of the frail light that gleams through the darkness, and of men's presence here.

The St. Lawrence is the friend and servant of man. The Fraser is forever hostile and beyond taming. No man can stand on the cliff and look down at the brown line of the river, or stand beside the vast swirl and look up at the chaos of the hills, without fear and loneliness. Men's villages at the canyon's edge will all disappear some day, an incident in this million years of struggle between stone and water. All men, all men's civilizations are but a moment in this contest—a brief gold rush, soon to ebb again.

Up among the Rockies the snow melts in the spring. At its edge, overnight, the yellow avalanche lily opens with a tiny

shout of joy. The green moss sucks up the moisture like a
sponge until it can hold no more, and a drip of cold water
rolls from the edge of the rock. Presently it is a trickle, then
a brook, and then a river, hurrying northward in the mountain trench, curving to the west, turning south again through
the cliffs of clay, gathering up its hourly tons of dirt. Now it
is rolling in color of treacle through the canyon, through the
terrible, unyielding gut of Hell's Gate, out into the broad
meadows, and into the sea. At last the brown swell of it cuts
the green salt water in clear, sharp line, as if they were divided
by a wall of steel.

It is Father Fraser, beside whom we have lived in this country since our first coming. Even before we came the Indians
clung to his unfriendly side, netting the salmon as they came
up for the autumn spawning. A slide of rock from the blast of
the railway builders blocked the channel years ago, and the
breeding fish were battered to pieces as they tried to stem the
current. By international treaty Canada and the United States
are trying to restore the remnant of the old hordes, but the
Indians with long nets and spears still take fish from the river
in the fall. You can follow the migration of the Fraser's fish,
the powerful sockeye, growing red in their last days, into the
remote streams of the interior. All life has traveled by this
channel through the mountains, as we traveled tonight.

Jean laughed. "Do you remember Percy?" I remembered
Percy, the old writing man. He had come here with us on our
first journey, when the new road was half finished, resolved to
take copious notes, so that he might write in detail of the road
and the river.

"And when Percy got home," Jean reminded me, "he looked
at his notebook to find out about the river and all he had
written was, 'It goes in and it comes out.' Poor Percy!"

"Well," I said, "what better can you say of the river? It
goes in and it comes out. Nobody knows any more about it

than that. Nobody will ever understand it. Nobody will be able to put it down in words, ever."

"It's like the countryside of England," Jean said. "Once you've seen it, you're never the same again. Percy was right. It goes in with the clouds and the wind and the rain and it comes out like this."

There it was, rolling below us, a flat glitter in the light of the October moon, like a stream of metal poured between the hills and already hardened in its mold. Beside it, the headlight of a train flashed around a curve, no larger than a glow worm. We caught the sound of the train's faint whistle, saw the green and red lights glow for a moment on the last car, and go out. The existence of Canada as a nation has always depended on the railway tracks in this canyon, the shuttle of goods back and forth from the coast. In good times the long wheat trains labored along the river. Tonight the overloaded flat cars carried lumber for the bombed-out cities of Britain.

We turned out to the Lillooet road now, and the Dry Belt grew more pungent in our nostrils—the pine trees of red bark, the clean, medicinal sage brush, and by the roadside the leaves of sumac spurting, like arterial blood, from the cracked clay banks. Around the narrow bends we crawled, the river straight below. We clung to the inward bank through the patches of mist. We groped, blind and terrified, but drawn on by the power of the old road and the promise of the Cariboo beyond.

Past Lillooet the dawn broke out of a pale eastward streak. Suddenly, almost in a moment, the flat hills took on shape, bulk, and dimension and seemed to rush at us—no longer the tortured mountains of the canyon but the rounded clay hills and rolling range of the Dry Belt. It was the Cariboo, and it was the autumn of the uplands. The poplar trees seemed to boil like yellow paint far across the hills, just before the fall of the leaves.

The smoke was pouring out of the tin chimney of Annie

Joseph's cabin as we passed through the Indian village. The aged Indian woman stood blinking in the doorway at us, her calf by her side. Always Annie had a calf, begged from some relative on the rancheree, fed on wisps of hay that she had swept up from the railway cars. She had lived for years in a shack made of coal-oil cans and cardboard boxes, but now she had this abandoned cabin beside the white church, considering it a life of luxury, with her calf under a sound roof with her at last. We waved to her and she raised a withered hand.

Then up the five miles of switch-back hill, up through dwarf pine and juniper, up a mile in the air above Vancouver until, rounding the last curve, we saw the ranch of the O'Sheas. Nothing had changed. Nothing ever would change—the huge house, the litter of fences, corrals, pens, and barns, all weathered until they seemed to grow out of the range and draw their life from it like a tree.

Milton John came out of the barn, rubbing sleep from his eyes, and his grin showed his teeth in solid row of gold. The little Indian, with lean monkey's face, seemed to live in the barn, in a confusion of old saddles, bridles, and leather chaps. A rusty six-shooter hung in its holster by the nail. David O'Shea had carried it in the gold rush. Two lines of horses chewed their hay with a cheerful morning sound. I could hear the black stallion pawing nervously in the box stall. "Klahowya!" said Milton John.

We went up to the kitchen. At his stove (like a small locomotive) Sam Kee was lighting the fire. The old Chinaman paused to shake hands with us and hurriedly boiled coffee. Michael O'Shea and the family were not awake. We sat drinking Kee's coffee and looking about the house as if we had never seen it before.

They built the first of it in 1860, before the Cariboo Road was finished, when the gold rush came north on the Lillooet trail, over Pavilion Mountain. Since then they had added so many wings to it, so many stairways, galleries, rooms, and cupboards that the house had a complicated geography and seemed to keep swelling and unfolding like some strange and fearful flower.

The broad bench by the kitchen door was worn in the middle where the Indian cowboys sat shyly, waiting for their orders. There were lassoes and chaps on the walls that had hung there, apparently, for half a century. The floor of the dining room, at the head of the long table, was double-grooved where the first O'Shea, Michael's grandfather, used to push back his chair after saying grace. His picture, a man bearded like a black bear, hung on the wall by his old place. Beside the stove of the living room, on the wooden wall, there was still a dark smudge from his lamp. Here he read the Bible and Shakespeare through the long winter nights, when the ranch was snowbound, the road closed, the nearest neighbor twenty-five miles off, and he sat up to keep the fires going.

Throughout that house was a tangible sense of habitation, the feeling of lives lived there, of women who had borne children, of men who had watched the spring come and the first winter snow and the cold sunset, of old folks who had died under this roof.

On the knoll above the house, by a single twisted pine tree, the first O'Shea lay with his wife and two sons. Martha long outlived him, riding side-saddle, screaming her orders to the hired hands, bellowing at the Chinese cook, nursing the wives of remote settlers. On the day they buried her in a homemade coffin, the whites and Indians came from hundreds of miles around, until all the food ran out. They filled the parlor to look at her, sang hymns while Miss Piddington played the squeaky organ, hauled her to the grave on a newly painted farm wagon, and waited while the minister from Lillooet read the service, his white surplice blowing in the cold March wind. When he had finished, the Indians, who had been Martha's friends, chanted their own service around the new mound of earth.

Now life went on much as ever except for the trucks and

gasoline tractors—still the bawling of sheep in the spring, the sick lambs lying around the kitchen stove, the first swallows building mud houses in the eaves, the cowboys cleaning the ditches to save every drop of the precious irrigation water, fresh from the snow. Then the summer harvest with gangs of Indians crowding about the table at noon. Then winter, with the roads blocked.

Still at Christmas all the O'Sheas arrived by train, automobile, sleigh, and horseback, Aunt Geraldine from Clinton with twenty pounds of fruit cake and her canary in a cage. On Christmas Eve the Indians rode up from their village, their children clinging behind them, to receive trinkets, candies, and plum puddings in the kitchen. They sang their carols, left their presents of buckskin gloves and knitted sweaters and rode off again under the bright stars, with clink of horseshoe on frozen ground, puffs of white breath in the cold air.

Always, winter and summer, the ranch lay in infinite space, the brown range running to the edge of the mountain and dropping off suddenly into the canyon. Beyond that only the hard sky, the ragged line of mountains, and straight down below, as if you could leap into them, a string of deep blue lakes, like tears in the wrinkles of the canyon. Here on the plateau of the O'Sheas you are on the very top of the world, which lies around you, washing the edge. Its waves break vainly on this safe island.

Michael and I rode out over the range. As always, I recognized the quiet success of this man's life and the failure of mine. Here was a man who had learned the satisfaction of land and space and had never known, in this stillness, the loneliness of cities. A man who knew crops and loved horses, who never went to bed without a last look into the barn, pausing there to listen to the steady chewing sound in the darkness, and speaking to his old saddle horse, Rags, who was too old to work. How surely Michael sat his roan horse, a huge figure with a shock of red hair, unconscious of his looks, simple with a simplicity which was wiser than wisdom and deeper than knowledge.

He showed me his cattle, his new irrigation ditches, the green smear on the brown range which had yielded its third crop of alfalfa. Then we rode off the range into the timber and over to the canyon of the Fraser. Everywhere the little round poplar leaves were spinning frantically, tugging at their twigs, and many of them lay already on the ground like gold coins. In a few days, Michael guessed, the first snow would come.

I remembered riding with him here in a blizzard, in search of lost cattle, riding old Baldy, who cunningly placed his feet in the tracks of Michael's roan. I could see nothing ahead that day but the roan's dim shape, until I thought we would never get out of it alive. Suddenly, at nightfall, the big barn loomed up, like land in a storm, and the precious gleam of a light shone through the snow.

Now we were out of the timber again and on a nose of clay straight above the river. From here the Fraser looked no broader than your hand. Around it the clay hills were rounded and grooved as if they had been kneaded by human fingers. A few green patches of irrigated land, the size of torn postage stamps, clung to the cliffs above the river, and we could have dropped a stone on them.

Down there, too small for us to see, the ferryman rowed his boat across the brown swell, living alone in awful communion with the river. Often he had found corpses floating down. One night a man came staggering to the ferry, his wife on his back. Crossing the river, they started to climb the goat's trail to the road. The woman bore her child there on the trail, and the man carried them up to a ranch house.

Many times I had stood here, looking down the trench of the Fraser until it disappeared into the mountains beyond. I had seen it in winter under snow. I had seen it in April when the green ice rolled along it, and spring marched up the valley at one stride in the night. You could almost see the hills turn green then, with the sprouting of the bunchgrass, and the willows seemed to catch fire and glow red beside the irrigation ditches, and the air was full of a hundred spring smells, newly released from the frozen ground. I had seen it in the baking summer when the brown earth cracked, the parched bunchgrass complained in dry whisper under the wind, and the hot pine trees sweated with pungent resin and gasped for breath. Riding home through the irrigated lands in the darkness, with the slosh of hoofs in the irrigation ditches, I had breathed the sweet, sensual smell of alfalfa bloom; and the stars, over the creased velvet of the hills, were just above the horses' heads.

Now, in the autumn, the hills lay silent and dead, waiting for the winter. A cold wind blew down the river trench, swishing the horses' manes. "Snow," Michael said. "Snow tomorrow, maybe. An early winter."

Vancouver was just rising now for breakfast. Let it rise. The world of men was a hundred thousand miles from us here, on another planet. The Cariboo had no concern with it and never yet had sensed its fearful change. Why tell it what had happened down the road?

Always the Cariboo has been like that, its own world, hearing only vague echoes of the world beyond the mountains. If beef prices are above six cents on the hoof at the P. G. E. Railway station, there is no need to worry; and even if they are down to three cents and below production cost in a world depression, Cariboo never seems to change its ways. The same unvarying life at the O'Sheas; in the big ranches of the Chilcotin Plateau to the west, where the cattle are thick on every hill; in the little towns; in Mackenzie's general store at Williams Lake (Rod Mackenzie founded his fortune by ordering English billiard tables in mistake for dinner tables and selling them to the bewildered South African farmers before the Boer War); in Ashcroft, where Mrs. Al Johnson's green parrot swears perpetually at the loungers outside the beer parlor; in the stopping house where the English hostess used to wear a London evening frock to serve your dinner.

Always the same. In more than twenty years, while the out-side world crumbled to pieces, I have observed only one real organic change in the life of the Cariboo. In the old stopping houses they used to make the women of the household eat in the kitchen, after the men had finished in the dining room. Now the women have been emancipated and eat with the men. Of this the old-timers properly take a dark view.

As Jean and I drove away we looked back from the height of land, over the miles of range, the patches of green alfalfa, the intricate crisscross pattern of yellow poplar, and behind it all the sharp teeth of the mountains. Far off, a mere dot, the great ranchhouse clung to the range. The world paused forever at the plateau edge. This land of the O'Sheas was safe.

The Cariboo Road winds endlessly into the north. It is more than a road. It is life. By it every tiny village, every ranch and settler lives. They cling to it like children to their mother, watch every rut in it, know every bump, ask news of its distant stretches. Each wayside house is marked and named by the milestone of the road. It is their servant and their master. Always it beckons them on. It is like a mistress to be loved.

Up to the north it goes through the naked hills of the Ash-croft country, where the tomatoes and potatoes grow on the irrigated benches through the hot night; up through the weary jackpine by the Hundred Mile; past the Hundred and Twenty-Two and the open valley of Lac La Hache and Murphy's and the Australian; through Quesnel, a-doze beside the Fraser, and eastward through narrow gorges to Barkerville.

When I first saw Barkerville it was a ghost to make you shudder deliciously. The single street of drunken cabins was crushed between the churned gravels of Williams Creek and the shoulder of the hill. No house was in place, none level, all mounted on tipsy stilts during the gold rush, because the gravel kept rising all around as it poured out of the sluice boxes. On a wet night the creek seemed to seep through the log dykes and flow down the empty street. The rain drummed on the broken roofs and creaking sidewalks, and trickled in eerie sound from the eaves. Every black cabin door was filled with presences that you did not seek to discover.

We fled from it to the big drum stove of Kelly's Hotel, and there was old Bill Brown sitting in the corner, behind his square yard of white beard, nearly a hundred years old now. He was the last of the originals of '62, the Argonauts. We had four men in our party, and Bill trudged out of town angrily, back to his lonely cabin in the hills. He said Barkerville was getting too crowded.

We sang hymns that night down at Tregillus' house, around an old organ, as was the custom of the household. We played billiards on a table carted on the backs of mules over the Cariboo Road. We slept in a huge mahogany bed. We bought nuggets of gold from a Chinaman in an evil-smelling store, who weighed them by dim lamplight on an ivory scales, and we watched a poker game which, they said, went on all winter. Another time we carried a piano along the flooded street and set it up with half a dozen oil lamps in the old opera house, and danced where they used to watch the melodramas and the dancing girls in the sixties.

Thousands of miners crowded the single street in those days, spilling their gold dust on the bars, drinking, fighting, whoring, and returning to the creeks, broke, to shovel gravel, to dig shafts, to build sluices. Always there was plenty more gold, another creek. Cariboo Cameron made a million, they say, not a quarter of mile from town and lost it and was buried on the hill above his claim. But the gold ran out at last.

Barkerville is no longer the ghost town we used to know. It has been repaired, reroofed, cleaned up, painted, so that only the old church at the end of the street, beautifully brown and weathered, remains as an authentic touch of the gold rush—

the church and the mounds of gravel for miles along the creek, where gold was washed.

Barkerville is now the ghost of a ghost, and we were glad we had seen it in the days of splendid poverty. Now Bill Brown was gone and Harry Jones and the Pack Rat, who had so filled his cabin with old papers, tin cans, scrap iron, and useless junk that there was hardly room for his stove and bed. But Tregillus was still there. A newcomer the Argonauts thought him. He had been here only fifty-odd years.

Tregillus was a hard-rock man from Devonshire, who had come long after the placer gold had been drained from the creeks. He spent his life picking holes into the solid hillside, searching for the mother lode of ore. A few years ago he found it, or something like it, and an American mining company paid him enough to keep him well the rest of his life, and his children after him. Tregillus did not go away or even change his house. This narrow gorge beside the creek, this crazy street, the vegetable garden twenty feet square which he packed in by wheelbarrow from the hills, are all he asks for a lifetime of toil and faith. The old man, with dark placid face and white whiskers, rocked contentedly in his chair now because he had found what he was looking for—not money but quartz gold, the lode from which, through incalculable ages, the nuggets and dust washed into the creeks. He had proved his theory among the men who scoffed at him, and he was satisfied.

Jack Song was there, too, cooking at Kelly's Hotel, very old now, ready to go back to China and die, as soon as the Japanese got out. Song walked up the road on foot from New Westminster fifty-seven or fifty-eight years ago (he couldn't be quite sure) and got a job cooking at Kelly's. He is there still, with the laughing eyes and utter serenity to be found only in old Chinamen. Soon he will be gone, too, and the lavish meals that he loves to spread all at once on the table in front of you.

Up in Stout's Gulch, which yielded millions of dollars in gold, two men were working now, young Swedes who shoveled over the old worked-out gravel and threw it into a rough sluice box. One of them held up a little pepper can for me to see. The bottom of the can was covered with small nuggets and gold dust. "Poor wages, that's all," he said.

Since 1862 men have turned this gravel over and over again. Farther up the gulch, on the Lowhee claims, a stream of water is channeled into narrowing pipes until it is compressed in hydraulic monitors like giant nozzles on a garden hose. Out of the monitors it gushes with force sufficient to tear away a hillside. With nothing but water the miners have bored thus since the sixties, until they have cut a new canyon for miles into the mountains. We looked down now on the water cannon blasting away the gravel, hurling down the boulders, and washing them into the sluice box, which coiled away and was lost in the gorge. From where we stood the men by the monitor were no larger than ants in the trench that they had cut.

A little way from Barkerville the old Richfield courthouse still stands. At Richfield, Judge Begbie (the terrible Hanging Judge) used to bring such justice into the gold rush that there was hardly any crime from one end of the road to the other. Nevertheless, four men, I once reported, had been hanged together behind the jail. Indignant at this slight on the lawful behavior of the old days, Jim Leighton wrote me that only three had swung from the gibbet. Only three. Mr. Leighton should know, the last living man who saw it, the only surviving Argonaut, now gone from the valley.

Justice still follows Begbie's stern principles. In a court down the road, I watched a young judge try a man who broke out of the Barkerville jail and shot at a policeman. Only the prisoner was there, the judge in black gown, a policeman, and I, in a sweltering room that smelled of pine resin. A cow grazed outside the window, her bell clanking. But every refinement of the law was observed, the prisoner given every protection, addressed courteously, offered counsel and a jury, and, pleading guilty, was sentenced to seven years in the penitentiary. It all took about fifteen minutes. In that hot courtroom, the cowbell clanking outside the window, you could see how justice has always followed the road; also what Canada is fighting the war for—the joint rights of society but the guaranteed rights of the individual who quarrels with it.

We drove away from Barkerville, secretly sad at its rebirth. In the graveyard above the creek a man was digging a new grave. Beside him, the wooden crosses of the gold rush, over the bones of the Argonauts, were rotting fast.

Down the road a piece is Wells, the brawling, raw, and friendly town that lode gold has built on the muskeg by Jack of Clubs Lake. It is a young man's town, the authentic modern mining camp, without a garden or a shade tree, with all modern conveniences suddenly dumped into the wilderness. Once a week, on Fridays, the ladies from the red-light district up the creek are allowed to come to town to see the doctor.

At Quesnel we stopped for two days of pony races and dancing. It was here we saw the Scottish piper leading a parade of Indians and heard the town band, of which a classic story is told. When "God Save the King" had been played and all the other instruments were silent, the drummer suddenly added a tremendous beat on his drum. "The trouble was," he explained to the band leader, "I was watching the music too close, and played a fly speck." It was here, too, that we watched the flaming sunset, which an old stage driver once declared was "pretty good for a little town of two thousand people."

North again to Prince George, and here, more than five hundred miles from Vancouver, we were still only halfway up to the top of British Columbia, not quite halfway from the Rockies to the coast. Half of the province to the north is almost empty, spanned nowadays by airplanes on their way to Alaska.

All this way that we had followed from Vancouver will be part of the road to Alaska some day, most of it through the empty, untouched wilderness of the north—a thousand new miles of road to build. Meanwhile Canada dots the wilderness with air fields, American bombers drop down into Prince George almost every day, and Canadians feel as never before the common partnership that defends America. Also, up here, it is a queer thing to observe an Indian who has never seen a railway or an automobile calmly board a plane with his sled dogs and pack, and settle down for a snooze.

At Prince George I always pause for a talk with Harry Perry, who writhes in agony of editorial composition so that the weekly *Citizen* may proclaim the truth of the world crisis, and very sagely. From Harry you can get rare stories of the old days (old not by years but by tradition and legend) when the railway came through. Like that exquisite and true tale of Prince George's first efforts to steal the lucrative whisky and red-light business away from South Fort George.

They persuaded a lady to build a luxurious house of pleasure in Prince George, gave a grand opening party with all prominent citizens invited, and next day the police, influenced by the commercial barons of South Fort George, promptly closed the resort. This was a commercial disaster for the new city, but it salvaged what it could. The abandoned palace of joy was used as the first city hall, worthy of the dignity of a new mayor.

The road goes west through the lake country, where you may travel by canoe three hundred miles without a portage, and into the Indian country.

At Fort St. James, where white men first grew crops on this side of the Rockies, you can watch the Indians weaving fish nets, tanning moose hides, sewing birchbark. They are quite unspoiled. Once I sat in a clean Indian house while the chief talked to the lieutenant-governor in the florid style of the old days—talked about his hunting rights, the poverty of his people, the duty of the Great White Father. Finally he presented a paddle to the visitor, who, with great presence of mind, handed over his silver-tipped walking stick in return. The whole thing was done with utmost dignity and no thought of publicity or effect.

Farther up the road we paused to make way for a curious procession of Indians, chanting in Latin, a priest in black gown in front, two men carrying a small, rough coffin, an Indian woman weeping behind it.

At an Indian school we drank tea at the table of an aged priest, with wonderfully serene eyes, who would have been happy among the Jesuits in the old Iroquois villages.

In Hazelton, further to the west, you are in an Indian trading post. The sidewalks are crowded with old men and their squaws. The stores are full of furs and trade goods and the smell of buckskin. These are no movie Indians or hangers-on to be dressed up for war dances on holidays. These are the same Indians who fought the white men because the white witchcraft had produced a fatal epidemic of measles. This is the country of Kitwancool Jim, who murdered a white man for his devil tricks and led an Indian war until the soldiers arrived from the coast. This is the town where Simon Peter Gunanoot shot a white man who had insulted his wife and hid out in the wilderness for fifteen years against all the powers of the Crown and its police. He finally surrendered, to be found innocent by a jury for lack of evidence, and to die respected by everyone.

In the evening we walked past the edge of the town, beside the Skeena. On the river bank Jean poked her head into a dark shack, and screamed. There in the dusk, with grinning face, wild hair, and horrid convulsion of limbs, was a dummy, dressed in white men's clothes—some kind of idol to be worshiped or feared. We went away from there. By the river an Indian woman squatted, smoking a short pipe, silhouetted black against the sunset and still as the idol.

We climbed up the hill to the graveyard of Hazelton. The "dead houses" are crowded together there in a village of their own, each crammed with the owner's possessions—a sewing machine, an old photograph, some boots or a chair. Gimcrack houses of fretwork and intricate fences, some with domes and minarets, some with little stone totem poles, carved at factories in the east and sanctified by the Christian church, which forbids the noble wooden poles of the old pagans.

Once, long ago, I stood here on the night of the year's longest day. At eleven o'clock in this latitude I could read a newspaper. Above me, almost within reach, was the perfect pyramid of Rocher de Boule, the mountain of the rolling rocks. Down below, the Bulkley and Skenna rivers joined abruptly, wedging in the narrow townsite of Hazelton. The air in that northern sunset was of a quality I had never seen before, as if fine specks of gold floated in it, as if you could sift them out with a net. In this graveyard with its dead houses, silent now in the twilight, there was a feeling of loneliness, of unseen presence and horror not to be described. Nothing Christian here, despite the crosses, no thought of Christian resurrection. It was the haunt of savages who would rise again in demon form.

An aged Indian, dressed in tweed sports coat, old-fashioned English knee breeches, and moccasins, and carrying a cane, came suddenly out of the bushes and stood looking intently at a grave with a carved headstone. As I learned afterwards, he was a rich man who had already raised his own monument, with his name and a recital of his virtues on it. He frequently came here to admire it in the quiet evening. But I didn't know that then. I only beheld this apparition in the shadows, among the houses of the dead. I got up and walked very quickly down the hill and felt foolish when I reached the bottom.

From the cliffs of the canyon of Hagwilget you can still see half a dozen broken posts wedged into the rock walls, or could when I was there last. They are all that is left of the suspension bridge which the Indians built of wire abandoned by the Overland Telegraph. (They made the squaws go out and dance on the bridge before the braves would cross it, but later on pack trains moved safely across the swaying cobweb.) Below the remains of the bridge are a few fish houses where some salmon hang in the smoke of damp wood. Perhaps an Indian will be standing by the side of the fast water, spear in hand.

Long ago a slide of rock blocked the channel of Hagwilget and stopped the salmon on their autumn migration. The terrible Babines from the north, blaming the Skeena people for lack of fish, came down here on the warpath. The few Skeenas who were left after the massacre fled into the wilderness. They called their new village Kispiox, "the town of the people who hid." It still stands where, at last, the road peters out and dies among the trees.

A little jungle of totem poles grows by the river, among the poor shacks of Kispiox. They are not painted like the totems of museums and tourist advertisements, but, rotting gradually in the weather, they still show the craftsmanship of the old carvers. A century ago, perhaps, they were dragged from the forest, with feasting and medicine making, and reared up here to tell the story of every house. The people with half a body each and no necks are carved there; the warrior who stood in the blood of his enemies up to the waist; the canoe which bore the Skeena woman after she had escaped from the Haidas, silencing her baby by cutting out her husband's tongue and thrusting it into the child's mouth; and the mosquito which will always sting a flirtatious girl.

That morning no one was to be seen in Kispiox. The shacks by the river, with their row of carved idols, seemed abandoned. After a while an old man came limping from a house. He had a massive head, a face of crumpled leather, and thick, gold-rimmed spectacles. Behind them there was a twinkle of humor in his eyes.

This was Chief Solomon Nalth, the leader of the people who hid. He could speak no English, but he called to a young man who translated for him. The chief would welcome us to Kispiox.

We sat on bare benches in the tribal hall until old Solomon was ready. He appeared after a while with a headdress of yellow rawhide, a demon's face on the front of it, strips of weasel skin dangling from it, and fringed with the whiskers of the sea lion. He still wore his white man's shirt and vest, for he had had little time to change, but wrapped around him like a kilt was a robe of buckskin. It was gay with beadwork and a hundred clattering bear claws. In either hand he carried a noisy rattle, carved in the shape of a bird and painted black and red.

His companion wore a top hat of enormous size, rammed down over his ears and decorated with a kind of medallion of gold braid, the size of a doughnut. Beneath the hat was a sad old face that never changed expression. This man stood as still as a cigar-store Indian in his black overcoat, which dangled beside his moccasins. Slung over one shoulder, like a military decoration, was a red silk sash. In one hand he carried a broomstick, which he began to hammer on the floor.

A few Indians had gathered shyly at the other side of the hall, each with a stick, and they hammered the floor in rhythm. Slowly Chief Solomon began his dance of welcome. Crouching, he walked up and down the hall on his toes, as if stalking an enemy. He began to move faster, speaking quickly in his own tongue. Now he was leaping wildly into the air, dashing at us and retreating, waving his rattles, twisting his frail body in ecstasy.

His weasel skins waved behind him, the bear claws tinkled. He talked now in deep gutturals and now shrieked in high-pitched falsetto. The sweat ran down his face and dropped on the floor.

Just as suddenly, he stopped, swaying weakly for a moment

in the middle of the floor. From a carved wooden box he took two handfuls of white feathers—down from the breast of an eagle—and running towards us, let them flutter from his trembling hands upon our heads. We were welcome now to fish and hunt all over the lands of his tribe.

We left him there, standing among his falling totem poles, a tired old man in gold-rimmed spectacles. From the fishermen's cottages of Nova Scotia, from the peasant houses of Quebec, from the towers of Ottawa, and the lonely prairies, we had come a long way. This was the end of the road, at Kispiox, where the people hid.

Index

375